Woodward's Historical Series.

No. V.

THE

Witchcraft Delusion

IN

NEW ENGLAND:

ITS

RISE, PROGRESS, AND TERMINATION,

AS EXHIBITED BY

DR. COTTON MATHER,

IN

THE WONDERS OF THE INVISIBLE WORLD;

AND BY

MR. ROBERT CALEF,

IN HIS

MORE WONDERS OF THE INVISIBLE WORLD.

WITH A

Preface, Introduction, and Notes,

BY SAMUEL G. DRAKE.

IN THREE VOLUMES.

VOL. I.

The Wonders of the Invisible World.

PRINTED FOR W. ELLIOT WOODWARD,
ROXBURY, MASS.
MDCCCLXVI.

EDITION IN THIS SIZE 280 COPIES.

MUNSELL, PRINTER.

TO

MY MORE THAN BROTHER,

HARLOW ROYS,

WHO AT ALL TIMES

ALIKE IN PROSPERITY AND ADVERSITY

HAS STOOD MY FRIEND,

WHO WHEN MY STEPS SEEMED RAPIDLY

DESCENDING INTO THE "DARK VALLEY"

AND

"THE RIVER" WITH THE "BOATMAN PALE"

WERE CLOSE BEFORE ME,

CHEERED ME BY HIS PRESENCE

AND HELD ME BACK BY THE GRASP OF HIS STRONG HAND,

WARM WITH LIFE AND LOVE,

IN TOKEN OF AN AFFECTION WHICH

STRONG AT FIRST,

AS YEARS PASS AND WE GROW OLDER

GROWS MORE INTENSE,

I DEDICATE THESE VOLUMES.

W.

PREFATORY.

THE Object in giving to the Public this new Edition of the *Wonders of the Invisible World*, is mainly to preserve an accurate Reprint of that *wonderful* Book. At the same Time it is intended to show that its Author has unjustly been singled out and held up to everlasting Scorn, as though he had been the Instigator of the whole Mischief; that from his high Standing socially he was more prominent than any other Man, and that this occasioned his being especially held responsible is clearly true. His ready Pen also largely contributed to place him in the front Rank of those whom that woeful Delusion led captive; he having written more largely upon the Subject than any other.

The firſt Edition of the *Wonders of the Inviſible World* was publiſhed in Boſton early in the Year 1693, at which Time *Witches* had begun to grow ſcarce; in other Words, Proſecutions had nearly ceaſed, and People were ſeriouſly looking about themſelves, and anxiouſly inquiring what they had been about? The ſerious Inquirers were thoſe (though few in Number) who had from the Beginning had Doubts as to the Reality of Witchcraft. When this Claſs began to reaſon, their Strength began to concentrate, and in due Time it put an End to the Horrors which had ſo ſtrongly tended to the Ruin of the whole Community. Until this Reaction was brought about, no Perſon was for a Moment ſafe. Notwithſtanding this frightful State of Things was thus brought to a Stand, a large Portion of the People retained all their Faith in the Reality of Witchcraft, and many of them exclaimed in Deſpair, that "the Kingdom of Satan had prevailed," and that they were a "God-forſaken People." In this latter Claſs was the Author of the *Wonders of the Inviſible World.* He never wavered in his Faith to the very End, becauſe his Conviction that he had eſpouſed the Truth was ſtronger than any Argument which could be brought againſt it. Some others of the Miniſters, and one or two of the Judges were equally ſanguine in their own Righteouſneſs. And yet we find the following cautious Piece of Advice given by "ſeveral Miniſters to his Excellency and the Honourable Council":---"We judge that in the Proſecution of theſe, and all ſuch Witchcrafts, there is Need of a very critical and exquiſite Caution, leſt by too much Credulity for Things received only upon the Devil's Authority, there be a Door opened for a long Train of miſerable Conſequences, and Satan get an Advantage over us, for we ſhould not be ignorant of his Devices." For all this it is not eaſy to diſcover the Practice of any of that "exquiſite Caution" in the Proceedings againſt thoſe accuſed.

No ſooner was the Edition of the *Wonders* printed in Boſton, than Copies were ſent to London and reprinted there with all Diſpatch, as will be ſeen by the "*Imprimatur*" in the Front of the Work. Mr. Deodat Lawſon's "*Brief and True Narrative*" of the ſame Affair was printed in Boſton in 1692, by Benj. Harris, and the next Year in London by John Dunton, in Connection with Dr. Increaſe Mather's "*Further Account of the Tryals of the New England Witches.*" A ſecond (in Fact, it was the third) Edition of Mr. Lawſon's Work was iſſued in London in 1704, which, though he calls it a *ſecond Edition* is quite a different Book from the firſt Edition. In the firſt he inſerted the Names of the Parties, while in the laſt, Daſhes ſtand in their Stead. It has two Dedications: one "To the Right Worſhipful and truly Honourable, Sir Henry Aſhhurſt, Barr[t]. and to His Truly Honourable and Religious Conſort, Lady Diana

Aſhhurſt, Barr[t] :" ſigned Deodat Lawſon. The other is "To the Worſhipful and Worthily Honoured *Bartholomew Gidney*, *John Hathorne*, and *Jonathan Corwin*, Eſqrs. Together with the Reverend *Mr. John Higginſon*, Paſtor, and Mr. *Nicholas Noyes* Teacher of the Church of Chriſt at Salem." Signed Deodat Lavſon. It ſhould be mentioned alſo that Dr. I. Mather's "*Further Account*," &c., contains Nothing beyond a Reprint of Lawſon's Book, (firſt Edition) except a "*Letter*" containing "*A further Account of the Tryals of the New England Witches*," ſent "*to a Gentleman in London*." This Letter was added at the End of the "*Further Account*." It was probably written by Mr. Mather to John Dunton, his Friend and Publiſher, and occupies about three additional Pages.

In this Reprint of the *Wonders* I have followed the ſecond Edition, preſuming that to be the moſt accurate, as the Copy from which it was printed was doubtleſs furniſhed by the Author.

Very few Copies of the original Edition are known to be in Exiſtence. I have never owned one, and am indebted to my Friend, GEORGE BRINLEY, Eſq., for the Uſe of his (rather imperfect) Copy. While this Preface was in the Hands of the Printer, my Publiſher, Mr. WOODWARD, has had the rare Fortune to obtain a very good one.

At this Period the Preſs literally ſwarmed with Works upon Witchcraft. Dunton printed in rapid Succeſſion all the Works from New England, and other Publiſhers were equally buſy. It would be a Matter of no little Curioſity if ſome one would collect the Titles of the Works on this Subject, and publiſh them in Book Form, with, or even without Abſtracts of their Contents. In a unique Volume now before me, belonging to Harvard College Library --- for the Loan of which I am indebted to the Kindneſs of Mr. SIBLEY, the Librarian --- there are ſeveral Tracts, the Titles of which are quite as ſingular as any of the Mathers.

One or two I will here extract. "The Lancasshire Levite Rebuk'd: or, a Vindication of the Dissenters from Popery, Superstition, Ignorance, and Knavery, unjustly Charged on them by Mr. Zachary Taylor in his Book, entitled, The Surry Impostor." Another runs thus: "The Devil turn'd Casuist or the Cheats of Rome laid open, in the Exorcism of a Despairing Devil, at the House of Thomas Pennington in Orrel in the Parish of Wigan in the County of Lancaster. By Zachary Taylor, M. A. Chaplin to the right reverend Father in God, Nicholas [Strafford] Lord Bishop of Chester, and Rector of Wigan."

Witch Books, as they were called, of the Father Land, must have been common among the People of New England, as will be seen by a Comparison of the Trials of Witches in both Countries. This Comparison shows that the accused in this Country were well acquainted with the ridiculous Nonsense of what had been and was passing at Witch Trials i

England. The ſame Cant and Incoherency are viſible at every Step. Inſomuch, that the Frivolity, Shallow-mindedneſs and Falſity were ſo apparent, that they remind one of the childiſh Nurſery Tales of Youth, and excite the moſt profound Wonder how they could have ever been viewed as Matter for ſerious Conſideration by any Perſons having any Pretenſions to common Senſe.

The original Records of the Court Proceedings againſt thoſe accuſed of Witchcraft were never fully given to the Public, until about two Years ago, Mr. W. Elliot Woodward, of Roxbury, cauſed a complete Tranſcript to be made of the whole, and printed them in two Volumes, ſmall Quarto, uniform with this Undertaking. Thoſe, with the preſent Volumes, will put the Student of New England Hiſtory in Poſſeſſion of nearly all the Materials exiſting upon this deeply intereſting, though humiliating, and in ſome reſpects, revolting Subject.

INTRODUCTORY.

AS a Belief in Witchcraft is not entirely exploded, it may be intereſting to examine a few of the early Definitions of it.

One of the earlieſt Lexicographers, or Expounders of Engliſh Words, was Edward Phillips, the Nephew of John Milton. It is ſaid that Phillips made up his Work from Milton's Preparation in the ſame Line. However that might be, it is quite clear that many of his Definitions have that Clearneſs and Preciſion for which Milton is ſo remarkable. Phillips's third (and I believe his laſt) Edition of "The New World of Words" was printed in 1671. In that we find Witchcraft thus defined: "A certain evill Art, whereby with the Aſſiſtance of the Devil, or evill Spirits, ſome Wonders may be wrought, which exceed the common Apprehension of Men: It cometh from the Dutch Word *Wiechelen*, that is, to divine, or gueſſe; it is called in Latin Veneficium, in Greek *Pharmaceia*, i.e. the Art of making Poiſons."

In 1706, John Kerſey publiſhed the ſixth Edition of Philips's Work, greatly augmented; though the Definition of *Witchcraft* is cut down to a few Words, thus: "The Black Art, whereby with the Aſſiſtance of the Devil, or evil Spirits, ſome Wonders may be wrought, which exceed the common Apprehenſions of Men."

Phillips does not define a *Witch*, but he ſays a "Wizard is a Witch, a cunning Man, one that telleth where things are that were loſt. Some think it comes from the Saxon Word *Witega*, i.e. a Prophet."

Kerſey defines a Witch, an old Hag, or Woman that deals with Familiar Spirits; and a Wizard "a Sorceror, or Inchanter; a Cunning Man," &c., as before.

In 1674, Thomas Blount publiſhed the fourth Edition of his "Gloſſographia, or Dictionary of hard Words." He ſays, "Witch is derived from the Dutch *Witchelen*, or *Wiichelen*, which properly ſignifies whinnyng and neighing like a Horſe;

alſo to foretell or prophecy; and *Wiichelen*, ſignifies a Soothſayer; for that the Germans (from whom our Anceſtors the Saxons uſually deſcended) did principally (as Tacitus tells us) divine and foretel Things to come by the whinnying and neighing of their Horſes; *Hinitus* and *Trenitus* are his Words."

Witchcraft is not defined by Blount himſelf, while under the Article *Witch*, he extracts from Maſter William Perkins: "Witchcraft is an Art ſerving for the working of Wonders by the Aſſiſtance of the Devil, ſo far as God will permit." To make the Definition of Witchcraft ſtill more plain, Mr. Blount extracts thus from an old Author named *Delrio*,[1] who defines Witchcraft to be "An Art, which by the Power of a Contract, entred into with the Devil, ſome Wonders are wrought, which paſs the common Underſtanding of Men."

As we approach a later Age, Lexicographers are pretty careful in their Definitions of Witchcraft. Bailey, in his folio Dictionary of 1730, ſays it is the Art of bewitching, enchanting, divining, &c."

[1] A Jeſuit of Loraine. His Book was a "Magical Diſquiſition."

Johnſon, though a Believer in Witchcraft, ſhirks the Definition of it thus: "The Practice of Witches. *Bacon.* Power, more than natural. *Sidney.*"

Noah Webſter publiſhed a Dictionary of the Engliſh Language in 1806, in which he ſays a *Witch* is "a Woman accuſed of magical Arts, a Hag." Witchcraft, "the Practice of Witches, a Charm." The great Lexicographer muſt have marvelled at theſe Definitions in his later Years; if ſo, he fails to make due Atonement in his incomparable "Unabridged." But the learned Editor of the "Imperial Dictionary,"[2] Dr. Ogilvie, appears to have taken ſuch Liberty with Dr. Webſter's Work as to bring it up to the Standard of the Times, eſpecially in that Claſs of Words in which *Witchcraft* is prominent. His Definition is ſo much to the Point, ſo clear, and ſo well expreſſed, that it is, though long, extracted entire: "WITCHCRAFT, the Practice of Witches; Sorcery; Enchantments; Intercourſe with the Devil; a ſupernatural Power, which Perſons were formerly ſuppoſed to obtain Poſſeſſion of by entering into Compact with the Devil. Indeed it was

[2] In three Volumes, royal Octavo, Glaſgow, 1856-9.

fully believed that they gave themſelves up to him, Body and Soul, while he engaged that they ſhould want for Nothing and be able to aſſume whatever Shape they pleaſed, to viſit and torment their Enemies, and accompliſh their infernal Purpoſes. As ſoon as the Bargain was concluded, the Devil was ſaid to deliver to the Witch an Imp or familiar Spirit, to be ready at call, and to do whatever it was directed. By the Aid of this Imp and the Devil together, the Witch, who was almoſt always an old Woman, was enabled to tranſport herſelf through the Air on a Broomſtick or a Spit, and to transform herſelf into various Shapes, particularly thoſe of Cats and Hares; to inflict Diſeaſes on whomſoever ſhe pleaſed, and to puniſh her Enemies in a Variety of Ways. The Belief of Witchcraft is very ancient. It was univerſally believed in Europe till the 16th Century, and even maintained its Ground with tolerable Firmneſs till the Middle of the 17th Century. Vaſt Numbers of reputed Witches were condemned to be burned every Year, ſo that in England alone it is computed that no fewer than 30,000 of them ſuffered at the Stake."

Dr. Ogilvie closes his Definition with one Extract from Shakespeare:

> "He hath a Witchcraft
> Over the King in's Tongue."

It cannot be denied that the Existence of Witchcraft is as fully taught in the Bible as Slavery. The Light of Science has extinguished the one, while the other yet struggles against Fate.[3] To urge the Authority of the Bible, that Slavery is a divine Institution, and therefore should be sustained, is just as reasonable as it would be to urge the Existence of Witches; and were there as many Interests at Stake in keeping alive Witchcraft, it would find as many Advocates, doubtless, as Slavery.

At first, Voices against Witchcraft were faint and few. Such was the Bewilderment of the human Mind in early Ages that Men hardly dared to think in Opposition to the Superstitions of the Multitude. Yet there were always some who doubted the delegated Power of the Devil, though they were not often lavish enough of their own Safety to let their Disbelief be known. Still, there are, no Doubt, some "dark Corners

[3] This Part of this Introduction was written not long before the Southern Rebellion began.

of the Earth" where it would not be entirely ſafe for one to declare publicly that there is no ſuch Matter as Witchcraft. Nor is this ſo much to be wondered at, when, at the preſent Day, and in a Portion of our own Country, a Man cannot ſpeak againſt Slavery, but at the Peril of his Life. This is no new Aſpect growing out of the preſent Rebellion, but it has been thus many Years.

Few Men dared to ſpeak boldly againſt the Exiſtence of Witchcraft before the Year 1700. Though they diſbelieved in it they were afraid to attack it. They began by endeavouring to ſhow the Inſufficiency of the Evidence relied upon in particular Caſes. In this Way, Frauds were detected and expoſed, and the Eyes of Judges were opened.

Among the early and ſucceſsful Combatants of Witchcraft in England was Sir Robert Filmer. This Gentleman, though he out-went Machiavel himſelf in Arguments to uphold Deſpotiſm, yet he entered a pretty effectual Demurrer againſt the Prerogative of the Devil, as attempted to be manifeſted in the Perſons of aged Matrons. Lancaſhire was diſtinguiſhed above all other Counties in England in Sir Robert's Time for its Production of Witches; but when his native County,

Kent, was ſcourged by the imaginary Arts of Satan, he thought it Time to make a public Declaration of his Views in Regard to the Nature of the Evidence made Uſe of for the Conviction of Witches. He therefore prepared a Treatiſe which he entitled "An Advertiſement to the Jury-men of England, touching Witches," printed in 1680, but whether it was ever printed before does not appear from this Impreſſion. In this Work he criticiſes the Productions of ſome of the prominent Authors in Favor of Witchcraft with much Ability.

To the Aſſertion that Witches act under a Contract with the Devil, Mr. Filmer obſerves, "That the Agreement between the Witch and the Devil they call a Covenant, and yet neither of the Parties are any Way bound to perform their Part; and the Devil, without Doubt, notwithſtanding all his Craft, hath far the worſt Part of the Bargain. The Bargain runs thus in Maſter Perkins's Work: 'The Witch as a Slave binds herſelf by Vow to believe in the Devil, and to give him either Body, or Soul, or both, under his Hand-writing, or ſome Part of his Blood. The Devil promiſeth to be ready at his Vaſſal's Command, to appear in the Likeneſs of any

Creature, to consult and to aid him for the procuring of Pleasure, Honor, Wealth, or Preferment; to go for him, to carry him any whither, and to do any Command.' Whereby we see the Devil is not to have Benefit of his Bargain till the Death of the Witch. In the Meantime, he is to appear always at the Witche's Command, to go for him [or her], to carry him any whither, and to do any Command; which argues the Devil to be the Witche's Slave, and not the Witch the Devil's Slave. And though it be true which Delrio affirmeth, 'That the Devil is at Liberty to perform or break his Compact, for that no Man can compel him to keep his Promise;' yet on the other Side, it is as possible for the Witch to frustrate the Devil's Contract, if he or she have so much Grace as to repent; the which there may be good Cause to do, if the Devil be found not to perform his Promise. Besides, a Witch may many Times require that to be done by the Devil, which God permits not the Devil to do; thus against his Will the Devil may lose his Credit, and give Occasion of Repentance, though he endeavor to the utmost of his Power to bring to pass whatsoever he hath promised; and so fail of the Benefit of his Bargain, though he have the

Hand-writing, or ſome Part of the Blood of the Witch for his Security, or the Solemnity before Witneſſes, as Delrio imagineth."

Thus much is given to ſhow in what Manner the Advocates of Witchcraft were combatted, without denying the actual Exiſtence of it. It was as much as could be ſafely advanced in the ſeventeenth Century. To have come out boldly, and denied the Thing altogether, would have been to proclaim a Diſbelief of the Teachings of the Bible; and this would have defeated the very Object ſought to be attained. It has, beyond Queſtion, occurred to all thinking Men in every Age, that Witches and Devils could not have a Being without God's Permiſſion; that if they did or do exiſt, it is his Pleaſure that they ſhould; that, therefore, if God wiſhed to deſtroy ſuch Miscreants he would do it by making War on them himſelf, inſtead of compelling Mankind to fight them blindfolded for all Eternity, or during the World's Exiſtence.

There are few Readers probably who have not heard of a Book upon Witchcraft by a royal Hand—a King of England. James I wrote a Book to which he gave the Title, *Dæmonologie.* To thoſe who have not ſtudied the State of Society in England for a Century or ſo before the Emigration of our Fathers to New England, and conſequently cannot comprehend the Kind and Degree of Knowledge and Intelligence poſſeſſed by the People; it will ſeem incredible how they were bound down by ſuch childiſh and utterly puerile Stuff as was put forth by James in his Work on Witchcraft. Nurſery Tales of a later Day are quite as eaſily believed to be realities as the Witch Stories of a former Age, and the Allegories of Bunyan are much eaſier transformed to Realities. That ſo weak and abſurd a Production as the *Dæmonologie* reflects the Underſtanding and Literature of our Fathers, muſt be not a little humiliating to their Deſcendants to the lateſt Poſterity. The *Dæmonologie* was printed at Edinburgh, in Quarto, ſix Years before James came to the Crown of England, namely, in 1593. His Work correſponded with the Times in which it was written. Here is a Specimen of its Contents: "The Devil teaches Witches how to make Pictures of Wax and Clay, that by the roaſting thereof, the Perſons that they bear the Name of, may be continually melted or dried away by continual Sickneſs . . . . not that any of theſe Means which he teacheth them (except Poiſons, which are composed of Things natural) can of themselves help any to these Turns they are imployed in. . . . . That Witches can bewitch, and take the Life of Men or Women by roasting of the Pictures [Images] which is very possible to their Master to perform; for although that Instrument of Wax have no Virtue in the Turn doing, yet may he not very well, by that same Measure that his conjured Slave melts that Wax at the Fire, may he not, I say, at these same Times, subtilly as a Spirit, so weaken and scatter the Spirits of Life of the Patient, as may make him on the one Part for Faintness to sweat out the Humours of his Body; and on the other Part, for the not concurring of these Spirits which cause his Digestion, so debilitate his Stomach, that his Humour radical continually sweating out on the one Part, and no new good Suck being put in the Place thereof for Lack of Digestion on the other, he at last shall vanish away even as his Picture will do at the Fire."

The Reader will hardly desire any more from such a royal Source; but even royal Nonsense may sometimes be Necessary upon historical Points, and we must listen to their incoherent Jargon, however much we hold them in Contempt. It was during the Reign of this King that New England began to be ſettled, and the Settlers were his Subjects, and with them came the Superſtitions common to the People of England.

In James's Book he lays down Rules for determining who were Witches, and great Numbers were executed in Purſuance of thoſe Rules. No ſooner was that benighted King ſeated upon the Engliſh Throne, but the following Statute was paſſed: "If any Perſon or Perſons ſhall uſe, practice, or exerciſe any Invocation, or Conjuration of any evil and wicked Spirit, or ſhall conſult, covenant with, entertain, employ, feed or reward any evil and wicked Spirit, to or for any Intent and Purpoſe: or take up any dead Man, Woman or Child, out of his, her or their Grave, or any other Place where the dead Body reſteth, or the Skin, Bone or any Part of the dead Perſon, to be employed or uſed in any Manner of Witchcraft, Sorcery, Charm, or Inchantment; or ſhall uſe, practice or exerciſe any Witchcraft; or ſhall uſe, practice or exerciſe any Witchcraft, Inchantment, Charm or Sorcery, whereby any Perſon ſhall be killed, deſtroyed, waſted, conſumed, pined or lamed in his or her Body, or any Part thereof; that then every ſuch Offender or Offenders, their

Aiders, Abettors, and Counſellors, being of any the ſaid Offenders duly and lawfully convicted and attainted, ſhall ſuffer Pains of Death as a Felon or Felons."

This Law does not materially differ from that enacted in the fifth Year of Elizabeth; yet there is a Clauſe in the older one, declaring that, "If any Perſon ſhall take upon him by Witchcraft, Inchantment, Charm or Sorcery, to tell or declare in what Place any Treaſure of Gold or Silver ſhould or might be found or hid in the Earth, or other ſecret Places, or where Goods, or Things loſt or ſtolen ſhould be found or be come: Or to the Intent to provoke any Perſon to unlawful Love, or whereby any Cattle or Goods of any Perſon ſhall be deſtroyed, waſted or impaired; or to deſtroy or hurt any Perſon in his, or her Body, though the ſame be not effected, &c. a Year's Impriſonment, and Pillory, &c. and the ſecond Conviction, Death."

In the early Laws of Maſſachuſetts, adopted in 1641, Witchcraft is thus briefly dealt with: "If any Man or Woman be a Witch (that is hath or conſulteth with a familiar Spirit) they ſhall be put to Death." Theſe Laws were called *The Body of Liberties*, and were drawn up by the famous Minifter of Bofton, John Cotton. He made them conform to the Bible, and Paffages of Scripture ftand againft each Law in the Margin. Againft this is found, Deut. xiii, 6, 10—xvii, 2, 6. Ex. xxii, 20.

In Plymouth Colony as late as 1671, nearly the fame Law was enacted. It differed only by faying, "If any Chriftian (fo called) be a Witch," &c.

If Sir Robert Filmer had feen our Laws, he would, perhaps, have indulged in a few Obfervations upon them. The Plymouth People feem to have looked a little farther than the learned Minifter of Bofton, as appears by the Provifo thrown in, that a *Chriftian* could not be a Witch. Of courfe the Judges were to determine the Point of Chriftian or no Chriftian, affuming that a Chriftian Judge could not err or be miftaken.

One of the Advocates of Witchcraft having afferted that a Perfon cannot make the neceffary Contract with the Devil to become a Witch, without renouncing God and Baptifm, "it will follow," fays Filmer, "that none can be Witches but fuch as have firft been Chriftians. And what fhall be faid then of all thofe idolatrous Nations, of Lapland, Finland, and divers Parts of Africa, and many other heathenish Nations, which Travellers report to be full of Witches? And indeed, what Need or Benefit can the Devil gain by contracting with those Idolators, who are surer his own than any Covenant can make them?"

Witchcraft, as formerly believed in, was the Art of working Wonders or Miracles, and some of its Expounders asserted, that the Power of effecting Wonders does not flow from the Skill of the Witch, but is derived wholly from the Devil, whom the Witch has Command over, by Virtue of a Contract. Whereupon Sir Robert Filmer sensibly remarks, "that the Devil is really the Worker of the Wonder, and the Witch but the Counsellor, Persuader or Commander of it, and only accessory before the Fact, and the Devil only Principal. Now the Difficulty will be, how the Accessory can be duly and lawfully convicted and attainted according as the Statute requires, unless the Devil, who is the Principle, be first convicted, or at least, outlawed; which cannot be, because the Devil can never be lawfully summoned according to the Rules of our Common Law."

In this Manner Witchcraft was successfully assailed, because it was a Species of reasoning that did not directly interfere with the Superstitions and Prejudices of the People. But the March of Mind amongſt the Maſſes was ſlow, and Trials for Witchcraft continued in England for twenty Years after Sir Robert Filmer wrote.

For one hundred Years, 1580 to 1680, in Germany alone, 1,000 Perſons a Year, on an Average, were, upon good Authority, ſaid to have ſuffered Death for the imaginary Crime of Witchcraft. Executions in that Country began to abate about 1694; the laſt Execution, being of a poor Nun, in 1749. And it may be remarked in this Connection, that immediately after the miſerable James publiſhed his Work on Witchcraft, 600 Perſons were put to a cruel Death for being Witches.

"Thou ſhalt not ſuffer a Witch to live," is a Command, and it was once conſidered as much to be regarded as any other Command in the Bible. That there were Witches in the World was as plain, and as much to be believed, as that there were Spirits of any Kind whatever. Whoever believed in the Immortality of the Soul, believed in the Immortality of bad Souls as well as good. Soul is another Word for Spirit; hence good Spirits and bad Spirits. Witches were bad Spirits, but whether they originated *in* Mankind, or whether they were ſent there to take Poſſeſſion of the human Body, and to exclude a better Tenant, has not been ſatisfactorily ſettled by Pſychologiſts and Metaphyſicians. But one Thing ſeems to be well eſtabliſhed, and that is, that quite as many bad Spirits find Habitations in the Sons and Daughters of theſe Days, as at any former Period. Fortunately it was found out, at length, that deſtroying the Tenement of a bad Spirit, did not deſtroy that Spirit. But this was not thought of until Thouſands had been put to Death.

It will doubtleſs be ſaid by many, that if ever there were Witches in the World, there are Witches now. This Point it is not intended to argue. There were always thoſe who denied the Exiſtence of Witches; or, what amounted to the ſame Thing, they would never allow that there was ſufficient Evidence produced to prove that *Craft* againſt any who were accuſed of it. Perſons who thus queſtion all Court Proceedings, where Witchcraft was attempted to be detected, were regarded as unfit for good Society, and unworthy of its Protection.

Thoſe who were for "ridding the Land" of Witches, thought thoſe who queſtioned the Legality of their Proceedings, were, at leaſt, Infidels, in the moſt obnoxious Senſe, and they were generally treated as ſuch, and were to be ſhunned by Society. Thus it fared with Mr. Robert Calef, who, during the Proſecutions and Executions of the People accuſed in Maſſachuſetts, as will be ſeen in the Progreſs of the preſent Work.

It is ſcarcely conceivable by even the partially enlightened of the preſent Age, that only one hundred and fifty Years ago our Anceſtors were, in ſome reſpects, ſo ſlightly removed from Barbarity and heathen Darkneſs. Superſtition will give Way only to mental Culture; but there may be conſiderable mental Culture, and alſo much Superſtition; for Perſons may be educated in many Things when thoſe very Things are founded in Error. Certain Premiſes are taken for granted, becauſe no Data exiſt, or at leaſt inſufficient Data, to inveſtigate them and the Foundations on which they reſt. This is ſtill the Caſe, but it was more ſo in Times paſt.

Barbarous Nations, as the Aborigines of any Country, are Slaves to the ſame Kind of Superſtition as that which cauſed the Executions for Witchcraft by the Governments of Old and New England. Even many of thoſe who oppoſed the Proſecutions for that imaginary Crime, were not free from the ſame Superſtitions with the Advocates of it. They believed in Witchcraft, and only argued the Want of Evidence againſt it. This gave them a decided Diſadvantage, becauſe the Evidence was, in many Caſes, apparently ſo overwhelming; inſomuch, that "the learned Baxter" wrote to Dr. Increaſe Mather, declaring, "The Evidence is ſo convincing, that he muſt be a very obdurate Sadducee who will not believe it." Hence if there were ſome Perſons who did not believe the ſtrange and unnatural Things alleged to have been performed by Perſons charged with Witchcraft they were treated as "obdurate Sadducees," whoſe Unbelief was only a Pretence. Times have ſo much changed, that it is not neceſſary to make the Admiſſions which the Oppoſers of Witchcraft formerly made. Then, to deny the Exiſtence of it was preciſely the ſame as to deny that the Bible was a Revelation from God. Therefore, as was before obſerved, thoſe who oppoſed the Proſecutions for Witchcraft, labored under a great Diſadvantage. The Belief in it being nearly univerſal, the ſolitary Individual who dared to ſtem ſo popular a Torrent, now looked upon clearly as a Deluſion, had nothing to expect on all Hands, but Obloquy, Deriſion and Contempt.

From all which, Nothing is eaſier to be diſcerned than this—wherever Ignorance is the greateſt, there Superſtition prevails moſt; that therefore it follows of courſe, that Ignorance and Superſtition are the Parents of Witchcraft.

It never occurred to Believers in Witchcraft, it would ſeem, that if Witches really exiſted, a Proſecution againſt them could no more reach them than it would the Air in a Bubble or the Breath which they breathed; for if they poſſeſſed the Power claimed for them, they alſo had the Power to abandon the Bodies they poſſeſſed the Moment it was decided to puniſh them in ſuch Bodies; and thus diſconcert all Attempts to obſtruct their Craft.

The Advocates of Witchcraft affirm that it is by Virtue of a League with the Devil that the Witch is enabled to carry on her Operations; and that the Devil, God's great Enemy, is allowed to commiſſion Witches, that they may alſo counteract his (God's) Purpoſes by enſnaring Souls, as though the Devil had not Power enough to do the whole Miſchief himſelf; and thus in a ſneakingly indirect Way make a Cats-paw of ſome demented old Woman, or other ſimple Perſon.

In the midſt of the Proceedings againſt the

People charged with being Witches, and while ſeveral Jails were crowded with thoſe unfortunate Perſons, a very ſerious Queſtion aroſe, which, of itſelf, was calculated to cauſe the moſt violent of the Proſecutors to ſtay their bloody Hands, and to aſk themſelves, what they had been doing? and if, after all, there was not a Poſſibility that they had been guilty of ſhedding innocent Blood? The Queſtion was a very ſimple and natural one, namely, Is it not poſſible for a Witch to appear in the Shape of an innocent Perſon? As ſoon as this Queſtion was ſtarted, there was quite a Shock in the Community, and the Men accounted the wiſeſt in the Land ſtood ſtill for a Time, and looked inquiringly upon one another. As long as the afflicted Perſons accuſed only the Poor and Friendleſs, Nothing appears to have been thought of the Poſſibility that ſuch Perſons could be innocent of the Charges preferred againſt them. But, when at length, Perſons conſidered of unblemiſhed Lives, ſtanding among the firſt in the Community, came to be accuſed, then the Caſe wore a different Aſpect; then it was that the before mentioned important Queſtion came up. This Queſtion divided the People, and from that Diviſion Safety reſulted. In this Inſtance, the common Order of Things was reverſed; Safety came from a Diviſion, and not from Union. Hence a new Proverb is derived—In Union there may be Error, while Diviſion may elicit the Truth.

The People, thus brought to a Stand, had a little Time for reflection. This, ſome improved to the Advantage of themſelves, while others improved it for the Advantage of the Public. Some had been ſo ſtrenuous in their Efforts to convict accuſed Perſons, that it was now very difficult for them, even to ſuſpend their Efforts without giving their Opponents an immediate Advantage over them; that even though the Judges of the Courts who tried the accuſed, had been guided mainly by "Mr. Perkins's Rules for the Diſcovery of Witches," on a careful Inſpection of thoſe Rules at this Day, it is difficult to ſee how Convictions were forced out of them.

Nevertheleſs, ſtrong Ground having been taken that Witches exiſted, and Perſons reputed Witches having been proſecuted with the utmoſt Rigor, and unrelenting Perſeverance for a long Time, the chief Agents in theſe bloody Proceedings, firm in their Convictions that they had done righteouſly, deemed it incumbent upon themſelves to keep the People to the ſame Opinions. This was the Origin of this unfortunate Book, "*The Wonders of the Inviſible World;*" the chief Part, or perhaps all of which, was compoſed while above one hundred poor People in and about Salem and Boſton were ſuffering a wretched impriſonment in the filthy and barbarous Jails of thoſe Days, to which Jails and Priſons of our Days are in Compariſon, Palaces. It was doubtleſs no ſooner determined that the Proceedings againſt the Witches ſhould be given to the World, than the Perſon was deſignated who ſhould perform that Service. And from the very opening of that Work it is at once diſcovered, that it was intended as a "Defence" of what had been already done, as well as to urge a Continuance of thoſe Proceedings, "until the Land was fully purged of the Demons which infeſted it."

For a long Period, the Publication of Books detailing the Doings and Proſecutions of Witches ſeems to have extended rather than abridged the Belief in Witchcraft. This may be accounted for in Part from the Conſideration that the Teachers of the People were themſelves groveling in the Mire of Superſtition. A more particular Reference to ſome of the Works beſt known ſomewhat more than two Centuries ago ſhall here follow.

One Thomas Cooper publiſhed in 1617, a Work of this Title, "The Myſtery of Witch-craft. Diſcouering, the Truth, Nature, Occaſions, Growth and Power thereof. Together with the Detection and Puniſhment of the ſame. As alſo, the Seuerall Stratagems of Sathan, enſnaring the poore Soule by this deſperate Practize of annoying the Bodie: with the ſeueral Vſes thereof to the Church of Chriſt. Very neceſſary for the redeeming of theſe atheiſticall and ſecure Times."

This Author dedicated his Work to the "Maior and Corporation of the Ancient Citie of Cheſter," &c., in which Dedication we find the following, which, throwing ſome Light on the reverend Dealer in Darkneſs, is extracted. He commences, "Diuers, and verie weighty haue been the Motiues (right Worſhipfull) to induce mee to the Dedication of theſe my Labors in this kinde vnto your Worſhips.

"The firſt is, becauſe my firſt Calling from the Vniverſitie, to employ my Miniſtrie for the Edification of the Saints, was by the Gouernors of your famous Citie, to ſucceed that painefull and profitable Teacher, Maister Harrison, who was thence called by the King's most Excellent Maiestie, to be one of the sixe Teachers to those barren and needfull Places of the Country of Lancashire. And therefore, hauing both kind intertainment among you; and by some of you being furthered to a more settled Pastorall Charge in that Countie, I could not but leave some Memoriall of my Thankefulnesse vnto you herein.

"Secondly, my free Admission to that Pastorall Charge, together with the singular Providence of God, in directing my Ministrie for the informing and reforming of that ignorant People, who never before enioyed any constant Ministrie, as also his admirable Protection and Deliuerance of me from vnreasonable Men, that vsed all their Force and Cunning to hinder the Proceedings of the Gospel of Christ."

These Extracts are made because they give a Glimpse of the Life and Character of an Author, second only to King James as a Cultivator of Witchcraft. His Book is a small Duodecimo of 368 Pages, in the Close of which he says, "to the wise and humble Reader, I am not ashamed to acknowledge, that which thou canst not but discerne; that I have borrowed most of my Grounds from his Maiesties Dæmonologie, Mr. Perkins, Mr. Gifford, and others." And this truly may be added, "the Blind were led by the Blind," in the fulleſt Senſe of the Maxim. Maſter Cooper further remarks upon the Labors of his royal Predeceſſor and others in theſe Words, "they have waded before mee heerein, to confirme the Authoritie thereof, againſt the Atheiſme of theſe evill Dayes: that ſo each might have the perfect Honour of their owne Paines.[4]

In his ſecond Chapter he ſays, "it is proued that there haue beene, are, and ſhall be Witches to the World's End: both by ſound Teſtimony, 1ſt, from the Word; 2d, from Antiquity; 3d, from pregnant Reaſons, and ſo ſuch Obiections anſwered, as ſeeme to contradict this Truth."

This moſt ſingularly ſuperſtitious Writer ſays there were good Witches as well as bad ones; that theſe good Witches are called the *unbinding* ones; becauſe they undo what the bad Witch does, and yet is allowed to do good Offices with the Conſent of the Devil.[5]

Good Witches performed wonderful Cures, according to the Belief of thoſe Days. Even

[4] *The Myſterie of Witchcraft*, P. 363. [5] Ibid, 211.

Burton[6] ſays, "they can effect ſuch Cures, the maine Queſtion is whether it be lawful in a deſperate Caſe, to crave their Help, or aſk a Wizard's Advice. 'Tis a common Practice of ſome Men to go firſt to a Witch, and then to a Phyſitian. If one cannot help the other ſhall." And Paracelſus declared, "that it mattered not whether a ſick Perſon were helped by God or Devil, ſo that he were eaſed." Some, however, demurred to this, and affirmed that it was better to die than be cured by a Witch or a Sorcerer.

Further to illuſtrate the Subject, I ſhall have Recourſe to Mr. Nathan Drake's *Shakeſpeare, and his Times.* That chief of Expounders of the "Immortal Bard," having had occaſion to review the Subject of Witchcraft, and having made ſo clear and valuable an Analyſis of it in his Examination of the Witches of Shakeſpeare, as is nowhere elſe to be found, I am, as will be the Readers of this Introduction, I apprehend, fortunate in being able to avail myſelf of the Labors of that eminent Scholar and able Antiquary.

The Play of Macbeth is founded on a Species of Superſtition that, during the Life-time of Shakeſpeare, prevailed in England and Scotland,

6 *Anatomy of Melancholy,* 221, Edition in Folio, 1651.

in a Degree until then unknown. In the 33d Year of Henry VIII, was enacted a Statute which adjudged all Witchcraft and Sorcery to be Felony without the Benefit of Clergy; but at the Commencement of the Reign of Elizabeth, the Evil seems to have been greatly on the Increase, for Bishop Jewel, preaching before the Queen, in 1558, tells her, "It may please your Grace to understand that Witches and Sorcerers within these few last Years are marvelously increased within your Grace's Realm. Your Grace's Subjects pine away, even unto the Death, their Colour fadeth, their Flesh rotteth, their Speech is benumbed, their Senses are bereft, I pray God they may never practice further then upon the Subject."[7] How prevalent the Delusion had become, in the Year 1584, we have the most ample Testimony in the ingenious Work of Reginald Scot, entitled "The Discoverie of Witchcraft," which was written as the sensible and humane Author has informed us, "in behalfe of the Poore, the Aged, and the Simple,"[8] and it reflects singular Discredit on the Age in which it was produced, that a Detection so complete, both with regard to Argument and Fact, should have failed in effecting its Purpose.

[7] Strype's *Annals*, I, P. 8.

[8] *Epistle to Sir Roger Manwood*, P. 1.

But the Infatuation had ſeized all Ranks, with an Influence which rivaled that reſulting from an Article of religious Faith, and Scot begins his Work with the Obſervation, that "the Fables of Witchcraft have taken ſo faſt hold and deepe Root in the Heart of Man, that fewe or none can, now adaies, with Patience indure the Hand and Correction of God. For if any Adverſitie, Greefe, Sickneſſe, Loſſe of Children, Corne, Cattell, or Libertie happen unto them; by and by they exclaime uppon Witches;—inſomuch as a Clap of Thunder, or a Gale of Wind is no ſooner heard, but either they run to ring Bells, or crie out to burne Witches;"[9] and in his ſecond Chapter, he declares, "I have heard to my greefe ſome of the Mineſterie affirme, that they have had in their Pariſh at one Inſtant xvij or xviij Witches: meaning ſuch as could work Miracles ſupernaturallie,"[10] a Declaration which, in a ſubſequent Part of his Book, he more particularly applies, when he informs us, that xvij or xviij were condemned at once at St. Oſees in the County of Eſſex, being a whole Pariſh, though of no great Quantitie."[11]

The Miſchief, however, was but in Progreſs,

[9] *Epiſtle to Sir Roger Manwood*, Chap. i, Pp. 1 and 2.

[10] Scot, *Diſcoverie*, Chap. ii, P. 4.

[11] *Diſcourſe of Devils and Spirits*, P. 543; annexed to the *Diſcoverie of Witchcraft.*

and received a rapid Acceleration from the Publication of the *Dæmonologie* of King James, at Edinburgh, in the Year 1597. The Origin of this very curious Treatife was probably laid in the royal Mind, in Confequence of the fuppofed Detection of a Confpiracy of 200 Witches with Dr. Fian, "Regifter to the Devil," at their Head, to bewitch and drown His Majefty, on his Return from Denmark, in 1590. James attended the Examination of thefe poor Wretches with the moft eager Curiofity, and the moft willing Credulity; and, when Agnis Tompfon confeffed, that fhe, with other Witches, to the Number juft mentioned, went altogether by Sea, each one in her Riddle, or Sieve, with Flagons of Wine, making merry and drinking by the Way, to the Kirk of North Berwick, in Lothian, where, when they had landed, they took Hands and danced, finging all with one Voice:

> "Commer [Goffip] go ye before, commer goe ye
> Gif ye will not go before, commer let me."

And "that Geilis Duncane did go before them, playing faid Reel on a Jew's Trump." James fent for Duncane, and liftened with Delight to his Performance of the Witches' Reel on the Jews-harp!

On Agnis, however, afferting, that the Devil had met them at the Kirk, His Majefty could not avoid expreffing fome Doubts; when, taking him afide, fhe "declared unto him the very Words which had paffed between him and his Queen on the firft Night of their Marriage, with their Anfwer each to other; whereat the King wondered greatly, and fwore by the living God, that he believed all the Devils in Hell could not have difcovered the fame."[12]

That the Particulars elicited from the Confeffions of thefe unfortunate Beings, which, it is faid, "made the King in a wonderful Admiration," formed the Bafis of the *Dæmonologie*, may be therefore readily admitted. It is alfo to be deplored, that, weak and abfurd as this Production now appears to us, its Effect on the Age of its Birth, and a Century afterwards, were extenfive and melancholy in the extreme. It contributed, indeed, more than any other Work on the Subject, to rivet the Fetters of Credulity; and fcarcely had a twelve month elapfed from its Publication, before its Refult was vifible in the Deftruction in

[12] See *Gent. Magz.*, XLIX, P. 449; Vol. VII, P. 556.

Scotland, of not leſs than 600 human Beings at once, for this imaginary Crime![13]

The Succeſſion of James to the Throne of Elizabeth ſerved but to propagate the Contagion; for no ſooner had he reached this Country, than his Dæmonologie reappeared from an Engliſh Preſs, being printed in London, in 1603, in Quarto, and with a Preface to the Reader, which commences by informing him of the "fearfull abounding at this Time in this Country, of theſe deteſtable Slaves of the Devel, the Witches, or Enchanters;"[14] a Declaration which, during the Courſe of the ſame Year, was accompanied by a new Statute againſt Witches, one Clauſe of which enacts, that, "Any one that ſhall uſe, practice, or exerciſe any Invocation or Conjuration of any evill or wicked Spirit, or conſult, covenant with, entertaine or employ, feede or reward, any evill or wicked Spirit, to or for any Intent or Purpoſe; or take up any dead Man, Woman or Child, out of his, her, or their Grave, or any other Place where the dead Body reſteth, or the Skin, Bone,

13 Naſhe's *Lenten Stuff,* 1599, as quoted by Reed, in his *Shakeſpeare,* Vol. X, Pp. 5, 11.

14 King James's *Works,* as publiſhed by James, Biſhop of Winton, Folio, 1616, P. 91.

or other Part of any dead Perſon, to be employed or uſed in any Manner of Witchcraft, Sorcery, Charme, or Enchantment; or ſhall uſe, practice, or exerciſe any Witchcraft, Enchantment, Charme, or Sorcery, whereby any Perſon ſhall be killed, deſtroyed, waſted, conſumed, pined, or lamed, in his or her Body, or any Part thereof, ſuch Offenders, duly and lawfully convicted and attainted, ſhall ſuffer Death."

This Act was not repealed until the Year 1736. (ix Geo. II.)

We cannot wonder if Meaſures ſuch as thoſe, which ſtamped the already exiſting Superſtitions with the renewed Authority of the Law, and with the Influence of regal Argument and Authority, ſhould render a Belief in the Exiſtence of Witchcraft almoſt univerſal; Faſhion and Intereſt on the one Hand, and Ignorance and Fear on the other, mutually contributing, by concealing and baniſhing Doubt, to diſſeminate Error, and preclude Detection.

Who thoſe were who, at this Period, had the Misfortune to be branded with the Appellation of Witches; what Deeds were imputed to them, and what was the Nature of their ſuppoſed Compact with the Devil, are Queſtions which will be moſt ſatisfactorily anſwered in the Words of

Reginald Scot, whose Book is not only extremely scarce, but highly curious and entertaining; and two or three Chapters from this copious Treasury of Superstition, with a very few Comments from other Sources, will exhaust this Part of the Subject.

"The Sort of such as are said to be Witches," writes Scot, "are Women which be commonly old, lame, bleare-eied, pale, fowle, and full of Wrinkles; poore, sullen, Superstitious, and Papists; or such as know no Religion; in whose drousie Minds the Divell hath gotten a fine Seat; so as, what Mischeefe, Mischance, Calamitie, or Slaughter is brought to passe, they are easilie persuaded the same is doone by themselves; imprinting in their Minds an earnest and constant Imagination thereof. They are leane and deformed, shewing Melancholie in their Faces, to the Horror of all that see them. They are doting, Scolds, mad, develish, and not much differing from them that are thought to be possessed with Spirits; so firme and stedfast in their Opinions, as whosoever shall onelie have respect to the Constancie of their Words uttered, would easilie beleeve they were true indeed.

"These miserable Wretches are so odious unto all their Neighbors, and so feared, as few dare offend them, or denie them anie Thing they aſke: whereby they take upon them; yea, and ſome Times thinke, that they can doo ſuch Things as are beyond the Abilitie of humane Nature. Theſe go from Houſe to Houſe, and from Doore to Doore for a Pot full of Milke, Yeſt, Drinke, Pottage, or ſome ſuch Reeleſe; without the which they could hardlie live: neither obtaining for their Service and Paines, nor by their Art, nor yet at the Divels Hands (with whome they are ſaid to make a perfect and viſible Bargaine) either Beautie, Monie, Promotion, Welth, Worſhip, Pleaſure, Honor, Knowledge, Learning, or any other Benefit whatſoever.

"It falleth out many Times, that neither their Neceſſities, nor their Expectation is anſwered or ſerved, in thoſe Places where they beg or borrowe; but ratheir Kindneſs is by their Neighbors reproved. And further, in Tract of Time the Witch weareth odious and tedious to her Neighbors; and they againe are deſpiſed and deſpited of hir; ſo as ſometimes ſhe curſeth one, and ſometimes another; and that from the Maiſter of the Houſe, his Wife, Children, Cattell, &c. to the little Pig that lieth in the Stie. Thus in Proceſſe of Time they have all diſpleaſed hir, and ſhe hath wiſhed evil Luck unto them all; perhaps with Curſes and Imprecations made in Forme. Doubtleſs (at Length) ſome of hir Neighbors die, or falle ſicke; or ſome of their Children are viſited with Diſeaſes that ver them ſtrangelie: as Apoplexies, Epilepſies, Convulſions, hot Fevers, Wormes, &c. Which by ignorant Parents are ſuppoſed to be the Vengeance of Witches. Yea and their Opinions and Conceits are confirmed and maintained by unſkilfull Phyſicians: according to the common Saieng; *Inſcitiæ Pallium Maleficium et Incantatio,* Witchcraft and Inchantment is the Cloke of Ignorance: whereas indeed evill Humors, and not ſtrange Words, Witches, or Spirits are the Cauſes of ſuch Diſeaſes. Alſo ſome of their Cattell periſh, either by Diſeaſe or Miſchance. Then they, upon whom ſuch Adverſities fall, weighing the Fame that goeth upon this Woman (hir Words, Diſpleaſure, and Curſes meeting ſo juſtly with their Misfortune) doo not onlie conceive, but are reſolved, that all their Miſhaps are brought to paſſe by hir onelie Means.

"The Witch on the other Side expecting hir Neighbors Miſchances, and ſeeing Things ſometimes come to paſſe according to hir Wiſhes,

Curſes, and Incantations (for Bodin himſelf conſeſſeth, that not above two in a hundred of their Witchings or Wiſhings take effect) being called before a Juſtice, by due Examination of the Circumſtances is driven to ſee hir Imprecations and Deſires, and hir Neighbors Harmes and Loſſes to concurre, and as it were to take effect: and ſo confeſſeth that ſhe (as a Goddes) hath brought ſuch Things to paſſe. Wherein, not onelie ſhe, but the Accuſer, and alſo the Juſtice are fowlie deceived and abuſed; as being thorough hir Confeſſion and other Circumſtances perſuaded (to the Injury of Gods Glorie) that ſhe hath doone, or can doo that which is proper onelie to God himſelfe.

"Another Sort of Witches there are, which be abſolutelie Cooſeners: Theſe take upon them, either for Glorie, Fame, or Gaine, to doo any Thing, which God or the Divell can doo: either for fortelling Things to come, bewraieng of Secrets, curing of Maladies, or working of Miracles."[15]

To this Chapter from Scot, which we have given entire, may be added the admirable Deſcription of the Abode of a Witch from the Pen

[15] *Diſcoverie of Witchcraft*, Vol. I, Chap. 3, Pp. 7-9.

of Spenſer, who as Warton hath obſerved, copied from living Objects, and had probably been ſtruck with ſeeing ſuch a Cottage, in which a Witch was ſuppoſed to live :

> "There is a gloomy hollow Glen ſhe found
> A little Cottage built of Sticks and Reeds
> In homely wiſe, and walled with Sods around;
> In which a Witch did dwell, in loathly Weedes.
> And wilful Want, all careleſſe of her Needes
> So chooſing ſolitarie to abide
> Far from all Neighbours, that her diviliſh Deeds
> And helliſh Arts from People ſhe might hide,
> And hurt far off unknowne whomever ſhe enviede."[16]

This very ſtriking Picture forever fixed the Character of the Habitation allotted to a Witch; thus in a ſingularly curious Tract, entitled, "Round about our Coal-Fire," publiſhed about the Cloſe of the ſeventeenth Century, and which details, in a pleaſing Manner, the Tradition of the olden Time, as a Source of Chriſtmas Amuſement, it is ſaid that "a Witch muſt be a hagged old Woman, living in a little rotten Cottage, under a Hill, by a Wood-ſide, and muſt be frequently ſpinning at the Door: ſhe muſt have a black Cat, two or three Broom-ſticks, an Imp

[16] Todd's *Spenſer*, iv, 480-1. *Faerie Queene*, B. iii, Cant. 7, Stan. 6.

or two, and two or three diabolical Teats to ſuckle her Imps."

Of the wonderful Feats which the various Kinds of Witches were ſuppoſed capable of performing, Scott has favored us with the following ſuccinct Enumeration. There are three Sorts of Witches he tells us, "one Sort can hurt and not helpe, the ſecond can helpe and not hurt, the third can both helpe and hurt. Among the hurtfull Witches there is one Sort more beaſtlie than any Kind of Beaſts, ſaving Wolves: for theſe uſually devour and eate young Children and Infants of their owne Kind. Theſe be they that raiſe Haile, Tempeſts, and hurtfull Weather; as Lightning, Thunder, &c. Theſe be they that procure Barrenneſſe in Man, Woman and Beaſt. Theſe can throwe Children in Waters, as they walk with their Mothers, and not be ſeene. Theſe can make Horſes kicke, till they caſt their Riders. Theſe can paſs from Place to Place in the Aire inviſible. Theſe can ſo alter the Mind of Judges, that they can have no Power to hurt them. Theſe can procure to themſelves and to others, Taciturnitie and Inſenſibilitie in their Torments. Theſe can bring trembling to the Hands, and ſtrike Terror into the Minds of them that apprehend them. Thefe can manifeft unto others, Things hidden and loft, and forefhow Things to come; and fee them as though they were prefent. Thefe can alter Men's Minds to inordinate Love or Hate. Thefe can kill whom they lift with Lightning and Thunder. Thefe can take away Man's Courage. Thefe can make a Woman mifcarrie in Childbirth, and deftroie the Child in the Mother's Wombe, without any fenfible Means either inwardlie or outwardlie applied. Thefe can with their Looks kill either Man or Beaft.

"Others doo write, that they can pull downe the Moone and the Starres. Some write that with wifhing they can fend Needles into the Livers of their Enemies. Some that they can transferre Corne in the Blade from one Place to another. Some, that they can cure Difeafes fupernaturallie, flie in the Aire, and danfe with Divels. Some write, that they can play the Part of *Succubus*, and contract themfelves to *Incubus*. Some faie they can tranfubftantiate themfelves and others, and take the Forms and Shapes of Affes, Woolves, Ferrets, Cowes, Affes, Horfes, Hogs, &c. Some fay they can keepe Divels and Spirits in the Likeneffe of Todes and Cats.

They can raiſe Spirits (as others affirme), drie up Springs, turn the Courſe of running Waters, inhibit the ſame, and ſtaie both Day and Night, changing the one into the other. They can go in and out at Awger Holes, and ſaile in an Egge Shell, a Cockle or Muſcle Shell, through and under the tempeſtuous Seas. They can bring Soules out of the Graves. They can teare Snakes in Pieces. They can alſo bring to paſs, that Churne as long as you liſt, your Butter will not come; *eſpecially, if either the Maids have eaten up the Cream; or the Good-wife have ſold the Butter before in the Market.*"[17]

The only material Acceſſion which the royal James has made to this curious Catalogue of the Deeds of Witchcraft, conſiſts in informing us, that theſe aged and decrepid Slaves of Satan, "make Picture of Waxe and Clay, that by the roaſting thereof, the Perſons that they bear the Name of, may be continually melted or dried away by continuall Sickneſſe;"[18] and his Mode of explaining how the Devil performs this Marvel, is a notable Inſtance both of his Ingenuity and his Eloquence. This Deed, he ſays, "is

[17] *Diſcoverie of Witchcraft*, Book i, Chap. 4, Pp. 9-11

[18] James's *Works*, by Winton, P. 116.

verie poſſible to their Maſter to performe; for although that Inſtrument of Waxe have no Vertue in that Turne doing, yet may he not very well, even by the ſame Meaſure, that his conjured Slaves melt that Waxe at the Fire, may be not, I ſay, at theſe ſame Times, ſubtily, as a Spirit, ſo weaken and ſcatter the Spirits of Life of the Patient, as may make him on the one Part, for Faintneſſe, to ſweat out the Humour of his Bodie, and on the other Part, for the not Concurrence of theſe Spirits, which cauſes his Digeſtion, ſo debilitate his ſtomache that this Humour radicall continually, ſweating out on the one Part, and no newe good ſucke being put in the Place thereof, for Lacke of Digeſtion on the other, he at laſt ſhall vaniſh away, even as his Picture will doe at the Fire? And that knaviſh and cunning Workman, by troubling him onely at ſometimes, makes a Proportion, ſo neere betwixt the working of the one and rhe other, that both ſhall end as it were at one Time."[19]

It remains to notice the Nature of the Compact or Bargain, which Witches were believed to enter into with their Seducer, and the Species of

[19] James's *Works*, by Winton, P. 117.

Homage which they were compelled to pay him; and here again we muſt have Recourſe to Scot, not only as the moſt compreſſed, but as the moſt authentic Detailer of this ſtrange Credulity of his Times. "The Order of their Bargaine or profeſſion," ſays he, "is double; the one ſolemne and publike; the other ſecret and private. That which is called ſolemne or publike, is where Witches come together at certaine Aſſemblies, at the Times prefixed, and doo not onelie ſee the Divell in viſible Forme; but confer and talke familiarlie with him. In which Conference the Divell exhorteth them to obſerve their Fidelitie unto him, promiſing them long Life and Proſperitie. Then the Witches aſſembled, commanded a new Diſciple (whom they call a Novice) unto him: and if the Divell find that young Witch apt and forward in the Renunciation of chriſtian Faith, in deſpiſing anie of the ſeven Sacraments, in treading upon Croſſes, in ſpetting at the Time of the Elevation, in breaking their Faſt on faſting Daies, and faſting on Sundaies: then the Devill giveth foorth his Hand, and the Novice joining Hand in Hand with him, promiſeth to obſerve and keepe all the Divels Commandments.

"This doone, the Divell beginneth to be more bold with hir, telling her plainlie, that all this will not ſerve his Turne: and therefore requireth Homage at hir Hands: yea he alſo telleth hir, that ſhe muſt grant him both hir Bodie and Soule to be tormented in everlaſting Fire; which ſhe yeeldeth unto. Then he chargeth hir to procure as manie. Men, Women and Children alſo, as ſhe can, to enter into this Societie. Then he teacheth them to make Ointments of the Bowels and Members of Children, whereby they ride in the Aire, and accompliſh all their Deſires. So as if there be anie Children unbaptized, or not garded by the Signe of the Croſſe, or Oriſons; then the Witches may and do catche them from their Mother's Sides in the Night, or out of their Cradles, or otherwiſe kill them with their Ceremonies; and after Buriall ſteale them out of their Graves, and ſeeth them in a Caldron, until their Fleſh be made potable. Of the thickeſt whereof they make Ointments, whereby they ride in the Aire; but the thinner Potion they put into Flaggons, whereof whoſoever drinketh, obſerving certain Ceremonies, immediatelie becometh a Maiſter or rather a Miſtreſſe in that Practice and Facultie.

"Their Homage with their Oth and Bargaine is received for a certeine Terme of Yeares; ſometimes forever. Sometimes it conſiſteth in the Deniall of the whole Faith, ſometimes in Part. And this is doone either by Oth, Proteſtation of Words, or by Obligation in writing, ſometimes ſealed with Wax, ſometimes ſigned with Blood, ſometimes by kiſſing the Divel's bare Buttocks.

"You muſt alſo underſtand, that after they have delicatelie banketted with the Divell and the Ladie of the Fairies; and have eaten up a fat Oxe, and emptied a Butt of Malmeſie, and a Binne of Bread at ſome noble Man's Houſe, in the Dead of the Night, nothing is miſſed of all this in the Morning. For the Ladie *Sibylla, Minerva*, or *Diana*, with a golden Rod ſtriketh the Veſſel and the Binne, and they are fully replenished againe." After mentioning that the Bullock is reſtored in the ſame magical Manner, he ſtates it as an "infallible Rule, that everie Fortnight, or at leaſt everie Month, each Witch muſt kill one Child at the leaſt for hir Part." He alſo relates from Bodin, that "at theſe magicall Aſſemblies, the Witches never faile to dance, and whiles they ſing and danſe, everie one hath a broome in hir Hand, and holdeth it up aloft."[20]

To theſe Circumſtances attending the Meetings of this unhallowed Siſterhood, King James adds, that Satan, in Order that "hee may the more vively counterfeit and ſcorne God, oft Times makes his Slaves to conveene in thoſe very Places, which are deſtinate and ordained for the conveening of the Servants of God (I meane by Churches) :—further, Witches oft times confeſſe, not only his conveening in the Church with them, but his occupying of the Pulpit."[21] For this Piece of Information James ſeems to have been indebted to the Confeſſions of Agnis Tompſon ; but he alſo relates, that the Devil, as ſoon as he has induced his Votaries to renounce their God and Baptiſm, "gives them his Marke upon ſome ſecret Place of their Bodie, which remaines ſoare unhealed, whileſt his next Meeting with them, and thereafter ever inſenſible, however it be nipped or pricked by any ;" a Seal of Deſtinction which, he tells us at the Cloſe of his Treatiſe, is of great Uſe in detecting them on their Trial, as "the finding of their Marke, and

20 *Diſcoverie of Witchcraft,* Book iii, Chap. 1, 2, Pp. 40-2.

21 *Works, apud* Winton, Pp. 112, 113.

the trying the Infenfiblenes thereof," was confi-dered as a pofitive Proof of their Craft. His Majefty, however, proceeds to mention another Mode of afcertaining their Guilt, terminating the Paragraph in a Manner not very flattering to his female Subjects, or very expreffive of his own Gallantry. "The other is," he tells us, "their fleeting on the Water: for as in a fecret Murther, if the dead Carkafe bee at any Time thereafter handled by the Murtherer, it will gufh out of Blood, as if the Blood were crying to the Heaven for Revenge of the Murtherer, God having appointed that fecret fupernaturall Signe, for Triall of that fecret unnaturall Crime, fo it appears that God hath appointed (for a fupernaturall Signe of the monftrous Impietie of Witches) that the Water fhall refufe to receive them in her Bofome, that have fhaken off them the facred Water of Baptifme, and wilfully refufed the Benefite thereof: No, not fo much as their Eyes are able to fhed Teares (threaten and torture them as you pleafe) while firft they repent (God not permitting them to diffemble their Obftinacie in fo horrible a Crime) albeit the Women-kind efpecially, be able otherwayes to fhed Teares at every light Occafion when they will, yea, although it were diſſembling like the Crocodiles."[22]

Such are the chief Features of this groſs Superſtition, as detailed by the Writers of the Period in which it moſt prevailed in this Country. *Scot* has taken infinite Pains in collecting, from every Writer on the Subject, the *minutiæ* of Witchcraft, and his Book is expanded to a thick Quarto, in Conſequence of his commenting at large on the Particulars which he had given in his initiatory Chapters, for the Purpoſe of their complete Refutation and Expoſure; a Work of great Labor, and which ſhows, at every Step, how deeply this Credulity had been impreſſed on the Subjects of Elizabeth. *James*, on the other Hand, though a Man of conſiderable Erudition, and, in ſome reſpects, of ſhrewd, good Senſe, wrote in Defence of this Folly, and, unfortunately for Truth and Humanity, the Doctrine of the Monarch was preferred to that of the Sage.

Fortunately the Time has arrived when the Belief of a King, or that of any other titled Perſonage, has very little Effect in faſtening upon the World at large any peculiar Opinions he may have formed upon any Subject not within the Province of Reaſon.

[22] King James's *Works, apud* Winton, Pp. 111, 135-6.

Spiritualifts and the Difciples of Mefmer have made the Difcovery that Witchcraft is fully explained by one or the other of the Myfteries taught by them. How much Truth there may be in the Affertion I cannot undertake to determine. But from a very limited Acquaintance with Myfteries in general, my Opinion is that the Application of Mefmerifm for the Explanation of Witchcraft, would partake very much of the Nature of applying one Abfurdity to the Explanation of another.

For the "thoufand and one" Examples of Witchcraft practiced by accufed Perfons in New England, an almoft exact Parallel may be found in Cafes which had previoufly occurred in Old England. And, in Proportion to the Number of Inhabitants in the refpective Countries, there were as many in New as in Old England who raifed their Voices againft Profecutions for the fuppofed Crime. Hence it is very obvious that mental Darknefs was as denfe in Old as in New England, at the Time of the Delufions of which we are fpeaking.

Superftition was then bounded only by the Limits of what was termed Civilization. The Light of Science for the laft two hundred Years has confiderably relieved Mankind from that deadly Incubus, and it is gratifying to believe that the March of Mind is onward and that a future of pure Light is before the World of Humanity. Like dark Spots on a Planet, fome Superftitions feem almoft as unaccountable, and their Removal appears about as difficult, fo long have we been accuftomed to tolerate them.

As late as 1668 it was afferted by an eminent Englifh Writer, a Member of the Royal Society,[23] that "*Atheifm* is begun in *Saducifm.* And thofe that dare not bluntly fay, *There* is NO GOD, content themfelves, (for a fair *Step*, and *Introduction*) to deny there are SPIRITS, or WITCHES. Which Sort of *Infidels*, though they are not ordinary among the *meer vulgar*, yet are they numerous in a little higher Rank of *Underftandings.* And thofe that know anything of the World, know, that moft of the loofer *Gentry*, and the fmall Pretenders to *Philofophy* and *Wit*, are generally Deriders of the *Belief* of *Witches*, and *Apparitions.*"

Hence there were but two Horns to the Dilemma in which every one found himfelf—he muft believe in Witchcraft and all the other

23 Jofeph Glanvill, in his *Blow at Modern Saducifm.*

degrading Attendants on that Belief, or he muſt be viewed and ſcorned as an Atheiſt, and as an Unbeliever in everything that was good!

It was difficult for People to diſtinguiſh between Miracles and Witchcraft, eſpecially when the moſt learned Men,[24] in Order to make the Miracle of the Aſcent of the Saviour appear reaſonable, argued that "He went as far towards Heaven as he could on Foot, even to the Top of Mount Olivet." And when Elijah was to faſt forty Days, "that there might be no Waſte of miraculous Power, God would have him eat a double Meal before entering upon the Term of faſting!" With ſuch wretched Abſurdities were the Minds of People of that Time enſlaved. The Superſtitions of the Greeks and Romans were not greater. And although there is a ſteady Progreſs in intellectual Improvement, and a Time is believed to be approaching when the World will be as free from the Cheats and Impoſtures of the preſent Day, as ſome of the preſent Day are of thoſe of previous Ages; yet it is in a Meaſure diſcouraging, when we ſee the Thouſands enſnared by ſuch tranſparent Jugglery

[24] Spencer's *Diſcourſe concerning Prodigies*, London, 1665.

as that which has peopled the Salt Lake Regions, and drawn other Thousands in our Midst to witness Feats that never did nor never will happen, except in the deluded Brains of those who desire to be thus deluded.

MEMOIR OF THE AUTHOR.

COTTON MATHER was born in Boſton, February 12th, 1662-3. In his Youth he was remarkable for his Progreſs in Knowledge, and ſoon became extenſively known for his varied Acquirements. At the Age of Twelve he entered Harvard College, and graduated in due Courſe. He was thrice married: 1ſt, when in his twenty-fourth Year, to Abigail, Daughter of Col. John Phillips, of Charleſtown; 2d, to Widow Elizabeth Hubbard, Daughter of Dr. John Clark; and 3d, to Lydia, Widow of Mr. John George, Daughter of the Rev. Samuel Lee, ſometime of Briſtol in Rhode Iſland. By the laſt Wife he had no Children, but by the others he had fifteen, nine of which were by the firſt.

The Father of Mr. Mather was Dr. Increaſe Mather, Paſtor of the North Church, of Boſton, of whom the Biographer of the former remarks, that, "as Preſident of Harvard College, by whoſe printed compoſures both Latin and Engliſh, and by whoſe Agency in the Courts of three Monarchs for his afflicted Country, have rendered him univerſally known."

His Mother was Maria, Daughter of Mr. John Cotton of Boſton, a Name as intimately aſſociated with the Hiſtory of New England as any other. And judging from the Portraits of the Grandſire and Grandſon, there was a very ſtrong Reſemblance of the one to the other.

Mr. Mather began to preach in 1680, and his firſt Sermon was delivered in Dorcheſter, on the 22d of Auguſt of that Year. In the following February he was invited to become an Aſſiſtant to his Father in the North Church in Boſton, which Invitation he accepted. About two Years later he was unanimouſly choſen Paſtor by the ſame Church, but was not ordained until May, 1684; his Ordination probably being deferred on Account of his Youth; being at the Time of his Ordination but twenty-one Years and three Months old. On that Occaſion he received the Right Hand of Fellowſhip from the venerable Mr. John Eliot, of Roxbury.

At an early Age he began to keep a Diary, and from the Paſſages we have from it we are convinced that its Entries were dictated by an honeſt Mind, and that Duplicity and evil Intentions could never find an abiding Place therein; that his ſole Aim was Goodneſs, and a ſtrong Deſire to lead a life of Purity, is manifeſt throughout.

Mr. Mather commenced Author at the Age of 23, and continued his Publications to the Year of his Deceafe; extending over a Period of about forty-two Years. In that Time he is faid by his Biographer to have iffued 383 Books; thus averaging about nine each Year. But many of his *Books* would in thefe Days be called Pamphlets, as they confifted of only a few Pages—a very few indeed containing Pages fufficient to give them the Character of a Book. A Lift of thefe 383 Works is given in his Life by his Son, but it is known to be incomplete. The Lift is very deficient in Refpect to the Titles of the Works, alfo, infomuch that their Contents cannot be determined from them.

There are feveral Biographies of Dr. Cotton Mather, all drawn mainly from that by his Son, Dr. Samuel Mather. An Abridgment of this was publifhed in England in 1744, in a fmall 12mo, by David Jennings. Mr. Jennings was inftigated to undertake the Abridgment by Dr. Ifaac Watts; the latter having confulted with Mr. Mather previoufly, and obtained his Confent to let his Work appear in an Abridgment. In giving his Confent for the abridged Edition, he thus apologizes for the original Undertaking: "The Life of my Father, as you have it in your Hands, was a youthful Attempt;[26] though I now plainly difcern my Defects in it, and am forry to

[26] He was only 23 when the Work was publifhed, which is indeed an Apology for its crude Style of Compofition.

ſee ſuch a Number of them, yet I can look on it with ſome Comfort; partly from a Conſciouſneſs of my honeſt Meaning in it, and partly becauſe I find ſeveral worthy Perſons approve of many Things in it, and have done me the Honour of expreſſing themſelves favourable about it."

The Mode of writing Biography has very much changed ſince the Life of Dr. Mather was firſt written. Thoſe written previous to, and at that Period, at leaſt many of them, might be reduced in Bulk from five to ſeven-eighths, without omitting anything of Value. This Remark is applicable to other Performances of that Time, and to ſome in theſe as well.

It may be juſtly ſaid of Cotton Mather, that he was one of the moſt remarkable Men of the Age in which he lived; not only remarkable on one, but on many Accounts; and for none, perhaps, more than for his wonderful Precociouſneſs, or the early Intuitiveneſs of his Mind. His Memory was likewiſe very extraordinary. The Acquirement of Knowledge ſeems to have been with him accompliſhed almoſt without Effort; and his Writings ſhow that they were generally drawn from the Storehouſe of his Mind, where, from Reading and Obſervation, they had been from Time to Time depoſited. Authors who write from this Source alone are generally diffuſe, and wanting in thoſe very eſſential and minute Particulars, which in theſe Days conſtitute ſo important a Part of every

Man's Writings. His Style is very peculiar; and no One who is acquainted with the Writings of "famous Thomas Fuller," can hardly doubt that Cotton Mather attempted to make that Writer's Compofition a Model for his own. Still he falls confiderably fhort of Fuller in his Attempts at witty Conceits; in them the latter is always happy, while the former often fails.

His Ability for acquiring Languages has probably been furpaffed by but very few, and he is faid to have been Mafter of more Languages than any other Perfon in New England in his Time. Thofe, efpecially the Latin, it muft be confeffed, he made a moft unreafonable Ufe of, bringing in Paffages from them at all Times, as though every Body underftood them, as well as himfelf.

So far as we now remember, Dr. Douglafs feems to have been the Author of the Fafhion or Practice, fo much of late Years in Vogue, of reviling Cotton Mather. It has been carried to fuch an Extent in fome Quarters, that any One who prefumes to mention his Name, does it at the Peril of coming in for a Share of Obloquy and Abufe himfelf. Some not only charge him with committing all Sorts of Errors and Blunders, but they bring againft him the more ferious Charge of mifreprefenting Matters of Fact. Now it would be well for thofe who bring thofe Charges to fcrutinize their own Works. It may be, if they cannot fee anything pedantic, puerile or falfe in them themfelves, others may come in

Contact with Errors even worſe than thoſe of Stupidity.

It is not to be denied that the Mind of Dr. Mather was ſingularly conſtituted; and whoever ſhall undertake an Analyſis of it will find a more difficult Taſk, we apprehend, than thoſe have found who content themſelves with nothing further than vituperative Denunciations upon its Productions. We owe a vaſt Deal to Cotton Mather; eſpecially for his hiſtorical and biographical Works. Were theſe alone to be ſtruck out of Exiſtence it would make a Void in theſe Departments of our Literature, that would probably confound any who affect to look upon them with Contempt. Even Dr. Douglaſs, although he has ſomewhere aſſerted, that, to point out all the Errors in the *Magnalia*, would be to copy the whole Book, is nevertheleſs, much indebted to him for Facts in many Parts of the very Work in which he has made that Statement; hence it would be very bad Logic that would not charge Dr. Douglaſs with copying Errors into his Work, knowing them to be Errors. It would be very eaſy for us to point to ſome Writers of our own Time equally obnoxious to the ſame plain Kind of Argument. And a late Writer of very good Standing has, with great apparent Deliberation ſaid, that, "it is impoſſible to deny, that the Reputation of Cotton Mather has declined of late Years." This, of courſe, was his Belief; but it ſtrikes us as very ſingular, that that ſame Author, ſhould, at the ſame Time, make the largeſt Book on the Life of a Man, in ſuch a *State of Decline*, that had hitherto appeared! But we are under no Concern for the Reputation of Cotton Mather, even in the Hands of his Enemies, and we have no Intention of ſetting up a ſpecial Defence of him or his Writings. We are willing the latter ſhould paſs for exactly what they are worth. All we deſign to do is to caution thoſe a little who need Caution, and ſave them, if we may, from having the Windows in their own Houſes broken, bythe very Miſſiles they themſelves have thrown.

But ſo far from the *Reputation* of Dr. Mather being in a *Decline*, his Writings have never been ſo much ſought after as at the preſent Time! So much ſo that even Reprints of ſuch of them as have been made are at once taken up, and at high Prices. Twenty Years ago, the *Magnalia* did not command above eight or ten Dollars, while Copies are at preſent rarely to be had for five Times their former Price. Reference is had to the original Edition, of courſe. This can hardly be taken as an Indication of a declining Reputation. The Style in all his Works, though peculiar to himſelf, is neverthelefs attractive, and never tedious, although often upon tedious Subjects. In Point of Scholarſhip, he was not excelled by any in the Country, and would not ſuffer by a Compariſon with the beſt of his Time in England.

The Charge of exceſſive Credulity has been brought againſt Dr. Mather, as though that Trait of Character were peculiar to him alone. There does not appear to be any Juſtice in ſingling him out as reſponſible for all the Credulity in the Country. That he was credulous no One will deny, nor will it be denied that he was ſurrounded by a credulous Community, the great Majority of which were equally credulous, and he was made to ſpeak for them. Hence he has become conſpicuous while others are nearly or quite forgotten. All Men are credulous in ſome Way and upon certain Things. Belief and Credulity are much the ſame. The Degree of Evidence required to convert the latter into the former has never been ſettled; nor can it be until all Minds are of the ſame Capacity. It requires a large Amount daily of Credulity to enable us to live in the tolerably good Opinion of our Companions in and out of Doors everywhere. Diſmiſs all of that liberal Sentiment from our Minds and we ſhould be diſmiſſed by the moſt of our Friends.

In the Reprints of ſome of the Works of Dr. Mather great Injuſtice has been done him, while, at the ſame Time, a Cheat has been put upon the Public. One Inſtance may be here given. In the Year 1815 there appeared a tolerably neat Edition of the *Chriſtian Philoſopher*,[27] in a Duodecimo of 324 Pages, printed at

27 Octavo, London, 1721. Printed for Emanuel Matthews, at the Bible *in* Pater-Noſter-Row.

Charleftown, for which a Copyright appears to have been taken out. On a curfory Examination we can difcover no Ground for copyrighting this Edition, except for making it unlike the Original in one Refpect only, namely, Omiffion of Important Matter. As an Example of the Omiffions the following may be taken: "We read of Heaven *giving Snow like Wool.* I have known it *give a Snow of Wool.* In a Town of *New England,* called *Fairfield,* in a bitter fnowy Night, there fell a Quantity of Snow, which covered a large frozen Pond, but of fuch a *woolen* Confiftence, that it can be called nothing but *Wool.* I have a Quantity of it, that has been thefe many Years lying by me."

Now, in the Edition of 1815, this important Paffage is entirely omitted! If Dr. Mather was impofed upon by fome ignorant and mifchievous Wight, that has nothing to do in excufing a Deception on the Part of a Publifher, who contracts to reprint a Work without any Refervation. If an Editor or Publifher thinks to fave the Credit of his Author by falfifying his Text, he can only be fure of one Thing, and that is, to bring difcredit upon himfelf.

I muft here difmifs the *Chriftian Philofopher;* but in another Work by our Author, of an earlier Date,[28] there is a fingular Story of Snow which may be noticed here: "It was credibly

[28] *Appendix Touching Prodigies* to his *Convention Sermon* of May 23, 1689.

affirmed, that in the Winter of the Year 1688, there fell a *Red Snow*, which lay like Blood on a Spot of Ground, not many Miles from Boſton; but the Diſſolution of it by a Thaw, which within a few Hours melted it, made it not capable of lying under the Contemplation of ſo many *Witneſſes* as it might be worthy of."

As the *Red Snow* did not come under the Doctor's immediate Obſervation, he has ſpoken of it with commendable Caution; inſomuch that his Character for Credulity is not enhanced by the Relation of the Story. Moreover it is a well known Fact that *Red Snow* is often mentioned by reputable northern Travelers. But we have never heard that it *ſnowed Wool* at any other Time and Place, except as mentioned above.

In 1692, Dr. Mather publiſhed his *Wonders of the Inviſible World.* This was the authorized Account of the Witchcraft Caſes of that Time. In this he laid himſelf open to the Charge of Credulity, which, it cannot be denied, has been pretty well ſuſtained ever ſince.

Many have reproached Dr. Mather, as though he was the Author of that diſmal and awful Deluſion. This is ſingularly unjuſt. He was himſelf one of the deluded; and this is the only Charge that can lie againſt him relative to it. All the World then believed in Witchcraft, and People entered into it according to their Temperament and Circumſtances. The Deluſion was not a Native of New England, but an Exotic from the Father Land; and it had been well if this had been the only one imported thence. Even when Profecutions had ceafed, there was not a Ceffation of a Belief in the Reality of Witchcraft; its Progrefs was ftayed from a very different Caufe, as is now too well known to be entered into or explained. Even to the prefent Day there are Thoufands who believe in its Reality; and that Belief can only be extirpated by the Progrefs of genuine Knowledge. Within our Remembrance we could ride from Bofton in a fingle Day, with a very moderate Horfe, into a New England Town where the Belief in Witchcraft was very general, and where many an old Horfe-fhoe could have been feen nailed to half the Bedfteads in the Town to keep away thofe imaginary Mifcreants who came riding through the Air upon Broomfticks, or acrofs the Lots upon the Back of fome poor old Woman, who perhaps from fome Malady had not left her Houfe for Years. How much fhort of a Day's Ride by Steam or otherwife it would now be neceffary to take to reach a Place where the Belief exifts, we fhall not undertake, but leave for others to determine.

Cotton Mather was undoubtedly the moft prominent Author who wrote on Witchcraft, and in the full Belief of it, in his Time, in this Country; this Circumftance accounts for his being fingled out by "one *Robert Calef*," who attacked him with fome Succefs, even then, in his Book which he called *More Wonders of the Invifible World*, &c., which he publifhed in London, in a quarto Volume, in the Year 1700. In his Book, Calef ftyles himfelf "Merchant, of *Bofton* in *New England*." Now in the Abfence of Proof to the contrary, it may not be unfair to prefume, that Calef iffued his Work quite as foon as he dared to, and quite as foon as public Opinion would tolerate a Work which had for its Aim a deadly Blow againft a Belief in the imaginary Crime of Witchcraft. For we know that as foon as Calef's Book did appear, fome of Dr. Mather's Friends came out with another Work againft that Author, from the Title of which alone its Contents can pretty well be judged of. It is *Some few Remarks upon a Scandalous Book written by one Robert Calef.* But this Book and its Authors are alike almoft unknown, while Calef occupies a confpicuous Place among the Benefactors of Mankind.

The foreign Correfpondence of Dr. Mather was very extenfive; "fo that," fays his Son, "I have known him at one Time to have above *fifty* beyond Sea." Among his Correfpondents were many of the moft learned and famous Men in Europe; as SIR RICHARD BLACKMORE, MR. WHISTON, DR. DESAGULIERS, MR. PILLIONERE, DR. FRANCKIUS, WM. WALLER, DR. CHAMBERLAIN, DR. WOODWARD, DR. JURIN, DR. WATTS, &c., &c. In a Letter which he wrote in 1743 Dr.

Watts ſays, "he had enjoyed a happy Correſpondence with Dr. Cotton Mather, for nearly twenty Years before his Death, as well as with the Rev. Mr. Samuel Mather, his Son, ever ſince."

In 1710 came out a Book from the Pen of our Author, which he entitled "*Bonifacius:* An Eſſay upon the Good to be deviſed by thoſe who would anſwer the great End of Life." In this Work are many good Maxims and Reflections, but its Popularity has probably been very much enhanced by what Dr. Franklin has ſaid of it. Dr. Mather was well acquainted with Franklin when the latter was a young Man; and when Franklin was an old Man, in the Year 1784, in writing to Samuel Mather, Son of our Subject, he thus alludes to it in his happy Style: "When I was a Boy, I met with a Book entitled, *Eſſays to do Good,* which I think was written by your Father. It had been ſo little regarded by a former Poſſeſſor, that ſeveral Leaves of it were torn out; but the Remainder gave me ſuch a Turn of thinking, as to have an Influence on my Conduct through Life; for I have always ſet a greater Value on the Character of a *Doer of Good* than on any other Kind of Reputation." In the ſame Letter is to be found that often told anecdote of an Interview he once had with Dr. Mather. This too, that it may loſe nothing at our Hands, we will give in the Author's own Words: "You mention being in your ſeventy-eighth Year; I am in my ſeventy-ninth; we are grown old together. It is now more than ſixty Years ſince I left Boſton, but I remember well both your Father and Grandfather; having heard them both in the Pulpit, and ſeen them in their Houſes. The laſt Time I ſaw your Father was in the Beginning of 1724, when I viſited him after my firſt Trip to Pennſylvania. He received me in his Library, and on my taking leave ſhowed me a ſhorter Way out of the Houſe through a narrow Paſſage, which was croſſed by a Beam overhead. We were ſtill talking as I withdrew, he accompanying me behind, and I turning partly towards him, when he ſaid haſtily, '*ſtoop, ſtoop!*' I did not underſtand him, till I felt my Head hit againſt the Beam. He was a Man that never miſſed any Occaſion of giving Inſtruction, and upon this he ſaid to me, '*You are young, and have the World before you;* STOOP *as you go through it, and you will miſs many hard Thumps,*' This Advice, thus beat into my Head, has frequently been of Uſe to me; and I often think of it, when I ſee Pride mortified, and Misfortunes brought upon People by their carrying their Heads too high." This Moral, ſo eſſentially good in itſelf, does not need the high Recommendation of a Franklin, though but for him it would not, probably, have been brought to the Knowledge of every Youth who has learned, or may yet learn to read.

The *Eſſay to do Good* has paſſed through many Editions, but how many it would be difficult to determine. It was ſeveral Times reprinted in London, once as late as 1807, under the Superviſion of the diſtinguiſhed Dr. George Burder. In this Country its Iſſue has not been confined to the Preſs of one Denomination.

It may be too much a Cuſtom for us to dwell on the Errors and Misfortunes of People while living; and to err, on the other Hand, by making their Characters appear too perfect after they have paſſed away; eſpecially if they have been ſufficiently conſpicuous in Life to require a written Memorial of them after their Deceaſe. Though Dr. Cotton Mather had Enemies while living, his Memory has been purſued with more Malignity ſince his Death, than has happened to that of moſt Men; and, as we conceive, without ſufficient Reaſon, and which could only be warranted by the moſt undoubted Proofs, that he has purpoſely led us into Errors, and that he acted falſely on the moſt important Occaſions; and that, finally, he was too bad a Man to make any Acknowledgment of all this, though conſcious of it when he took his final Departure with the Meſſenger of his laſt Summons.

He had vituperative Enemies in his Lifetime, from ſome of whom he received abuſive anonymous Letters. Theſe Letters he carefully filed, and wrote upon them ſimply the Word "Libels," which was all the Notice he took of them. It was an invariable Rule with him, that if he was obliged to ſpeak of the evil Ways of People to do ſo in Humility and Regret, and never in a Manner that could be offenſive. In his Diary he ſpeaks of *Pride* as a Sin, "which all are ſubject unto, and more eſpecially Miniſters," and ſtill more eſpecially was it "the beſetting Sin of young Miniſters." Had he lived in theſe latter Days that Annoyance might have been leſs on Account of its Univerſality.

Mr. Mather's Time was that of long Sermons, and we are told that he uſually cloſed them with the *fourteenth* Diviſion of his Diſcourſes. Beſides his Labors on Sundays, he ſometimes preached eleven Sermons in one Week beſides. He alſo conſtantly had Students with him whom he inſtructed in various Branches of Knowledge.

Of the Part Dr. Mather took in State Affairs, his Biographer ſays he was not at Liberty to omit an Account, although it was a difficult Section; and that he was "more at a Loſs what to do about it than any one in the whole Book." The Author, however, concludes, as he could not omit the Subject, to treat it "in ſuch a general Way as to give no One any Offence." And as it is a *Section* of the Doctor's Life of great Intereſt, it will here be given entire in the Language of his Biographer, who wrote ſo near the Time that his Account carries its Readers back to thoſe ſtirring Scenes of the Revolution of 1688, and furniſhes a Picture, life-like, of the every-day Manners of our Fathers on that memorable and novel Event.

The Account follows: "My Country is very ſenſible that in the Year 1688 (when one of the moſt wicked Kings was on the Britiſh Throne) Andros and his Crew were very violent, illegal and arbitrary in their Proceedings. I need not give any Narrative of their Managements here, becauſe there has been an Account of them already given to the World.[29]

"While theſe roaring Lions and ranging Bears were in the midſt of their Ravages; it was in the Month of April when we had News by the Edges concerning a Deſcent made upon England by the Prince of Orange for the Reſcue of the Nations from Slavery and Popery; then a ſtrange Diſpoſition entred into the Body of our People to aſſert our Liberties againſt the arbitrary Rulers that were fleecing them. But it was much feared by the more ſenſible Gentlemen at Boſton, that an unruly Company of Soldiers, who had newly deſerted the Service in which they had bin employed for the Eaſtern War, by the gathering of their Friends to them to protect them from the Governor, who, they tho't, intended Nothing but Ruine to them, would make a great Stir, and produce a bloody Revolution. And therefore the principal Gentlemen in Boſton met with Mr. Mather to conſult what was beſt to be done; and they all agreed, if poſſible, that they would extinguiſh all Eſſays in our People to an

[29] Referring doubtleſs to *New England Juſtified*, publiſhed by the Author's Grandfather.

Inſurrection; but that, if the country People to the Northward, by any violent Motions puſh'd on the Matter ſo far as to make a Revolution unavoidable, then to prevent the ſhedding of Blood by an ungoverned Multitude, ſome of the Gentlemen preſent would appear in the Head of what Action ſhould be done; and a Declaration was prepared accordingly.

"On April 18, the People were ſo driving and furious, that unheaded they began to ſeize our public Oppreſſors: upon which the Gentlemen aforeſaid found it neceſſary to appear that by their Authority among the People the unhappy Tumults might be a little regulated. And thro' the Goodneſs of God, although the whole Country were now in a moſt prodigious Ferment and Thouſands of exaſperated People in Arms were come into Boſton, yet there was no Manner of Outrage committed; only the *Public Robbers* that had lorded it over Us were confined. 'Twas then Mr. Mather appeared—He was the Inſtrument of preventing the Exceſſes into which the *Wrath of Man* is too ready to run. He came, and like a Neſtor or Uliſſes reaſoned down the Paſſions of the Populace. Had he liſped a Syllable for it, perhaps the People would, by a ſudden Council of War, have try'd, judg'd and hang'd thoſe ill Men who would have treated him otherwiſe. Neverthleſs he ſet himſelf both publicly and privately to hinder the Peoples proceeding any further than to reſerve the Criminals for the Juſtice of the Engliſh Parliament.

"Now the Perſecution which was intended for Mr. Mather was diverted; for on that very Day that he was to be committed to *Half a Year's Impriſonment*,[30] thoſe that would have wrong'd him were juſtly taken into Cuſtody: And yet ſo generous was he as not only to expoſe his Name, but even his Life unto the Rage of the Multitude for the ſaving of ſome that would have hurt him: Tho' he had no Thanks for his Ingenuity.

"The Spirit which acted him in theſe Matters is expreſſed in a Sermon he preached to the Convention of the Colony from 2 Chron. xv, 2. It was printed under the Title of, *The Way to Proſperity*.

"A few Days before this, the Inhabitants of Boſton aſſembling together to chuſe Repreſentatives for that Convention, it was apprehended, that the different Perſuaſions of the People, about the next Steps to be taken for our Settlement, would have produced a Fury near to Bloodſhed; and therefore Mr. Mather was deſired to be at their Meeting. The Meeting began with dangerous and horrible Paroxyſms, which when he ſaw, he upon it made an affectionate and moving Speech to them, at which many fell into Tears and the whole Body of the People preſent im-

30 It would ſeem from this that Mr. Mather had been proſecuted, tried and ſentenced to ſix Months' Impriſonment, but there appears no other Intimation of it.

mediately united in the Methods of Peace Mr. Mather propoſed unto them."

From what is here given it is not difficult to decide whether Mr. Mather was for or againſt Andros and his Government. It is a Pity the Author did not reviſe his Work in his mature Years, as well for his own Credit as a Writer as for his Father's Honor. It is the pooreſt of all his Performances.

The Convention before mentioned having ordered a Thankſgiving, for that "It having pleaſed the God of Heaven to mitigate his many Frowns upon us in the Summer paſt, with a Mixture of ſome very ſignal Favours, and in the midſt of Wrath ſo far to remember Mercy; That our Indian Enemies have had a Check put upon their Deſigns of Blood and Spoil, ... and eſpecially in the happy Acceſſion of Their Majeſties our Sovereigns, King William and Queen Mary to the Throne. It was therefore ordered that Thurſday the 19th of December, 1689, be kept as a Day of Thankſgiving." This Order was dated Dec. 3d, 1689.

On this Thankſgiving Occaſion Dr. Mather delivered one of his moſt elaborate Sermons, occupying, with a brief Appendix, *ſixty-two Pages*, 16mo. In it he refers to the Revolution under various Heads; comparing it to an Earthquake, one having then but recently nearly deſtroyed Lima. And more terrible Pictures it would be difficult to conceive of, than he has drawn, of what would have been the Condition of New England, had not the Revolution ſucceeded.

The next great Event in the Life of our Author was the Witchcraft Deluſion. As his own Work upon that memorable Chapter in New England's Annals is to be given in Connection with this Biography, any Apology or Remarks upon his Participation in it from the Editor could be of but little Value or Intereſt, no more will be done here than to extract what his Biographer-Son has favored the World with. That, as will be ſeen, is apologetical, and is far better told than the Part he took in the Revolution. It is indeed about all that can be ſaid in Extenuation of one thus circumſtanced.

"The Summer of the Year 1692, was a very doleful Time unto the whole Country. The Devils, after a moſt præternatural Manner by the dreadful Judgements of Heaven took a bodily Poſſeſſion of many People in our Salem, and Places adjacent; where the Houſes of the poor People began to be filled with the Cries of Perſons tormented by evil Spirits. There ſeemed to be an execrable Witchcraft in the Foundation of this wondrous Affliction; many Perſons of divers Characters being accuſed, apprehended, proſecuted upon the *Viſions* of the afflicted.

"Mr. Mather, for his Part, was always afraid of proceeding to convict and condemn any Perſon as a *Confederate* with afflicting Dæmons upon ſo feeble an Evidence as a *ſpectral Repreſentation.* Accordingly he ever teſtified againſt it both publicly and privately, and particularly in his Letter to the Judges, he beſought them that they would by no Means admit it; and where a conſiderable Aſſembly of Miniſters gave in their Advice about the Matter, he not only concurred with the Advice but he drew it up.

"Neverthelеſs, on the other Side, he ſaw in moſt of the Judges a charming Inſtance of Prudence and Patience; and as he knew their exemplary Piety, ſo he obſerved the Agony of Soul with which they ſought the Direction of Heaven, above moſt other of our People who were enchanted into a raging, railing and unreaſonable Diſpoſition. For this Cauſe, tho' Mr. Mather could not allow the Principles ſome of the Judges had eſpouſed, he could not however but ſpeak honorably of their Perſons on all Occaſions; and his Compaſſion upon the Sight of their Difficulties, which Compaſſion was raiſed by his Journeys to Salem the chief Seat of theſe diabolical Vexations, cauſed him ſtill to go to the Place. And merely for this Reaſon, ſome mad People in the Country (from whom one or two credulous Foreigners have dared to publiſh the abuſive Story) under a Faſcination of their *Spirits* equal to what our *Energumens* had upon their *Bodies*, reviled Mr. Mather as if he had been the Doer of the hard Things that were done in the Proſecution of the Witchcraft.

"In this evil Time Mr. Mather offered at the Beginning, that if the *poſſeſſed People* might be ſcattered far aſunder, he would ſingly provide for ſix of them; and he with ſome others would ſee whether without more bitter Methods, *Prayer* and *Faſting* would not put an End unto theſe heavy Trials: But his offer was not accepted.

"However for a great Part of the Summer he did almoſt every Week ſpend a Day by himſelf in the Exerciſe of a ſecret Faſt before the Lord. On theſe Days he cried unto God, not only for his own Preſervation from the Malice and Power of the evil Angels, but alſo for a good Iſſue of the Calamities in which he had permitted the evil Angels to enſnare the miſerable Country. He alſo beſought the Lord that he would enable him, proſper, direct, and accept him in publiſhing ſuch Teſtimonies for Him as were proper, and would be ſerviceable unto his Intereſts on that Occaſion.

"And that a right Uſe might be made of the prodigious Things which had been happening among us, he now compoſed and publiſhed his Book entituled, *The Wonders of the Inviſible World*, which was reprinted ſeveral Times in London: In the Preface he ſpeaks of, '*the heart-breaking Exerciſes*', he went thro' in writing it. There was a certain Diſbeliever of Witchcraft who wrote againſt this Book; but as the Man is dead, his Book died long before him.[31]

31 Calef's *More Wonders of the Inviſible World* is the Book aſſerted to have died *long before its Author.* However that might have been

"But having ſpoken eno' of the more publick Witchcraft, I think I will hale in here an Account of a Witchcraft happening in one private Family at Boſton, two or three Years before the general one. 'Twas, I think, in the Year 1689, in the Winter, that ſeveral Children belonging to a pious Family at the South End of Boſton were horribly bewitch'd and poſſeſſed.[32]

"Mr. Mather tho't it would be for the Glory of God, if he not only pray'd with as well as for the Children; but alſo took an Account of the extraordinary Symptoms which attended them, with ſufficient Atteſtations to confound the Sadduciſm and Atheiſm of a debauched Age."

An Accouut of the Caſe of the Goodwin Family was ſeparately publiſhed, and was noticed with Commendation by the "learned and pious Baxter," which has been often referred to as a Proof that other great Men, as well as Mr. Mather, were Believers in Witchcraft.

The Novelty and Singularity of a Thing was no Cauſe of its Rejection by Mr. Mather, and we next find him advocating Inoculation for the Small-pox; and, according to his Biographer he was the Cauſe of its Introduction into this

conſidered 30 Years after the *More* Wonders was printed, it is far from being Dead in this Age. Remarks will be more in Order when we come to *introduce* the Work.

[32] It is rather ſurpriſing that the Author ſhould ſpeak doubtfully of the Caſe of this Family as to the Time of its Occurrence, when the *Magnalia* was at his Hand, giving Date and Details of the Affair. See that Work, B. vi, Page 71.

Country. But in that, as in many other Things, too much is claimed for him. I have elſewhere given a Hiſtory of its being put in Practice in Boſton.[33]

In 1714 Dr. Mather was choſen a Member of the Royal Society of London; upon which Event his Biographer remarks: "The Reſpect which the Royal Society paid him, did alſo very much encourage him, and fortify him in his Eſſays to do Good, while it added to the ſuperior Circumſtances in which he was placed above the Contempt of Envious Men."

This laſt remark will apply to ſome of our own Times; who, if their Power were equal to their Envy, few beſides themſelves would be allowed to poſſeſs much in the Way of Honors without their Permiſſion. It was probably on this Occaſion, that ſome Individuals circulated the Report that the Doctor was not a Member of the Royal Society. Whereupon a Letter from the Secretary of that Society was produced, in which this Paſſage occurs: "As for your being choſen a Member of the Royal Society, that has been done, both by the Council and Body of the Society: only the Ceremony of Admiſſion is wanting; which you being beyond Sea, cannot be performed." This having been promulgated, the envious Detractors were ſilenced in that Age, and it is rather ſurpriſing that Ignorance and Malice ſhould attempt to revive it in this. As Mr. Mather never viſited

[33] See *Hiſtory and Antiquities of Boſton*, 561-3.

England, he of courſe never attended a Meeting of the Royal Society. But this did not affect his Memberſhip. That this did not affect his Memberſhip may be mentioned as pretty good Evidence, the Fact that ſome of his Works were ſoon after publiſhed in London, in the beſt Style of the Day, having appended to his Name in their Title-Pages, "D. D. and Fellow of the Royal Society." Now ſuch an Aſſumption would have been an Offence of a ſerious Character, had it been merely an Aſſumption; and a Rebuke would have gone forth from the Royal Society, and would ever ſince have been a Matter of Record and Notoriety. But Nothing of the Kind is heard ot, plainly becauſe Dr. Mather ſtood right with the Records of the Royal Society.

Nobody will charge the REV. THOMAS PRINCE with Inſincerity in what he has ſaid of his Colaborers, and HE ſays, "Dr. Cotton Mather, though born and conſtantly reſiding in this remote corner of America, has yet for near theſe forty Years made ſo riſing and great a Figure in the learned World, as has attracted to him while alive, the Eyes of many at the furtheſt Diſtance; and now deceaſed, can't but raiſe a very general Wiſh to ſee the Series, and more eſpecially the domeſtic Part of ſo diſtinguiſhed a Life exhibited. His printed Writings ſo full of Piety and various Erudition, his vaſt Correſpondence, and the continual Reports of Travellers who had converſed with him, had ſpread his Reputation into other Countries. And when, about fourteen Years ago, I travelled abroad, I could not but admire to what Extent his Fame had reached, and how inquiſitive were Gentlemen of Letters to hear and know of the moſt particular and lively Manner, both of his private Converſation and public Performances among us."

Dr. Colman ſpeaks in the higheſt Terms of Dr. Mather, in his Funeral Sermon. "His printed Works," he ſays, "will not convey to Poſterity, nor give to Strangers a juſt Idea of the real Worth and great Learning of the Man." To this and a great deal more equally commendatory, Mr. Prince ſubſcribes in theſe Words: "Every one who intimately knew the Doctor will readily aſſent to this Deſcription."

It would be difficult, perhaps, to produce an Example of Induſtry equal to that of which we are ſpeaking. In one Year, it is ſaid he kept ſixty Faſts and twenty vigils, and publiſhed fourteen Books—all this beſides performing his miniſterial Duties; which, in thoſe Days, were Something more than *nominal.* He kept a Diary, which has been extenſively uſed by ſome of his Biographers, but we have not ſought after it, as it is ſaid to be ſcattered in different Places! How this happened we have not been informed. Notwithſtanding he publiſhed ſo many Works, he left nearly as much unpubliſhed in Manuſcript; the principal Part of which is entitled, *Biblia Americana,* or *The Sacred Scriptures of the Old and New Teſtament Illuſtrated.* For the Publication of this Work

Propoſals were iſſued ſoon after its Author died, but Nothing further ſeems to have been done about it. Of the *Biblia Americana*, the Doctor's Son remarks, "*That* is a Work, the writing of which is enough conſtantly to employ a Man, unleſs he be a Miracle of Diligence, the Half of the three Score Years and ten, the Sum of Years allowed to us."

It remains now to mention the Book by which Dr. Mather is beſt known, and which will make his Name prominent through all coming Time—the Reader's Mind is already in Advance of the Pen—the *MAGNALIA CHRISTI AMERICANA.* This was printed in London, in 1702, in a moderate ſized folio Volume, the Aggregate of its Pages being 794. It is chiefly a Collection of what the Author had before printed on hiſtorical and biographical Subjects. The Value of its Contents has been variouſly eſtimated. Some decrying it below *any* Value, while others pronounce it "the only Claſſic ever written in America." At the Hazard of incurring the Charge of Stupidity, we are of the decided Opinion that it has a Value between thoſe Extremes. But we have ſufficiently expreſſed our Mind on the Value of the Author's Works before.

Until about the Year 1853 there had been but two Editions of the *Magnalia.* The Work was then ſtereotyped and iſſued in two handſome octavo Volumes, by the late Mr. Silas Andrus, extenſively known among the Publiſhers of the

Country. This was the third Edition of the Work, and poſſeſſed the Advantage of Tranſlations of the Quotations from the dead Languages with which the Work abounds. About two Years later an Edition was iſſued from the ſame ſtereotype Plates, and was accompanied by an Index. This, tho' very incomplete, rendered the Work much more valuable. The Plates we are informed are now in the Hands of Mr. William Gowans of New York, who is preparing to bring out a ſumptuous Edition of it with a new and complete Index. About thirty-two Years had elapſed between the ſecond and third Editions, though they were by the ſame Publiſher. The Date of the ſecond was 1820.

Unfortunately, this Edition was printed from a Copy of that in Folio, which had not the Errata, and conſequently abounds with all the Errors contained in the original Edition. To thoſe who do not underſtand the Matter, this printing an Edition of the *Magnalia* without correcting its Errata, may ſeem to incur for the Publiſher ſevere Reprehenſion. But the Truth appears to be, that the Copy uſed in printing the new Edition had not the complete Errata attached to it; and that in Fact, but very few Copies of the original Edition can be found to which it is attached. Now we account for its Rarity in this Way. Dr. Mather, living in Boſton while his Work was printing in London, could make no Corrections while it was paſſing through the Preſs; but when he received his

Copies afterwards, he found ſo many Errors that he was induced to print an extra Sheet of Corrections. This extra Sheet may not have been ſtruck off until moſt of the Copies of the *Magnalia* which had been ſent to New England were diſtributed. Thus we account for the rare Occurrence of Copies of the *Magnalia* containing the Errata; and hence we think the Publiſher of the Edition of 1820 ſhould not be too ſeverely cenſured. That our Solution is correct, we would mention that out of a great many Copies of the folio Edition imported by ourſelf and others from England, not one of them contained the Errata in Queſtion.

On the laſt Page of the *Magnalia*, the following are the laſt three Lines: "ERRATA. Reader, Carthagenia was of the Mind, that unto thoſe *three Things* which the Ancients held impoſſible, there ſhould be added this *fourth*, to find a Book printed without *Erratas*. It ſeems the Hands of *Briareus*, and the Eyes of *Argus* will not prevent them." And the additional Errata of which we have been ſpeaking, the Author thus prefaces: "The *Holy Bible* it ſelf, in ſome of its Editions, hath been affronted with ſcandalous Errors of the *Preſs-work*; and in one of them, they ſo printed thoſe Words, Pſalms cxix, 161, '*Printers have perſecuted me*,'" &c.

When the *Magnalia* was publiſhed, Dr. Mather's old Schoolmaſter, among others, wrote commendatory Poetry upon it, which was, according to the

Faſhion of the Day, inſerted in its introductory Pages. The following brief Specimen by TOMPSON may not be thought inappropriate to be extracted here:

"Is the bleſſ'd MATHER Necromancer turn'd,
To raiſe his Country's Father's Aſhes urn'd?
Eliſha's Duſt, Life to the Dead imparts;
This Prophet by his more familiar Arts,
Unſeals our Hero's Tombs, and gives them Air;
They riſe, they walk, they talk, look wondrous fair;
Each of them in an Orb of Light doth ſhine,
In Liveries of Glory moſt divine.
When ancient Names I in thy Pages meet,
Like Gems on Aaron's coſtly Breaſt-plate ſet;
Methinks Heaven's open, while great Saints deſcend,
To wreathe the Brows, by which their Acts were penned."

Few Miniſters preached a greater Number of Funeral Sermons than Dr. Mather; and when he died his Cotemporaries ſeemed to have vied with each other in performing the ſame Office for him. Several of their Sermons were printed. Some of theſe with their quaint Titles are now before us. Foremoſt among them appears that of the excellent MR. PRINCE; he entitled his, "The Departure of ELIJAH lamented.—A Sermon occaſioned by the great and publick Loſs in the *Deceaſe* of the very REVEREND and LEARNED COTTON MATHER, D.D., F.R.S., and Senior Paſtor of the *North Church* in Boſton. Who left this Life on *Feb.* 13th, 1727,8. The Morning after he finiſhed the LXV. Year of his Age." From 2 Kings ii, 12, 13. The Imprint of this Sermon is, "BOSTON in *New England:* Printed for *D. Henchman,* near the Brick Meeting Houſe in Cornhill. MDCCXXVIII."

The running Title of Dr. Colman's Sermon on the ſame Occaſion is "The holy Walk and glorious Tranſlation of bleſſed *ENOCH.*" His Text was Gen. v. 24. It would be difficult to find anything of the Kind, either before or ſince, which, in our Judgment, is ſuperior to this Diſcourſe of Dr. Colman; but valuable as it is, we cannot introduce Extracts from it here. His Alluſion, however, to the then paſt and preſent State of Things connected with his Subject, is ſo happy that we cannot overlook it.

"Dr. Mather's Brethren in the Miniſtry here," he ſays, "are bereaved and weak with him. God has taken their Father as well as his, from their Heads this Day. He was a Paſtor in the Town when the eldeſt of the preſent Paſtors were but Children, and long before moſt of them were born. They are weak indeed when he that is now ſpeaking to them is the *firſt* in Years among them, in all reſpects elſe the leaſt," &c.

The REV. JOSHUA GEE, Colleague with Dr. Mather, alſo preached a Funeral Sermon on his departed Friend, entitled, "ISRAEL'S *Mourning* for AARON'S *Death.*" In this Diſcourſe there is the following important Note: "Within a few Months paſt, we have been called to lament the Deaths of two ſuch aged Servants of the LORD. The Rev. *Mr. Samuel Danforth* of Taunton, who died Nov.

14. And my honored Father-in-law, the Rev. *Mr. Peter Thatcher* of Milton, who died Dec. 17, 1727: while the Days of mourning were ſcarce over in this Town for my dearly beloved Friend and Brother, the Rev. *Mr. William Waldron*, who died Sept. 11, 1727."

Dr. Mather's Son and Biographer, "SAMUEL MATHER, M. A., and Chaplain at CASTLE WILLIAM," alſo preached a Funeral Sermon on his Father's Death. "The *Departure* and *Character* of ELIJAH conſidered and improved," was its running Title. Only about five Years before, the deceaſed preached a Sermon on the Death of his Father; in the Title-page of which, when printed, inſtead of the Author's Name we read, "By one who, as a SON with a *FATHER*, ſerved with him in the Goſpel."

Dr. Mather died inteſtate, and the Order of the Judge of Probate for the Diſtribution of his Eſtate is as follows: "One third to his Widow, Lydia Mather; two ſingle Shares or fourth Parts to Samuel Mather, Clerk, only ſurviving Son, and one Share each to the Reſt of his Children, viz., Abigail Willard, deceaſed, Wife of Daniel Willard, alſo deceaſed, their Children and legal Repreſentatives, and Hannah Mather, Spinſter." Dated, 25th May, 1730.

The Portrait now in Circulation of Dr. Mather was engraved from a beautiful *Mezzotinto*, half Size, with the following Inſcription underneath it:

"Cottonus Matherus S. Theologiæ Doctor Regiæ Societatis Londiniensis Socius, et Eccelsiæ apud Bostonum Nov = Anglorum nuper Præpositus.

Ætatis Suæ LXV. MDCCXXVII.

P. Pelham ad vivum pinxit ab Origin Fecit."

Those desiring genealogical Information of the Mather Family, I must refer to the Pedigree printed in Connection with Dr. I. Mather's *Brief History*, &c.

The Wonders of the Invisible World.

OBSERVATIONS

As well *Hiſtorical* as *Theological*, upon the NATURE, the NUMBER, and the OPERATIONS of the

DEVILS.

Accompany'd with

I. Some Accounts of the Grievous Moleſtations, by DÆMONS and WITCHCRAFTS, which have lately annoy'd the Countrey; and the Trials of ſome eminent *Malefactors* Executed upon occaſion thereof: with ſeveral Remarkable *Curioſities* therein occurring.

II. Some Counſils, Directing a due Improvement of the terrible things, lately done, by the Unuſual & Amazing Range of EVIL SPIRITS, in Our Neighbourhood: & the methods to prevent the *Wrongs* which thoſe *Evil Angels* may intend againſt all ſorts of people among us; eſpecially in Accuſations of the Innocent.

III. Some Conjectures upon the great EVENTS, likely to befall, the WORLD in General, and NEW-ENGLAND in Particular; as alſo upon the Advances of the TIME, when we ſhall ſee BETTER DAYES.

IV. A ſhort Narrative of a late Outrage committed by a knot of WITCHES in *Swedeland*, very much Reſembling, and ſo far Explaining, *That* under which our parts of *America* have laboured!

V. THE DEVIL DISCOVERED: In a Brief Diſcourſe upon thoſe TEMPTATIONS, which are the more Ordinary *Devices* of the Wicked One.

By Cotton Mather.

Boſton Printed, and Sold by *Benjamin Harris*, 1693.

PUbliſhed by the Special Command of His EXCELLENCY, the Governour of the Province of the Maſſachuſetts-Bay in New-England.

The Wonders of the Invifible World:

Being an Account of the

T R Y A L S

OF

Several Witches,

Lately Excuted in

N E W - E N G L A N D:

And of feveral remarkable Curiofities therein Occurring.

Together with,

I. Obfervations upon the Nature, the Number, and the Operations of the Devils.

II. A fhort Narrative of a late outrage committed by a knot of Witches in *Swede-Land*, very much refembling, and fo far explaining, that under which *New-England* has laboured,

III. Some Councels directing a due Improvement of the Terrible things lately done by the unufual and amazing Range of *Evil-Spirits* in *New-England*.

IV. A brief Difcourfe upon thofe *Temptations* which are the more ordinary Devices of Satan.

By *COTTON MATHER*.

Publifhed by the Special Command of his EXCELLENCY the Govenour of the Province of the *Maffachufetts-Bay* in *New-England*.

Printed firft, at *Boftun* in *New-England;* and Reprinted at *London*, for *John Dunton*, at the *Raven* in the *Poultry*. 1693.

Imprimatur.
Decmb. 23.
1692.

EDMUND BOHUN.[34]

34 Edmund Bohun was himſelf a Writer of conſiderable Note. The Work by which he is beſt known is probably that entitled *The Character of Queen Elizabeth*, a ſizable Octavo, printed in 1693. His Writings are ſaid to be Voluminous, yet but few of them are met with at this Day. One of the firſt Gazetteers was by him in a thick Octavo, 1688. He does not, however, call it a Gazetteer, but a Geographical Dictionary. His Deſcriptions compare ſingularly with thoſe of the ſame Articles in Works of later Times: as for Example, he ſays Columbus diſcovered America in 1499. All the Notice Boſton receives at his Hands is at the Cloſe of an Article on Boſton in Lincolnſhire—"there is another Place in *New England* of the ſame Name." Under the Head of New England he gives it a much larger Notice; calls New England *a Colony*, "and they have built ſeven great Towns, the Chief of which is Boſton, which in 1670, had fifty Sail of Ships belonging to it." He was Author of a Life of Biſhop Jewell, and was living in 1700.

THE

Author's Defence.

IS, as I remember, the Learned *Scribonius*,[35] who reports, that One of his Acquaintance, devoutly making his Prayers on the behalf of a Person molested by *Evil Spirits*, received from those *Evil Spirits* an horrible Blow over the Face: And I may my self expect not few or small Buffetings from Evil Spirits, for the Endeavours wherewith I am now going to encounter them. I am far from Insensible that at this extraordinary Time of the *Devils coming down in great Wrath upon us*, there are too many Tongues and Hearts thereby *set on fire of Hell;* that the various Opinions about the Witchcrafts which of later Time have troubled us, are maintained by some with so much cloudy Fury, as if they could never be suf-

35 The only known Work of "Learned Scribonius" is that entitled *De Compositione Medicamentorum* Liber," the best Edition of which is said to be that of Padua, 1655, in 4to, with Notes by Rhodius. He was of Rome in the Time of Claudius. His Book is a Sort of Repository of Prescriptions, which Prescriptions were of about as much value, in a medical Point of View, as later ones were for determining what Persons were Witches. *Nouveau Dict. Hist. a Lyon*, 1804.

O

ficiently ſtated, unleſs written in the Liquor wherewith Witches uſe to write their Covenants; and that he who becomes an Author at ſuch a time, had need be *fenced with Iron, and the Staff of a Spear*. The unaccountable Frowardneſs, Aſperity, Untreatableneſs, and Inconſiſtency of many Perſons, every Day gives a viſible Expoſition of that paſſage, *An evil ſpirit from the Lord came upon Saul;* and Illuſtration of that Story, *There met him two poſſeſſed with Devils, exceeding fierce, ſo that no man might paſs by that way.* To ſend abroad a Book, among ſuch Readers, were a very unadviſed thing, if a Man had not ſuch Reaſons to give, as I can bring, for ſuch an Undertaking. Briefly, I hope it cannot be ſaid, *They are all ſo;* No, I hope the Body of this People, are yet in ſuch a Temper, as to be capable of applying their Thoughts, to make a *Right Uſe* of the ſtupendous and prodigious Things that are happening among us: And becauſe I was concern'd, when I ſaw that no abler Hand emitted any Eſſays to engage the Minds of this People, in ſuch holy, pious, fruitful Improvements, as God would have to be made of his amazing Diſpenſations now upon us. THEREFORE it is, that One of the Leaſt among the Children of *New-England*, has here done, what is done. None, but *the Father, who ſees in ſecret*, knows the Heart-breaking Exerciſes, wherewith I have compoſed what is now [vi] going to be expoſed, leſt I ſhould in any one thing miſs of doing my deſigned Service for his Glory, and for his People; but I am now ſomewhat comfortably aſſured of his favourable acceptance; and, *I will not fear; what can a Satan do unto me!*[36]

Having performed ſomething of what God required, in labouring to ſuit his Words unto his Works, at this Day among us, and therewithal handled a Theme that has been ſometimes counted not unworthy the Pen, even of a King,[37] it will eaſily be perceived, that ſome ſubordinate Ends have been conſidered in theſe Endeavours.

I have indeed ſet myſelf to countermine the whole PLOT of the Devil, againſt *New-England*, in every Branch of it, as far as one of my *darkneſs*, can comprehend ſuch a *Work of Darkneſs*. I may add, that I have herein alſo aimed at the Information and Satisfaction of Good Men in another Country, a thouſand Leagues off, where I have, it may be, more, or however, more conſiderable Friends, than in *My Own;* And I do what I can to have that Country, now, as well as always, in the beſt Terms with *My Own*. But while I am doing theſe things, I have been driven a little to do ſomething likewiſe for myſelf; I mean, by taking off the falſe Reports, and hard Cenſures about my Opinion in theſe Matters, the *Parters Portion* which my *purſuit of Peace* has procured me among the *Keen*. My hitherto *unvaried Thoughts* are here publiſhed; and I believe,

36 This Self Complacency is ſomewhat ſurpriſing, conſidering this Record was made while above an hundred poor Wretches were lying in the Jails of Boſton and Salem!

37 The Author doubtleſs has Reference to the *Dæmonology* of James I. See *Introduction*.

they will be owned by moſt of the Miniſters of God in theſe Colonies; nor can amends be well made me, for the wrong done me, by other ſorts of *Repreſentations.*

In fine; For the *Dogmatical*[38] part of my Diſcourſe, I want no Defence; for the *Hiſtorical* part of it, I have a very Great One; the Lievtenant-Governour of *New-England*[39] having peruſed it, has done me the Honour of giving me a *Shield*, under the Umbrage whereof I now dare to walk Abroad.

38 It is ſaid that the learned Joſeph Glanvil was made a "Fellow of the Royal Society" for an elaborate Treatiſe which he wrote on "The Vanity of *Dogmatizing*." If that entitled the ſaid Joſeph to be thus diſtinguiſhed, no one ought any longer to queſtion our Author's Claim to the ſame Diſtinction. Glanvil was as earneſt a Defender of Witchcraft in his Time as Doctor Mather was a few Years later; and his Books, like this of the Doctor's, are entirely neglected except by the curious Inveſtigators of the Progreſs of Society.

39 Thus ſpeaking of New England was ſtrictly correct then, though it reminds us of what our Engliſh Brethren uſed to ſay at a much later Period in Reference to Boſton,—ſpeaking of it as "the Colony of Boſton," "the Colony of New England," &c.

[vii] Reverend and Dear SIR,

YOU very much gratify'd me, as well as put a kind Reſpect upon me, when you put into my hands, your elaborate and moſt ſeaſonable Diſcourſe, entituled, The Wonders of the Inviſible World. *And having now peruſed ſo fruitful and happy a Compoſure, upon ſuch a Subject, at this Juncture of Time; and conſidering the place that I hold in the Court of* Oyer *and* Terminer, *ſtill labouring and proceeding in the Trial of the Perſons accuſed and convicted for Witchcraft, I find that I am more nearly and highly concerned than as a meer ordinary Reader, to expreſs my Obligation and Thankfulneſs to you for ſo great Pains; and cannot but hold myſelf many ways bound, even to the utmoſt of what is proper for me, in my preſent publick Capacity, to declare my* ſingular Approbation *thereof. Such is your Deſign, moſt plainly expreſſed throughout the whole; ſuch your Zeal for God, your Enmity to Satan and his Kingdom, your Faithfulneſs and Compaſſion to this poor People; ſuch the Vigour, but yet great Temper of your Spirit; ſuch your Inſtruction and Counſel, your* Care of Truth, *your Wiſdom and Dexterity in allaying and moderating that among us, which needs it; ſuch your clear diſcerning of Divine*

Providences and Periods, now running on apace towards their Glorious Iſſues in the World; and finally, ſuch your good News of The Shortneſs of the Devil's Time,[40] *that all Good Men muſt needs deſire, the making of this your Diſcourſe publick to the World; and will greatly rejoyce, that the* Spirit of the Lord *has thus enabled you to* lift up a Standard *againſt the Infernal Enemy, that hath been* coming in like a Flood upon us. *I do therefore make it my particular and earneſt Requeſt unto you, that as ſoon as may be, you will commit the ſame unto the* PRESS *accordingly. I am,*

Your aſſured Friend,

WILLIAM STOUGHTON.[41]

40 This has Reference to what is intimated in that Part of the preſent Volume, entitled—"The Devil Diſcovered."

41 The Writer of the above Letter (Judge Stoughton) was 61 Years old at the Time; and it may reaſonably be ſuppoſed was in the full Enjoyment of his intellectual Faculties. And as he was one of the ableſt Men of his Day, ſuch an Indorſement of the Author's Work was no mean Fortification from behind which to defend even a very bad Cauſe. Stoughton lived ſeveral Years after he had ceaſed trying Witches,—dying in 1701, at the the Age of 70. He was Son of Mr. Iſrael Stoughton of Dorcheſter, a Captain in the Pequot War, and Colonel afterwards in the Parliamentary Army in England.

[viii][42] I LIVE by *Neighbours* that force me to produce theſe undeſerved Lines. But now, as when Mr. Wilſon[43] beholding a great Muſter of Souldiers, had it by a Gentleman then preſent, ſaid unto him, *Sir, I'll tell you a great Thing: Here is a mighty Body of People; and there is not* Seven *of them all, but what loves Mr.* Wilſon. That gracious Man preſently and pleaſantly re-ply'd: *Sir, I'll tell you as good a thing as that; here is a mighty Body of People, and there is not ſo much as* One *among them all, but Mr.* Wilſon *loves him.* Somewhat ſo: 'Tis poſſible, that among this Body of People, there may be few that love the Writer of this Book; but give me leave to boaſt ſo far, there is not one among all this Body of People, whom this *Mather* would not ſtudy to ſerve, as well as to love. With ſuch a *Spirit of Love,* is the Book now before us written: I appeal to all *this World;* and if *this* World will deny me the Right of acknowledging ſo much, I appeal to the *other*, that it is *not written with an Evil Spirit:* for which cauſe I ſhall not wonder, if *Evil Spirits* be exaſperated by what is written, as the *Sadduces* doubtleſs were with what was diſcourſed in the Days of our Saviour. I only demand the *Juſtice*, that others *read* it, with the ſame Spirit where-with I *writ* it.

42 No Paging thus far in the Original.

43 John Wilſon, the firſt Miniſter of Boſton. He died Auguſt 7th 1667, aged 78. See the *Biographical Dictionaries*, Eliot and Allen.

[5] ENCHANTMENTS ENCOUNTER'D.

§ I. IT was as long ago, as the Year 1637, that a Faithful Minifter of the Church of *England*, whofe Name was Mr. *Edward Symons*,[44] did in a Sermon afterwards Printed, thus exprefs himfelf; 'At *New-England* 'now the Sun of Comfort begins to appear, and 'the glorious Day-Star to fhow it felf;—*Sed* '*Venient Annis Sæculæ Seris*, there will come 'Times in after Ages, when the *Clouds will over-* '*fhadow and darken the Sky there.* Many now 'promife to themfelves nothing but fucceffive 'Happinefs there, which for a time through God's

[44] Probably the fame whofe Name appears in fundry Publications as *Symmonds*. Walker, *Sufferings of the Clergy*, ii, 361, calls him *Simmons*, and fpeaks very dubioufly of him, as though he was a great Sufferer both for, and for not being a Puritan. See alfo *Ibid*, Part i, 67, 68. Neale, *Hift. Puritans*, ii, 19-20. Brooks's *Lives*, iii, 110-11. Old Thomas Fuller was well acquainted with Mr. Symonds, and gives an Anecdote or two about him in his *Worthies*, and tells us he died *about* 1649, in London. He died in 1649, in London.

'Mercy they may enjoy; and I pray God, they 'may a long time; but in this World there is no 'Happineſs perpetual.' An *Obſervation*, or I had almoſt ſaid, an *Inſpiration*, very diſmally now verify'd upon us! It has been affirm'd by ſome who beſt knew *New-England*, That the World will do *New-England* a great piece of Injuſtice, if it acknowledge not a meaſure of Religion, Loyalty, Honeſty, and Induſtry, in the People there, beyond what is to be found with any other People for the Number of them.[45] When I did a few years ago, publiſh a Book, which mentioned a few memorable Witchcrafts, committed in this country; the excellent *Baxter*, graced the Second Edition of that Book, with a kind Preface, wherein he ſees cauſe to ſay, *If any are Scandalized, that* New-England, *a place of as ſerious Piety, as any I can hear of, under Heaven, ſhould be troubled ſo much with Witches; I think, 'tis no wonder: Where will the Devil ſhow moſt Malice, but where he is hated, and hateth moſt:* And I hope, the Country will ſtill deſerve and anſwer the Charity ſo expreſſed by that Reverend Man of God.[46] Whoſoever travels over this Wilderneſs,

[45] As to the *Loyalty* profeſſed, *that* required pretty ſtrong Aſſurances on the Part of the prominent Men of New England, to gain it Credence among the Officials in Old England; for not long before an Agent of Maſſachuſetts had aſſerted that "the Acts of that Colony were not ſubject to any reëxamination in England;" and a Writer of 1688 that "till the Reign of his preſent Majeſty, Jame II, New England would never ſubmit to any Governor ſent from England, but lived like a Free State."

[46] The Work here referred to

will ſee it richly beſpangled with Evangelical Churches, whoſe Paſtors are holy, able, and painful Overſeers of their Flocks, lively Preachers, and vertuous Livers; and ſuch as in their ſeveral Neighbourly Aſſociations, have had their Meetings whereat Eccleſiaſtical Matters of common Concernment are conſidered: *Churches*, whoſe Communicants have been ſeriouſly examined about their Experiences of Regeneration, as well as about their Knowledge, and Belief, and blameleſs Converſation, before their Admiſſion to the Sacred Communion; although others of leſs but hopeful Attainments in Chriſtianity are not ordinarily deny'd Baptiſm for themſelves and theirs; Churches, which are ſhye of uſing any thing in the Worſhip of God, for which they cannot ſee a Warrant of God; but with whom yet the Names of *Congregational*, *Preſbyterian*, *Epiſcopalian*, or *Antipædobaptiſt*, are ſwallowed up in that of *Chriſtian;* Perſons of all thoſe Perſwaſions being taken into our [6] Fellowſhip, when viſible Goodlineſs has recommended them:[47] Churches, which uſually do within themſelves manage their

was publiſhed in 1689. Its Title abridged was—*Memorable Providences relating to Witchcrafts and Poſſeſſions, with ſome Sermons annexed.* Its being republiſhed and commended by Baxter, only ſhows that that great Man was as much benighted as the Reſt of the World, ſo far as the Matter in Hand is concerned.

[47] This Amalgamation of Creeds was often attempted by the more catholic Portion of the Community, and as often defeated by the more dogmatical Part, from the firſt Setttlement of the Country to this Day. When there is but one Intereſt to ſerve, and when that one Intereſt is agreed upon, then will a millenial Amalgamation of Creeds take place.

own Difcipline, under the Conduct of their Elders; but yet call in the help of *Synods* upon Emergencies, or Aggrievances; *Churches*, Laftly, wherein Multitudes are growing ripe for Heaven every day; and as faft as thefe are taken off, others are daily rifing up. And by the Prefence and Power of the Divine Inftitutions thus maintained in the Country. We are ftill fo happy, that I fuppofe there is no Land in the Univerfe more free from the debauching, and the debafing Vices of Ungodlinefs. The Body of the People are hitherto fo difpofed, that *Swearing*, *Sabbath-breaking*, *Whoring*, *Drunkennefs*, and the like, do not make a Gentleman, but a Monfter, or a Goblin, in the vulgar Eftimation.[48] All this notwithftanding, we muft humbly confefs to our God, that we are miferably degenerated from the firft Love of our Predeceffors; however we boaft our felves a little, when Men would go to trample upon us, and we venture to fay, *Wherein foever any is bold (we fpeak foolifhly) we are bold alfo.*[49]

[48] In the firft Settlement of the Country, when all, or nearly all were within the Pale of the Church, or directly under the Eye of the Minifter or a Magiftrate, there was little Need of Courts, Conftables and Lawyers; but in a growing Community thofe Days muft neceffarily be of limited Duration; and as there never was a Community of any confiderable Numbers, in Times paft, wherein there were no *Monfters or Goblins*, fuch a Community is hardly to be expected to be found in Time to come.

[49] It is human Nature for People to refent being taunted with Faults, whether they be real or imaginary. While a few will reform the many will cling to Error with more Tenacity. Thus the enormous Crime of Slavery—few Men were fo depraved by Nature as to maintain that it was right, in reafoning with themfelves; while, when it was harfhly denounced as a vile Felony,

The firſt Planters of theſe Colonies were a choſen Generation of Men, who were firſt ſo pure, as to diſreliſh many things which they thought wanted Reformation elſewhere; and yet withal ſo peaceable, that they embraced a voluntary Exile in a ſqualid, horrid, *American* Deſart,[50] rather than to live in Contentions with their Brethren. Thoſe good Men imagined that they ſhould leave their Poſterity in a place, where they ſhould never ſee the Inroads of Profanity, or Superſtition: And a famous Perſon returning hence, could in a Sermon before the Parliament profeſs, *I have been ſeven Years in a Country, where I never ſaw one Man drunk, or heard one Oath ſworn, or beheld one Beggar in the Streets all the while.*[51] Such great Perſons as *Budæus*, and others, who miſtook Sir *Thomas Moor's* UTOPIA, for a Country really exiſtent, and ſtirr'd up ſome Divines charitably to

Anger took the Place of Reaſon in the Slaveholder, and here Argument only ſerved to rivet firmer the Fetters intended to be removed. So it was with other leſs heinous Offences.

50 This and ſimilar Expreſſions were in frequent Uſe by nearly all the early Writers on American Affairs. "In this Howling Wilderneſs," "in theſe goings down of the Sun," &c., &c.

51 This "famous Perſon" was Mr. Giles Firmin. See *N. E. Hiſt. and Gen. Reg.* iv, 11; *alſo* Felt, *Eccl. Hiſt. N. Eng.*, ii, 48. Nathaniel Ward has a very ſimilar Paſſage: "I thank God that I have lived in a Colony of many thouſand Engliſh almoſt theſe twelve Years, am held a very ſociable Man, yet I may conſiderately ſay, I never heard but one Oath ſworne, nor never ſaw one Man drunk, nor never heard of three Women Adultereſſes in all this time, that I can call to mind."—*Simple Cobber,* 67, Pulſifer's *Edition,* 1843. The Reader will find much that is highly intereſting reſpecting the Worthies mentioned in this Note in Mr. J. Ward Dean's *Life of Nathaniel Ward,* now ready for Publication.

undertake a Voyage thither, might now have certainly found a Truth in their Miſtake; *New-England* was a true *Utopia*. But, alas, the Children and Servants of thoſe old Planters muſt needs afford many degenerate Plants, and there is now riſen up a Number of People, otherwiſe inclined than our *Joſhua's*, and the Elders that out-liv'd them. Thoſe two things our holy Progenitors, and our happy Advantages make Omiſſions of Duty, and ſuch Spiritual Diſorders as the whole World abroad is overwhelmed with, to be as provoking in us, as the moſt flagitious Wickedneſſes committed in other places; and the Miniſters of God are accordingly ſevere in their Teſtimonies: But in ſhort, thoſe Intereſts of the Goſpel, which were the Errand of our Fathers into theſe Ends of the Earth, have been too much neglected and poſtponed, and the Attainments of an handſome Education, have been too much undervalued, by Multitudes that have not fallen into Exorbitances of Wickedneſs; and ſome, eſpecially of our young Ones, when they have got abroad from under the Reſtraints here laid upon them, have become extravagantly and abominably Vicious. Hence 'tis, that the Happineſs of *New-England* has been but for a time, as it was foretold, and not for a long time, as has been deſir'd for us. A Variety of Calamity has long follow'd this Plantation; and we have all the Reaſon imaginable to aſcribe it unto the Rebuke of Heaven upon us for our manifold *Apoſtaſies*; we make no right uſe of our Diſaſters: If we do not, *Remember whence we are fallen, and repent, and do the firſt Works.* But yet our Afflictions may come under a further Conſideration with us: There is a further Cauſe of our Afflictions, whoſe due muſt be given him.

[7] § II. The *New-Englanders* are a People of God ſettled in thoſe, which were once the *Devil's* Territories; and it may eaſily be ſuppoſed that the *Devil* was exceedingly diſturbed, when he perceived ſuch a People here accompliſhing the Promiſe of old made unto our Bleſſed Jeſus, *That He ſhould have the Utmoſt parts of the Earth for his Poſſeſſion.*[52] There was not a greater Uproar among the *Epheſians*, when the Goſpel was firſt brought among them, than there was among, *The Powers of the Air* (after whom thoſe *Epheſians* walked) when firſt the *Silver Trumpets* of the Goſpel here made the *Joyful Sound.* The Devil thus Irritated, immediately try'd all ſorts of Methods to overturn this poor Plantation: and ſo much of the Church, as was *Fled into this Wilderneſs*, immediately found, *The Serpent caſt out of his Mouth a Flood for the carrying of it away.* I believe, that never were more *Satanical Devices* uſed for the Unſetling of any People under the

[52] Ideas ſimilar to theſe are often met with in the *Magnalia* and other Writings of the Author. But he was by no means ſingular in his Notions regarding the Devil. Moſt of the Divines of Dr. Mather's Day inculcated the ſame Sentiments, to ſay nothing of thoſe of a later Day.

Sun, than what have been Employ'd for the Extirpation of the *Vine* which God has here *Planted, Caſting out the Heathen, and preparing a Room before it, and cauſing it to take deep Root, and fill the Land, ſo that it ſent its Boughs unto the* Atlantic *Sea* Eaſtward, *and its Branches unto the* Connecticut *River* Weſtward, *and the Hills were covered with the ſhadow thereof.* But, All thoſe Attempts of Hell, have hitherto been Abortive, many an *Ebenezer* has been Erected unto the Praiſe of God, by his Poor People here; and, *Having obtained Help from God, we continue to this Day.* Wherefore the Devil is now making one Attempt more upon us; an Attempt more Difficult, more Surprizing, more ſnarl'd with unintelligible Circumſtances than any that we have hitherto Encountred;[53] an Attempt ſo *Critical*, that if we get well through, we ſhall ſoon Enjoy *Halcyon* Days with all the *Vultures* of Hell *Trodden under our Feet*. He has wanted his *Incarnate Legions* to Perſecute us, as the People of God have in the other Hemiſphere been Perſecuted: he has therefore drawn forth his more *Spiritual* ones to make an Attacque upon us. We have been adviſed by ſome Credible Chriſtians yet alive, that a Malefactor, accuſed of *Witchcraft* as well as *Murder*, and Executed in this place more than Forty Years ago, did then give Notice of, *An*

[53] This frank Acknowledgment that Witchcraft was "ſnarl'd" and "unintelligible," would ſeem to have been a ſufficient Reaſon for letting it alone. But Reaſon and Superſtition cannot exiſt together.

Horrible PLOT *against the Country* by WITCHCRAFT, *and a Foundation of* WITCHCRAFT *then laid, which if it were not seasonably discovered, would prbably Blow up, and pull down all the Churches in the Country.*[54] And we have now with Horror seen the *Discovery* of such a *Witchcraft!* An Army of *Devils* is horribly broke in upon the place which is the *Center*, and after a sort, the *First-born* of our *English* Settlements: and the Houses of the Good People there are fill'd with the doleful Shrieks of their Children and Servants, Tormented by Invisible Hands, with Tortures altogether preternatural. After the Mischiefs there Endeavoured, and since in part Conquered, the terrible Plague, of *Evil Angels*, hath made its Progress into some other places, where other Persons have been in like manner Diabolically handled. These our poor Afflicted Neighbours, quickly after they become *Infected* and *Infested* with these *Dæmons*, arrive to a Capacity of Discerning those which they conceive the *Shapes* of their Troublers; and notwithstanding the Great and Just Suspicion, that the *Dæmons* might Impose the *Shapes* of Innocent Persons in their *Spectral Exhibitions* upon the Sufferers, (which may perhaps prove no small part of the *Witch-Plot* in the issue) yet many of the Persons thus Represented, being Examined, several of

[54] It is not very clear to what particular Case the Author refers. See *Hist. and Antiqs. Boston*, 283, 309. "More than forty Years ago" is too indefinite for present historical Purposes.

them have been Convicted of a very Damnable *Witchcraft:* yea, more than One *Twenty* have *Confessed*, that they have Signed unto a *Book*, which the Devil show'd them, and Engaged in his Hellish Design of *Bewitching*, and *Ruining* our Land. *We* [8] know not, at least *I* know not, how far the *Delusions* of Satan may be Interwoven into some Circumstances of the *Confessions;* but one would think, all the Rules of Understanding Humane Affayrs are at an end, if after so many most Voluntary Harmonious *Confessions*, made by Intelligent Persons of all Ages, in sundry Towns, at several Times, we must not Believe the *main strokes* wherein those *Confessions* all agree: especially when we have a thousand preternatural Things every day before our eyes, wherein the *Confessors* do acknowledge their Concernment, and give Demonstration of their being so Concerned. If the Devils now can strike the minds of men with any *Poisons* of so fine a Composition and Operation, that Scores of Innocent People shall Unite, in *Confessions* of a Crime, which we see actually committed, it is a thing prodigious, beyond the Wonders of the former Ages, and it threatens no less than a sort of a Dissolution upon the World. Now, by these *Confessions* 'tis Agreed, *That* the Devil has made a dreadful Knot of *Witches* in the Country, and by the help of *Witches* has dreadfully increased that Knot: *That* these *Witches* have driven a Trade of Commissioning their *Confederate Spirits*, to do all sorts of Mischiefs to the

Neighbours, whereupon there have enſued ſuch Miſchievous conſequences upon the Bodies and Eſtates of the Neighbourhood, as could not otherwiſe be accounted for: yea, *That* at prodigious *Witch-Meetings*, the Wretches have proceeded ſo far, as to Concert and Conſult the Methods of Rooting out the Chriſtian Religion from this Country, and ſetting up inſtead of it, perhaps a more groſs *Diaboliſm*, than ever the World ſaw before. And yet it will be a thing little ſhort of *Miracle*, if in ſo *ſpread* a Buſineſs as this, the Devil ſhould not get in ſome of his Juggles, to confound the Diſcovery of all the reſt.[55]

§ III. Doubtleſs, the Thoughts of many will receive a great Scandal againſt *New-England*, from the Number of Perſons that have been Accuſed, or Suſpected, for *Witchcraft*, in this Country: But it were eaſie to offer many things, that may Anſwer and Abate the Scandal. If the Holy God ſhould any where permit the Devils to hook two or three wicked *Scholars* into *Witchcraft*, and then by their Aſſiſtance to Range with their *Poiſonous Inſinuations* among Ignorant, Envious, Diſcontented People, till they have cunningly decoy'd them into ſome ſudden *Act*, whereby the Toyls of Hell ſhall be perhaps inextricably caſt

[55] It has long been perfectly clear that the Devil *did get in his Juggles*, and that he *did* ſucceed, almoſt beyond Belief, in confounding the Underſtanding of the whole Community, and particularly that of our Author. Reſpecting Witchcraft in Sweden, &c., conſult Dr. Anthony Horneck's *Relation of the Swediſh Witches.*

over them: what Country in the World would not afford *Witches*, numerous to a Prodigy? Accordingly, The Kingdoms of *Sweden*, *Denmark*, *Scotland*, yea and *England* it ſelf, as well as the Province of *New-England*,[56] have had their Storms of *Witchcrafts* breaking upon them, which have made moſt Lamentable Devaſtations: which alſo I wiſh, may be *The Laſt*. And it is not uneaſie to be imagined, that God has not brought out all the *Witchcrafts* in many other Lands with ſuch a ſpeedy, dreadful, deſtroying *Jealouſie*, as burns forth upon ſuch *High Treaſons*, committed here in *A Land of Uprightneſs*: Tranſgreſſors may more quickly here than elſewhere become a Prey to the Vengeance of Him, *Who has Eyes like a Flame of Fire*, and, *who walks in the midſt of the Golden Candleſticks*. Moreover, There are many parts of the World, who if they do upon this Occaſion inſult over this People of God, need only to be told the Story of what happen'd at *Loim*, in the Duchy of *Gulic*, where a Popiſh Curate having ineffectually try'd many Charms to Eject the Devil out of a Damſel there poſſeſſed, he paſſionately bid the Devil come out of her into himſelf; but the Devil anſwered him, *Quid mihi Opus, eſt eum tentare, quem Noviſſimo die, Jure Optimo, ſum poſſeſſurus?* That is, *What need I meddle*

[56] It is not ſtrange that Engliſh Writers talk about the "Colony of Boſton," when our own beſt informed Natives ſpeak in this careleſs Manner about the "Province of New-England."

with one whom I am ſure to have, and hold at the Laſt-day as my own for ever!

[9] But beſides all this, give me leave to add, it is to be hoped, That among the Perſons repreſented by the *Spectres* which now afflict our Neighbours, there will be found *ſome* that never explicitly contracted with any of the *Evil Angels*. The Witches have not only intimated, but ſome of them acknowledged, That they have plotted the Repreſentations of *Innocent Perſons*, to cover and ſhelter themſelves in their Witchcrafts; now, altho' our good God has hitherto generally preſerved us from the Abuſe therein deſign'd by the Devils for us, yet who of us can exactly ſtate, *How far our God may for our Chaſtiſement permit the Devil to proceed in ſuch an Abuſe?* It was the Reſult of a Diſcourſe, lately held at a Meeting of ſome very Pious and Learned Miniſters among us, *That the Devils may ſometimes have a permiſſion to Repreſent an Innocent Perſon, as Tormenting ſuch as are under Diabolical Moleſtations: But that ſuch things are Rare and Extraordinary; eſpecially when ſuch matters come before Civil Judicature.*[57] The Opinion expreſſed with ſo much Caution and Judgment, ſeems to be the prevailing Senſe of many others, who are men Eminently Cautious and Judicious; and have both *Argument* and *Hiſtory* to Countenance them in it. It is *Rare*

[57] The ſerious Conſideration of this Poſtulate was the primary Cauſe of the Reaction which followed the Proſecutions. See Dr. I Mather's *Caſes of Conſcience.* MS. in the Editor's Poſſeſſion.

and Extraordinary, for an Honeſt *Naboth* to have his Life it ſelf Sworn away by two *Children of Belial*, and yet no Infringement hereby made on the Rectoral Righteouſneſs of our Eternal Sovereign, whoſe *Judgments are a Great Deep*, and who *gives none Account of His matters*.[58] Thus, although the Appearance of Innocent Perſons in *Spectral Exhibitions* afflicting the Neighbourhood, be a thing *Rare and Extraordinary;* yet who can be ſure, that the great *Belial* of Hell muſt needs be always *Yoked* up from this piece of Miſchief? The beſt man that ever lived has been called a *Witch:* and why may not this too uſual and unhappy Symptom of A *Witch*, even a Spectral Repreſentation, befall a perſon that ſhall be none of the worſt? Is it not poſſible? The *Laplanders* will tell us 'tis poſſible: for Perſons to be unwittingly attended with officious *Dæmons*, bequeathed unto them, and impoſ'd upon them, by Relations that have been *Witches*.[59] *Quæry*,

[58] The Incomprehenſibleneſs of the Creator is nowhere more ſtrikingly expreſſed than in the following old Lines:

What mortal Man can with a Span
  mete out Eternity?
Or fathom it by Depth of Wit
  or Strength of Memory?
The lofty Sky is not ſo high,
  Hell's Depth to this is ſmall;
The World ſo wide is but a Stride,
  compared therewithal.
It is a main great Ocean,
  withouten Bank or Bound:
A deep Abyſs, wherein there is
  no Bottom to be found.

Day of Doom, Edit. 1715, P. 51.

[59] In the Notes of Butler and Dr. Naſh to *Hudibras* the Reader will find ſome Amuſement reſpecting the Witches of Lapland. Although the Laplanders are deſcribed as a miſerable Race, they could not have been much behind the Engliſh in Matters of Superſtition at this Period. Dr. Heylyn ſays the Laplanders, "at their firſt going out of their Doores in a Morning vſe to giue worſhip and diuine honour all the Day following, to that liuing Creature what ere it be, which they ſee at their firſt going out." *Mikrokoſmos*, 328, Edit. 1624, 4to.

alſo, Whether at a Time, when the Devil with his Witches are engag'd in a War upon a people, ſome certain ſteps of ours, in ſuch a War, may not be follow'd with our appearing ſo and ſo for a while among them in the Viſions of our afflicted *Forlorns!* And, Who can certainly ſay, what other Degrees or Methods of ſinning, beſides that of a *Diabolical Compact*, may give the Devils advantage to act in the Shape of them that have miſcarried? Beſides what may happen for a while, to try the *Patience* of the Vertuous. May not ſome that have been ready upon feeble grounds uncharitably to Cenſure and Reproach other people, be puniſhed for it by *Spectres* for a while expoſing them to Cenſure and Reproach? And furthermore, I pray, that it may be conſidered, Whether a World of Magical Tricks often uſed in the World, may not inſenſibly oblige *Devils* to wait upon the Superſtitious Uſers of them. A Witty Writer againſt *Sadduciſm* has this Obſervation, That perſons who never made any expreſs Contract with *Apoſtate Spirits*, yet may Act ſtrange Things by *Diabolick Aids*, which they procure by the uſe of thoſe wicked *Forms* and *Arts*, that the Devil firſt imparted unto his Confederates. And he adds, *We know not but the Laws of the Dark Kingdom may Enjoyn a particular Attendance upon all thoſe that practice their Myſteries, whether they know them to be theirs or no.* Some of them that have been cry'd out upon as *Employing Evil Spirits* to hurt our Land, have been known to be moſt bloody *Fortune-Tellers;* and ſome of them have confeſſed, That when they told *Fortunes,* they would pretend the Rules of *Chiromancy* and the like Ignorant Sciences, but indeed they had no Rule (they ſaid) [10] but this, *The things were then Darted into their minds. Darted!* Ye Wretches;[60] By whom, I pray? Surely by none but the *Devils;* who, tho' perhaps they did not exactly *Foreknow* all the thus Predicted Contingencies; yet having once *Foretold* them, they ſtood bound in Honour now to uſe their Intereſt, which alas, in *This World,* is very great, for the Accompliſhment of their own Predictions. There are others, that have uſed moſt wicked *Sorceries* to gratifie their unlawful Curioſities, or to prevent Inconveniencies in Man and Beaſt; *Sorceries,* which I will not *Name,* leſt I ſhould by naming, *Teach them.*[61] Now, ſome *Devil* is evermore Invited into the Service of the Perſon that ſhall Practiſe theſe *Witchcrafts;* and if they have gone on Impenitently in theſe Communions with any *Devil,* the *Devil* may perhaps become at laſt a *Familiar* to them, and ſo aſſume their *Livery,* that they cannot ſhake him off in any way, but that One, which I would moſt heartily preſcribe unto them, Namely, That of a

60 It does not appear to have occurred to the Doctor that a *good Spirit* might have been the Author of ſuch *darting* Operations.

61 It would have been gratifying to at leaſt ſome of the Author's Readers if he had informed them how, where and when he became poſſeſſed of the Art of Sorcery, and as he acknowledges having the Art, how he eſcaped Proſecution. This is *parum claris lucem dare* indeed.

deep and long *Repentance*. Should theſe *Impieties* have been committed in ſuch a place as *New-England*, for my part I ſhould not wonder, if when *Devils* are Expoſing the *Groſſer* Witches among us, God permit them to bring in theſe *Leſſer* ones with the reſt for their perpetual Humiliation. In the Iſſue therefore, may it not be found, that *New-England* is not ſo ſtock'd with *Rattle Snakes*, as was imagined.[62]

§ IV. But I do not believe, that the progreſs of *Witchcraft* among us, is all the Plot which the Devil is managing in the *Witchcraft* now upon us. It is judged, That the Devil raiſ'd the Storm, whereof we read in the Eighth Chapter of *Matthew*, on purpoſe to over-ſet the little Veſſel wherein the Diſciples of Our Lord were Embarqued with Him. And it may be fear'd, that in the *Horrible Tempeſt* which is now upon ourſelves, the deſign of the Devil is to ſink that Happy Settlement of Government, wherewith Almighty God has graciouſly enclined Their Majeſties to favour us.[63] We are bleſſed with a GOVERNOUR, than whom no man can be more willing to ſerve Their Majeſties, or this their

[62] This Hopefulneſs occaſionally breaks out. It ill agrees with the doleful Tone often expreſſed, in various Parts of the Doctor's Writings—that "New England is on the broad Road to Perdition."

[63] This has Reference to the Favor expected at the Hands of William and Mary. The new Charter granted by them was received in Boſton on the 14th of May, 1692. Sir Wm. Phipps came over at the ſame Time and aſſumed the Office of Governor.

Province: He is continually venturing his *All* to do it:. and were not the Interefts of his Prince dearer to him than his own, he could not but foon be weary of the *Helm*, whereat he fits. We are under the Influence of a LIEUTENANT GOVERNOUR,[64] who not only by being admirably accomplifhed both with Natural and Acquired Endowments, is fitted for the Service of Their Majefties, but alfo with an unfpotted Fidelity applies himfelf to that Service. Our COUNCELLOURS are fome of our moft Eminent Perfons, and as Loyal Subjects to the Crown, as hearty lovers of their Country.[65] Our Conftitution alfo is attended with fingular Priviledges; All which Things are by the Devil exceedingly *Envy'd* unto us. And the Devil will doubtlefs take this occafion for the raifing of fuch complaints and clamours, as may be of pernicious confequence unto fome part of our prefent Settlement, if he can fo far *Impofe*. But that which moft of all Threatens us, in our prefent Circumftances, is the *Mifun-*

64 William Stoughton, afterwards Governor.

65 Thefe were to be 28 in Number. As the early Hiftories do not name them I copy them here from the Charter as printed in 1726: "Simon Broadftreet, John Richards, Nathanael Saltonftall, Wait Winthrop, John Philips, James Ruffell, Samuel Sewall, Samuel Appleton, Bartholomew Gedney, John Hathorn, Elifha Hutchinfon, Robert Pike, Jonathan Corwin, John Jolliffe, Adam Winthrop, Richard Middlecot, John Fofter, Peter Sergeant, Jofeph Lynd, Samuel Heyman, Stephen Mafon, Thomas Hinkley, William Bradford, John Walley, Barnabas Lothrop, Job Alcot, Samuel Daniel, and Silvanus Davis, Efquires." Ifaac Addington was appointed Secretary. Nearly all noticed in Allen's *Amer. Biog. Dict.*

derſtanding, and ſo the *Animoſity*, whereunto the *Witchcraft* now Raging, has Enchanted us. The Embroiling, firſt, of our *Spirits*, and then of our *Affairs*, is evidently as conſiderable a Branch of the Helliſh Intrigue which now vexes us as any one Thing whatever. The Devil has made us like a *Troubled Sea*, and the *Mire* and *Mud* begins now alſo to heave up apace. Even Good and Wiſe Men ſuffer themſelves to fall into their *Paroxyſms*; and the Shake which the Devil is now giving us, fetches up the *Dirt* which before lay ſtill at the bottom of our ſinful Hearts. If we allow the Mad Dogs of Hell to poyſon us by biting us, [11] we ſhall imagine that we ſee nothing but ſuch things about us, and like ſuch things fly upon all that we ſee. Were it not for what is IN US, for my part, I ſhould not fear a thouſand Legions of Devils: 'tis by our Quarrels that we ſpoil our Prayers; and if our humble, zealous, and united Prayers are once hindred: Alas, the *Philiſtines* of Hell have cut our Locks for us; they will then blind us, mock us, ruine us: In truth, I cannot altogether blame it, if People are a little tranſported, when they conceive all the ſecular Intereſts of themſelves and their Families at the Stake; and yet at the ſight of theſe Heartburnings, I cannot forbear the Exclamation of the Sweet-ſpirited *Auſtin*, in his Pacificatory Epiſtle to *Jerom*, on the Conteſt with *Ruffin*, *O miſera & miſeranda Conditio!* O Condition, truly miſerable! But what ſhall be done to cure theſe Diſtractions? It is wonderfully neceſſary, that ſome healing Attempts be made at this time: And I muſt needs confeſs (if I may ſpeak ſo much) like a *Nazianzen*, I am ſo deſirous of a ſhare in them, that if, being thrown overboard, were needful to allay the *Storm*, I ſhould think Dying, a Trifle to be undergone, for ſo great a Bleſſedneſs.[66]

§ V. I would moſt importunately in the firſt place, entreat every Man to maintain an holy Jealouſie over his own Soul at this time, and think; May not the Devil make me, though ignorantly and unwillingly, to be an Inſtrument of doing ſomething that he would have to be done? For my part, I freely own my Suſpicion, leſt ſomething of Enchantment, have reach'd more Perſons and Spirits among us, than we are well aware of. But then, let us more generally agree to maintain a kind Opinion one of another. That Charity without which, even our giving our Bodies to be burned would profit nothing, uſes to proceed by this Rule; It is kind, it is not eaſily provok'd, it thinks no Evil, it believes all things, hopes all things. But if we diſregard this Rule of Charity, we ſhall indeed give our Body Politick to be burned.[67] I have heard it affirmed, That in the

[66] The horrible Picture drawn in this long Paragraph has Reference eſpecially to the ſtill deep Current among the few who did not believe in Witchcraft, or at leaſt who did not believe in extreme Meaſures againſt thoſe accuſed of it.

[67] Strange Source, indeed, whence to hear a Plea for Charity!

late great Flood upon *Connecticut*, thofe Creatures which could not but have quarrelled at another time, yet now being driven together very agreeably ftood by one another.[68] I am fure we fhall be worfe than *Bruitifh* if we fly upon one another at a time when the Floods of Belial make us afraid. On the one fide; [Alas, my Pen, muft thou write the word, *Side* in the Bufinefs?] There are very worthy Men, who, having been call'd by God, when and where this Witchcraft firft appeared upon the Stage to encounter it, are earneftly defirous to have it fifted unto the bottom of it. And I pray, which of us all that fhould live under the continual Impreffions of the Tortures, Outcries, and Havocks which Devils confeffedly Commiffioned by Witches make among their diftreffed Neighbours, would not have a Biafs that way beyond other Men? Perfons this way difpofed have been Men eminent for Wifdom and Vertue, and Men acted by a noble Principle of Confcience. Had not Confcience (of Duty to God) prevailed above other Confiderations with them, they would not for all they are worth in the World have medled in this Thorny bufinefs. Have there been any difputed Methods ufed in difcovering the Works of Darknefs? It may be none but what have had great Precedents in other parts of the World; which may, though not altogether juftifie, yet much alleviate a Miftake in

[68] Did this Fact fuggeft the Idea of the *Happy Family* to the Keepers of modern Menageries? The Frefhet is not mentioned by the Chroniclers.

us if there ſhould happen to be found any ſuch miſtake in ſo dark a Matter.[69] They have done what they have done, with multiplied Addreſſes to God for his Guidance, and have not been inſenſible how [12] much they have expoſed themſelves in what they have done. Yea, they would gladly contrive and receive an expedient, how the ſhedding of Blood, might be ſpared, by the Recovery of Witches, not gone beyond the Reach of Pardon. And after all, they invite all good Men, in terms to this purpoſe, 'Being amazed at the 'Number and Quality of thoſe accuſed of late, we 'do not know but Satan by his Wiles may have 'enwrapped ſome innocent Perſons; and therefore 'ſhould earneſtly and humbly deſire the moſt 'Critical Enquiry upon the place, to find out the 'Falacy; that there may be none of the Servants 'of the Lord, with the worſhippers of *Baal.* I may alſo add, That whereas, if once a Witch do ingeniouſly confeſs among us, no more *Spectres* do in their Shapes after this, trouble the Vicinage; if any guilty Creatures will accordingly to ſo good purpoſe confeſs their Crime to any Miniſter of God, and get out of the Snare of the Devil, as no Miniſter will diſcover ſuch a Conſcientious Confeſſion, ſo I believe none in the Authority will preſs him to diſcover it; but rejoyc'd in a Soul ſav'd from Death. On the other ſide [if I muſt

[69] There was a Propoſition, it is ſaid, to ſend to England to engage one Matthew Hopkins, a profeſſed Witch-finder, then in high repute in that Country. See *Hiſtory and Antiquities of Boſton*, 309.

again uſe the word *Side*, which yet I hope to live to blot out] there are very worthy Men, who are not a little diſſatisfied at the Proceedings in the Proſecution of this Witchcraft. And why? Not becauſe they would have any ſuch abominable thing, defended from the Strokes of Impartial Juſtice. No, thoſe Reverend Perſons who gave in this Advice unto the Honourable Council; 'That Preſumptions, whereupon Perſons may be 'Committed, and much more Convictions, where-'upon Perſons may be Condemned, as guilty of 'Witchcrafts, ought certainly to be more conſi-'derable than barely the Accuſed Perſons being 'repreſented by a *Spectre* unto the Afflicted; Nor 'are Alterations made in the Sufferers, by a Look 'or Touch of the Accuſed, to be eſteemed an 'infallible Evidence of Guilt; but frequently 'liable to be abuſed by the Devils Legerdemains: I ſay, thoſe very Men of God moſt conſcientiouſly Subjoined this Article to that Advice,—'Never-'theleſs we cannot but humbly recommend unto 'unto the Government, the ſpeedy and vigorous 'Proſecution of ſuch as have rendred themſelves 'Obnoxious; according to the beſt Directions 'given in the Laws of God, and the wholſome 'Statutes of the *Engliſh* Nation for the Detection 'of Witchcraft. Only 'tis a moſt commendable Cautiouſneſs, in thoſe gracious Men, to be very ſhye leſt the Devil get ſo far into our Faith, as that for the ſake of many Truths which we find he tells us, we come at length to believe any

Lyes, wherewith he may abuſe us: whereupon, what a Deſolation of Names would ſoon enſue, beſides a thouſand other pernicious Conſequences? and leſt there ſhould be any ſuch Principles taken up, as when put into Practice muſt unavoidably cauſe the *Righteous to periſh with the Wicked;* or procure the Bloodſhed of any Perſons, like the *Gibeonites,* whom ſome learned Men ſuppoſe to be under a falſe Notion of Witches, by *Saul* exterminated.

They would have all due ſteps taken for the Extinction of Witches; but they would fain have them to be ſure ones; nor is it from any thing, but the real and hearty goodneſs of ſuch Men, that they are loth to ſurmiſe ill of other Men, till there be the fulleſt Evidence for the ſurmiſes. As for the Honourable Judges that have been hitherto in the Commiſſion, they are above my Conſideration: wherefore I will only ſay thus much of them, That ſuch of them as I have the Honour of a Perſonal Acquaintance with, are Men of an excellent Spirit; and as at firſt they went about the work for which they were Commiſſion'd, with [13] a very great averſion, ſo they have ſtill been under Heart-breaking Solicitudes, how they might therein beſt ſerve both God and Man? In fine, Have there been faults on any ſide fallen into? Surely, they have at worſt been but the faults of a well-meaning Ignorance. On every ſide then, why ſhould not we endeavour with amicable Correſpondencies, to help one another out of the Snares wherein the Devil would involve us? To wrangle the Devil out of the Country, will be truly a New Experiment: Alas! we are not aware of the Devil, if we do not think, that he aims at inflaming us one againſt another; and ſhall we ſuffer our ſelves to be Devil-ridden? or by any unadvisableneſs contribute unto the Widening of our Breaches?

To ſay no more, there is a publiſhed and credible Relation; which affirms, That very lately in a part of *England*, where ſome of the Neighbourhood were quarrelling, a *Raven* from the Top of a Tree very articulately and unaccountably cry'd out, *Read the Third of Colloſſians and the Fifteenth!* Were I my ſelf to chuſe what ſort of Bird I would be transformed into, I would ſay, *O that I had wings like a Dove!* Nevertheleſs, I will for once do the Office, which as it ſeems, Heaven ſent that *Raven* upon; even to beg, *That the Peace of God may Rule in our Hearts.*

§ VI. 'Tis neceſſary that we unite in every thing: but there are eſpecially two Things wherein our Union muſt carry us along together. We are to unite in our Endeavours to deliver our diſtreſſed Neighbours, from the horrible Annoyances and Moleſtations with which a dreadful Witchcraft is now perſecuting of them. To have an hand in any thing, that may ſtifle or obſtruct a Regular Detection of that Witchcraft, is what we may well with an holy fear avoid. Their Majeſties good Subjects muſt not every day be torn to pieces by horrid Witches, and thoſe bloody Felons, be left wholly unproſecuted. The Witchcraft is a buſineſs that will not be ſham'd, without plunging us into ſore Plagues, and of long continuance.[70] But then we are to unite in ſuch Methods for this deliverance, as may be unqueſtionably ſafe, leſt *the latter end be worſe than the beginning*. And here, what ſhall I ſay? I will venture to ſay thus much, That we are ſafe, when we make juſt as much uſe of all Advice from the inviſible World, as God ſends it for. It is a ſafe Principle, That when God Almighty permits any Spirits from the unſeen Regions, to viſit us with ſurprizing Informations, there is then ſomething to be enquired after; we are then to enquire of one another, What Cauſe there is for ſuch things? The peculiar Government of God, over the unbodied Intelligences, is a ſufficient Foundation for this Principle. When there has been a Murder committed, an Apparition of the ſlain Party accuſing of any Man, altho' ſuch Apparitions have oftner ſpoke true than falſe, is not enough to Convict the Man as guilty of that Murder; but yet it is a ſufficient occaſion for Magiſtrates to make a particular Enquiry, whether ſuch a Man

[70] It is at every Step ſurpriſing to obſerve how the Writer aſſumes to be the Judge, in this at the ſame Time "dark and incomprehenſible Buſineſs," as it is frequently acknowledged by him to be.

have afforded any ground for ſuch an Accuſation. Even ſo a Spectre exactly reſembling ſuch or ſuch a Perſon, when the Neighbourhood are tormented by ſuch Spectres, may reaſonably make Magiſtrates inquiſitive whether the Perſon ſo repreſented have done or ſaid any thing that may argue their confederacy with Evil Spirits, altho' it may be defective enough in point of Conviction; eſpecially at a time, when 'tis poſſible, ſome overpowerful Conjurer may have got the ſkill of thus exhibiting the Shapes of all ſorts of Perſons, on purpoſe to ſtop the Proſecution of the Wretches, whom due Enquiries thus provoked, might have made obnoxious unto Juſtice.

[14] *Quære*, Whether if God would have us to proceed any further than bare *Enquiry*, upon what Reports there may come againſt any Man, from the World of *Spirits*, he will not by his Providence at the ſame time have brought into our hands, theſe more evident and ſenſible things, whereupon a man is to be eſteemed a Criminal. But I will venture to ſay this further, that it will be ſafe to account the Names as well as the Lives of our Neighbors; two conſiderable things to be brought under a Judicial Proceſs, until it be found by Humane Obſervations that the Peace of Mankind is thereby diſturbed. We are Humane Creatures, and we are ſafe while we ſay, they muſt be Humane Witneſſes, who alſo have in the particular Act of Seeing, or Hearing, which enables them to be Witneſſes, had no more than

Humane Aſſiſtances, that are to turn the Scale when Laws are to be executed. And upon this Head I will further add: A wiſe and a juſt Magiſtrate, may ſo far give way to a common Stream of Diſſatisfaction, as to forbear acting up to the heighth of his own Perſwaſion, about what may be judged convictive of a Crime, whoſe Nature ſhall be ſo abſtruſe and obſcure, as to raiſe much Diſputation. Tho' he may not do what he ſhould leave undone, yet he may leave undone ſomething that elſe he could do, when the Publick Safety makes an *Exigency*.

§ VII. I was going to make one Venture more; that is, to offer ſome ſafe Rules, for the finding out of the Witches, which are at this day our accurſed Troublers: but this were a Venture too *Preſumptuous* and *Icarian* for me to make; I leave that unto thoſe Excellent and Judicious Perſons, with whom I am not worthy to be numbred: All that I ſhall do, ſhall be to lay before my Readers, a brief *Synopſis* of what has been written on that Subject, by a Triumvirate of as Eminent Perſons as have ever handled it. I will begin with,

AN ABSTRACT OF MR. PERKINS'S[71] WAY FOR THE DISCOVERY OF WITCHES.

I. THERE *are* Presumptions, *which do at least probably and conjecturally note one to be a* Witch.

[71] The same "Master William Perkins," I suppose, who wrote the three stout Folios of Puritan Theology, published in 1606, besides many smaller Works. The earliest Notice I find of him is by another equally famous and voluminous Puritan, the Rev. Samuel Clark, in his *Marrow of Ecclesiastical History*, published in 1650. Mr. Clark informs us that William Perkins was born at Marston in Warwickshire, in 1558, was educated at "*Christ's* College in *Cambridg*," and that in the 24th of *Elizabeth*, he was chosen a Fellow of that College, and that "hee was very wilde in his Youth." From his Professorship, "hee was chosen to *Saint Andrews* Parish in *Cambridg*, where he preached all his Life after. His Sermons were not so plain, but the piously learned did admire them; nor so learned, but the plain did understand them: Hee brought the Schools into the Pulpit, and unshelling their Controversies out of their hard School-tearms, made thereof plain and wholsom Meat for his People: He was an excellent Chirurgion at the jointing of a broken Soul, and at stating of a doubtful Conscience. In his Sermons hee used to pronounce the Word *Damn* with such an Emphasis, as left a dolefull Echo in his Auditor's Ears a good while after: and when hee was Catechist in Christ's College, in expounding the Commandments, hee applied them so Home to the Conscience as was able to make his Hearers Harts fall down, and their Hairs almost to stand upright."

On Reference to the Works of famous Thomas Fuller, it will be found, that in his Life of Perkins he has substantially the same Account. From that Author Mr. Clark doubtless borrowed the Expressions used by him, as Fuller's Work was published several Years before, and they seem peculiar to that highly talented Writer. Clark is followed because he was of the same religious Denomination as Mr. Perkins. Mr. Clark continues: "In his Life hee was so pious and spotless, that Malice was afraid to bite at his Credit, into which shee knew that her Teeth could not enter: Hee had a rare Felicitie in reading

Theſe give occaſion to Examine, yet they are no ſufficient Cauſes of Conviction.

of Books, and as it were but turning them over would give an exact account of all that was conſiderable therein: hee peruſed Books ſo ſpeedily that one would think that hee read nothing, and yet ſo accurately that one would think he read all: Beſides his frequent Preaching, hee wrote manie excellent Books, both Treatiſes, and Commentaries, which for their Worth were manie of them tranſlated into Latine, and ſent beyond Sea, where to this Daie they are highly prized, and much ſet by, yea ſome of them are tranſlated into *French*, *High-Dutch*, and *Low-Dutch*: and his reformed Catholick was tranſlated into *Spaniſh*; yet no Spaniard ever ſince durſt take up the Gantlet of Defiance caſt down by this Champion."

But there is one Fact mentioned by Fuller which Mr. Clark omits: "There goeth," he ſays, "an uncontrolled Tradition, that Perkins, when a young Scholar, was a great Studier of Magic, occaſioned perchance by his Skill in the Mathematics. For, ignorant People count all Circles above their own Sphere to be Conjring; and preſently cry out, 'thoſe Things are done by Black Art' for which their dim Eyes can ſee no Colour in Reaſon. And in ſuch Caſe, when they cannot fly up to Heaven to make it a Miracle, they fetch it from Hell to make it Magic, though it may lawfully be done by natural Cauſes."

Mr Perkins died "in the fourtieth Year of his Age, *Anno* 1602, being born the firſt, and dying the laſt Year of [the Reign of] Elizabeth: He was of a ruddie Complexion, fat and corpulent: Lame of his right Hand, yet this *Ehud* with a left-handed Pen did ſtab the Romiſh Caus—as one ſaith: [Hugh Holland]

'Though Nature thee of thy right Hand bereft.
'Right well thou writeſt with thy Hand that's left.'

"Hee was buried with great Solemnity at the ſole Charges of Chriſts College, the Univerſitie, and Town ſtriving which ſhould expreſs more Sorrow thereat: Doctor *Montague*, afterwards Biſhop of Winchester preached his Funeral Sermon."—*Marrow of Eccleſiaſtical Hiſtorie*, 414-417, and Fuller's *Holy and Profane State*, 80-84.

The well known Rev. Mr. Job Orton ſpeaks of the Folios of Perkins with Delight, and adds: "What led me more particularly to read him was, that his Elder Brother was one of my Anceſtors, from whom I am in a direct Line, by my Mother's Side deſcended."—Orton, in *Brook's Lives*, ii, 135. In his Will, dated 16 Oct., 1602, he mentions, among others, Nathaniel Cradock, his Brother-in-law, Wife Timothye, Father and Mother Thomas and Anna Perkins, Son-in-law, John Hinde, and Brethren and Siſters, but not by Name.—*Ibid.*

II. *If any Man or Woman be notoriouſly defamed for a* Witch, *this yields a ſtrong Suſpition. Yet the Judge ought carefully to look, that the Report be made by* Men *of Honeſty and Credit.*

III. *If a* Fellow-Witch, *or* Magician, *give Teſtimony of any Perſon to be a* Witch ; *this indeed is not ſufficient for Condemnation ; but it is a fit Preſumption to cauſe a ſtraight Examination.*

IV. *If after Curſing there follow Death, or at leaſt ſome miſchief : for* Witches *are wont to practiſe their miſchievous Facts by Curſing and Banning : This alſo is a ſufficient matter of Examination, tho' not of Conviction.*

V. *If after Enmity, Quarrelling, or Threatning, a preſent miſchief does follow ; that alſo is a great Preſumption.*

[15] VI. *If the Party ſuſpected be the Son or Daughter, the man-ſervant or maid-ſervant, the Familiar Friend, near Neighbor, or old Companion, of a known and convicted Witch ; this may be likewiſe a Preſumption ; for Witchcraft is an Art that may be learned, and conveyed from man to man.*

VII. *Some add this for a Preſumption : If the Party ſuſpected be found to have the Devil's mark ; for it is commonly thought, when the Devil makes*

I have been more particular in this Notice of Perkins for two Reaſons ; firſt, becauſe of his Puritaniſm he was ſelected as a prime Authority in Matters of Witchcraft by our Author; and ſecond, becauſe he ſeems to have been a Man poſſeſſing that Precocity of Mind, and in other reſpects was ſimilarly gifted. To thoſe deſirous of learning more of that noted Puritan Leader will find Gratification in the excellent and elaborate Life of him in Brook's *Lives of the Puritans.*

his Covenant with them, he alwaies leaves his mark behind them, whereby he knows them for his own:— a mark whereof no evident Reason in Nature can be given.

VIII. *Lastly, If the party examined be Unconstant, or contrary to himself, in his deliberate Answers, it argueth a Guilty Conscience, which stops the freedom of Utterance. And yet there are causes of Astonishment, which may befal the Good, as well as the Bad.*

IX. *But then there is a* Conviction, *discovering the* Witch, *which must proceed from just and sufficient proofs, and not from bare presumptions.*

X. *Scratching of the suspected party, and Recovery thereupon, with several other such weak Proofs; as also, the fleeting of the suspected Party, thrown upon the Water; these Proofs are so far from being sufficient, that some of them are, after a sort, practices of Witchcraft.*

XI. *The Testimony of some Wizzard, tho' offering to shew the Witches Face in a Glass: This, I grant, may be a good Presumption, to cause a strait Examination; but a sufficient Proof of Conviction it cannot be. If the Devil tell the Grand Jury, that the person in question is a Witch, and offers withal to confirm the same by Oath, should the Inquest receive his Oath or Accusation to condemn the man? Assuredly no. And yet, that is as much as the Testimony of another Wizzard, who only by the Devil's help reveals the Witch.*

XII. *If a man, being dangerously sick, and like to*

dy, upon Suſpicion, will take it on his Death, that ſuch an one hath bewitched him, it is an Allegation of the ſame nature, which may move the Judge to examine the Party, but it is of no moment for Conviction.

XIII. *Among the ſufficient means of Conviction, the firſt is, the free and voluntary Confeſſion of the Crime, made by the party ſuſpected and accuſed, after Examination. I ſay not, that a bare confeſſion is ſufficient, but a Confeſſion after due Examination, taken upon pregnant preſumptions. What needs now more witneſs or further Enquiry?*

XIV. *There is a ſecond ſufficient Conviction, by the Teſtimony of two Witneſſes, of good and honeſt Report, avouching before the Magiſtrate, upon their own Knowledge, the two things: either that the party accuſed hath made a League with the Devil, or hath done ſome known practices of witchcraft. And,* all Arguments that do neceſſarily prove either of theſe, *being brought by two ſufficient Witneſſes, are of force fully to convince the party ſuſpected.*

XV. *If it can be proved, that the party ſuſpected hath called upon the* Devil, *or deſired his Help, this is a pregnant proof of a League formerly made between them.*

XVI. *If it can be proved, that the party hath entertained a Familiar Spirit, and had Conference with it, in the likeneſs of ſome viſible Creatures; here is Evidence of witchcraft.*

XVII. *If the witneſſes affirm upon Oath, that the ſuſpected perſon hath done any action or work which necessarily infers a Covenant made, as, that he hath used En-*[16]*chantments, divined things before they come to pass, and that peremptorily, raised Tempests, caused the Form of a dead man to appear; it proveth sufficiently, that he or she is a* Witch.[72] This is the Substance of Mr. *Perkins.*

'Take next the Sum of Mr. *Gaules*[73] Judgment 'about the Detection of Witches. 1. Some 'Tokens for the Trial of Witches are altogether 'unwarrantable. Suchare the old Paganish Sign, 'the Witches *Long Eyes*; the Tradition of Witches

[72] On perusing these Articles for the Detection of Witches, one cannot escape the Conviction that on their being sifted by the ordinary Rules of Common-sense, they actually amount to nothing at all. Thus in Article VI it is laid down, that "Witchcraft is an Art, that may be learned, and conveyed from Man to Man." This Postulate follows of course, previously assuming that the Occult Sciences originate in Mathematics; and further, that Mathematical Calculations are inseparable from the Laws that govern the whole System of the Universe, and hence emanate from, or are a Part of the Creator himself. Whence then, with this inevitable Conclusion, does the "Art" originate? Nothing can be clearer, therefore, than this,—if those learned Plodders of Master Perkins's Time had followed out the most simple Rules of Logic, they would have had neither Witch nor Devil wherewith to addle their own Brains, or to confound those of the unlearned Multitude. This Question being disposed of, all others having Dependence on it, or traceable to it, effectually dispose of the whole Question of Witchcraft.

[73] John Gaule has not, so far as ascertained, been stumbled on by any Makers of Biographical Dictionaries, and Bibliographers are almost equally silent. How many Works he was Author of is not known. The Title of one is *Distractions, or Holy Madness*, 12mo, 1629. He wrote other theological Works, but their Titles have not come to the Annotator's Knowledge.

'not weeping; the caſting of the Witch into the 'Water, with Thumbs and Toes ty'd a-croſs. And 'many more ſuch Marks, which if they are to 'know a Witch by, certainly 'tis no other Witch, 'but the Uſer of them. 2. There are ſome 'Tokens for the Trial of Witches, more probable, 'and yet not ſo certain as to afford Conviction. 'Such are ſtrong and long Suſpicion: Suſpected 'Anceſtors, ſome appearance of Fact, the Corps 'bleeding upon the Witches touch, the Teſti-'mony of the Party bewitched, the ſuppoſed 'Witches unuſual Bodily marks, the Witches 'uſual Curſing and Banning, the Witches lewd 'and naughty kind of Life. 3. Some Signs there 'are of a Witch, more certain and infallible. As, '*firſtly*, Declining of Judicature, or faultering, 'faulty, unconſtant, and contrary Anſwers, upon 'judicial and deliberate examination. *Secondly*, 'When upon due Enquiry into a perſon's Faith 'and Manners, there are found *all* or *moſt* of the 'Cauſes which produce Witchcraft, namely, '*God* forſaking, *Satan* invading, particular *Sins* 'diſpoſing; and laſtly, a compact compleating all. '*Thirdly*, The Witches free Confeſſion, together 'with full Evidence of the Fact. *Confeſſion* with-'out *Fact* may be a meer Deluſion, and *Fact* 'without *Confeſſion* may be a meer Accident. '*4thly*, The ſemblable Geſtures and Actions of 'ſuſpected Witches, with the comparable Ex-'preſſions of Affections, which in all Witches have 'been obſerv'd and found very much alike. '*Fifthly*, The Teſtimony of the Party bewitched, 'whether pining or dying, together with the joynt 'Oaths of ſufficient perſons, that have ſeen certain 'prodigious Pranks or Feats, wrought by the Party 'accuſed. 4. Among the moſt unhappy circum-'ſtances to convict a Witch, one is, a maligning 'and oppugning the Word, Work, and Worſhip 'of God, and by any extraordinary ſign ſeeking 'to ſeduce any from it. See *Deut.* 13. 1, 2, '*Mat.* 24. 24. *Act.* 13. 8, 10. 2 *Tim.* 3. 8. Do 'but mark well the places, and for this very 'Property (of thus oppoſing and perverting) they 'are all there concluded arrant and abſolute 'Witches. 5. It is not requiſite, that ſo *palpable* '*Evidence of Conviction* ſhould here come in, as in 'other more ſenſible matters; 'tis enough, if there 'be but ſo much *circumſtantial* Proof or Evidence, 'as the Subſtance, Matter, and Nature of ſuch an 'abſtruſe Myſtery of Iniquity will well admit. [*I ſuppoſe he means, that whereas in other Crimes we look for more direct proofs, in this there is a greater uſe of conſequential ones.*] 'But I could 'heartily wiſh, that the Juries were empanell'd 'of the moſt eminent Phyſicians, Lawyers, and 'Divines that a Country could afford. In the 'mean time 'tis not to be called a Toleration, if 'Witches eſcape, where Conviction is wanting. 'To this purpoſe our *Gaule*.

I will tranſcribe a little from one Author more,

'tis the Judicious *Bernard* of *Batcomb*,[74] who in his *Guide to grand Jurymen*, after he has mention'd ſeveral things that are ſhrewd Preſumptions of a Witch, proceeds to ſuch things as are the *Convictions* of ſuch an one. And he ſays, '*A witch* '*in league with the* Devil *is convicted by* [1][75] *theſe* '*Evidences;* I. By a witches *Mark;* which is on 'the Baſer ſort of Witches; and this, by the Devils 'either Sucking or Touching of them. *Tertullian* 'ſays, *It is the Devils cuſtome to mark his.* And 'note, That this mark is *Inſenſible*, and being 'prick'd it will not Bleed. Sometimes, its like a '*Teate;* ſometimes but a *Blewiſh Spot;* ſometimes 'a *Red* one; and ſometimes the *fleſh Sunk:* but 'the Witches do ſometimes cover them. II. By 'the Witches *Words*. As when they have been 'heard calling on, ſpeaking to, or Talking of 'their *Familiars;* or, when they have been heard '*Telling* of *Hurt* they have done to man or 'beaſt: Or when they have been heard *Threatning* of ſuch Hurt; Or if they have been heard

[74] As there is more than one *Batcomb* in England "Judicious Bernard's" being *of* that Place is not much of a Guide to any looking after his Biography. Fortunately, or unfortunately for him, his Portrait was engraved, and that cauſed him to be noticed by Granger. His Name was Richard, and he was Paſtor of "Batcombe" in Somerſetſhire. The Work extracted from by our Author was publiſhed in 1627. He was Author of a Concordance to the Bible, though it was not ſo entitled; alſo of a Work called the *Threefold Treatiſe of the Sabbath*, in 1641, in which Year he died. His Portrait by Hollar firſt appeared in this Work.—*Biog. Hiſt. England*, ii, 369. He was perhaps the Author of *The Iſle of Man; or the Legal Proceedings in Man-Shire againſt Sinne*, 12mo, 1635.

[75] Here the paging begins anew, in the Edition followed.

'Relating their *Tranſportations.* III. By the 'Witches *Deeds.* As when they have been *ſeen* 'with their Spirits, or ſeen ſecretly Feeding any 'of their *Imps.* Or, when there can be found 'their Pictures, Poppets, and other Helliſh Com-'poſitions. IV. By the Witches *Extaſies:* With 'the Delight whereof, Witches are ſo taken, that 'they will hardly conceal the ſame: Or, however 'at ſome time or other, they may be found in 'them. V. By one or more *Fellow-Witches,* 'Confeſſing their own Witchcraft, and bearing 'Witneſs againſt others; if they can make good 'the Truth of their Witneſs, and give ſufficient 'proof of it. As, that they have ſeen them with 'their Spirits or, that they have Received Spirits 'from them; or that they can tell, when they 'uſed Witchery-Tricks to Do Harm; or, that 'they told them what Harm they had done; or 'that they can ſhow the mark upon them; or, 'that they have been together in their Meetings; 'and ſuch like. VI. By ſome *Witneſs of God* 'Himſelf, happening upon the Execrable Curſes 'of Witches upon themſelves, Praying of God to 'ſhow ſome Token, if they be Guilty. VII. By 'the Witches own *Confeſſion,* of Giving their Souls 'to the Devil. It is no Rare thing, for Witches 'to Confeſs.

They are Conſiderable Things, which I have thus Recited; and yet it muſt be with *Open Eyes,* kept upon *Open Rules,* that we are to follow theſe things.

S. 8. But *Juries* are not the only Inſtruments to be imploy'd in ſuch a Work; all *Chriſtians* are to be concerned with daily and fervent *Prayers*, for the aſſiſting of it. In the Days of *Athanaſius*, the Devils were found unable to ſtand before that *Prayer*, however then uſed perhaps with too much of Ceremony, *Let God Ariſe, Let his Enemies be ſcattered. Let them alſo that Hate Him, flee before Him.*

O that inſtead of letting our Hearts *Riſe* againſt one another, our Prayers might *Riſe* unto an high pitch of Importunity, for ſuch a *Riſing* of the Lord! Eſpecially, Let them that are *Suffering* by *Witchcraft*, be ſure to *ſtay* and *pray*, and *Beſeech the Lord thrice*, even as much as ever they can, before they complain of any Neighbour for afflicting them. Let them alſo that are *accuſed* of *Witchcraft*, ſet themſelves to *Faſt* and *Pray*, and ſo ſhake off the *Dæmons* that would like *Vipers* faſten upon them; and get the *Waters of Jealouſie* made profitable to them.

And Now, O *Thou Hope of* New-England, *and the Saviour thereof in the Time of Trouble; Do thou look mercifully down upon us, & Reſcue us, out of the Trouble which at this time do's threaten to ſwallow us up. Let Satan be ſhortly bruiſed under our Feet, and Let the Covenanted Vaſſals of Satan, which have Traiterouſly brought him in upon us, be Gloriouſly Conquered, by thy Powerful and Gracious Preſence in the midſt of us. Abhor us not, O God, but cleanſe us, but heal us, but ſave us, for the ſake of thy Glory. Enwrapped in our Salvations. By thy Spirit, Lift up a ſtandard againſt our infernal adverſaries, Let us quickly find thee making of us glad, according to the Days wherein we have been afflicted. Accept of all our Endeavours to glorify thee, in the Fires that are upon us; and among the reſt, Let theſe my poor and weak eſſays, compoſed with what Tears, what Cares, what Prayers, thou* only *knoweſt, not want the Acceptance of the Lord.*

[2] A DISCOURSE ON THE WONDERS OF THE INVISIBLE WORLD.[76]

UTTERED (IN PART) ON AUG. 4, 1692.

Ecclefiaftical Hiftory has Reported it unto us, That a Renowned Martyr at the Stake, feeing the Book of the REVELATION thrown by his no lefs Profane than Bloody Perfecutors, to be Burn'd in the fame Fire with himfelf, he cryed out, *O Beata Apocalypfis; quam bene mecum agitur, qui tecum Comburar!* BLESSED REVELATION! faid he, *How Bleffed am I in this Fire, while I have Thee to bear me Company.*[77] As for our felves this Day, 'tis a Fire of fore Affliction and Confufion, wherein we are Embroiled; but it is no inconfiderable Advantage

[76] This was printed at the Time (1692) in a feparate Tract.

[77] Whoever has the Inclination to turn over the Pages of the Martyrology may perhaps find who this "Renowned Perfon" was.

U

unto us, that we have the Company of this Glorious and Sacred Book the REVELATION to aſſiſt us in our Exerciſes. From that Book there is one Text, which I would ſingle out at this time to lay before you; 'tis that in

REVEL. xii. 12.

Wo to the Inhabitants of the Earth, and of the Sea; for the Devil is come down unto you, having great Wrath; becauſe he knoweth, that he hath but a ſhort time.

THE Text is Like the Cloudy and Fiery Pillar, vouchſafed unto *Iſrael,* in the Wilderneſs of old; there is a very *dark ſide* of it in the Intimation, that, *The Devil is come down having great Wrath;* but it has alſo a *bright ſide,* when it aſſures us, that, *He has but a ſhort time;* Unto the Contemplation of *both,* I do this Day Invite you.

We have in our Hands a Letter from our Aſcended Lord in Heaven, to Adviſe us of his being ſtill alive, and of his Purpoſe e're long, to give us a Viſit, wherein we ſhall ſee our Living *Redeemer, ſtand at the latter day upon the Earth.* 'Tis the laſt Advice that we have had from Heaven, for now ſixteen Hundred years; and the ſcope of it, is, to repreſent how the Lord Jeſus Chriſt having begun to ſet up his Kingdom in the World, by the preaching of the Goſpel, he would from time to time utterly break to pieces all Powers that ſhould make Head againſt it, until, *The Kingdoms of this World are become the Kingdomes of our Lord, and of his* [3] *Chriſt, and he ſhall Reign for ever and ever.* 'Tis a Commentary on what had been written by *Daniel,* about, *The fourth Monarchy;* with ſome Touches upon, *The Fifth;* wherein, *The greatneſs of the Kingdom under the whole Heaven, ſhall be given to the people of the Saints of the moſt High:* And altho' it have, as 'tis expreſſed by one of the Ancients, *Tot Sacramenta quot verba,* a Myſtery in every Syllable, yet it is not altogether to be neglected with ſuch a Deſpair, as that, *I cannot read, for the Book is ſealed.* It is a REVELATION, and a ſingular, and notable *Bleſſing* is pronounced upon them that humbly ſtudy it.

The Divine Oracles, have with a moſt admirable Artifice and Carefulneſs, drawn, as the very pious *Beverley,* has laboriouſly Evinced, an exact LINE OF TIME, from the firſt Sabbath at the *Creation* of the World, unto the great Sabbatiſm at the *Reſtitution* of all Things. In that famous *Line of Time,* from the Decree for the Reſtoring of *Jeruſalem,* after the *Babyloniſh* Captivity, there ſeem to remain a matter of *Two Thouſand and Three Hundred Years,* unto that *New Jeruſalem,* whereto the Church is to be advanced, when the Myſtical *Babylon* ſhall be *fallen.* At the Reſurrection of our Lord, there were ſeventeen or eighteen Hundred of thoſe Years, yet upon the Line, to run unto, *The reſt which remains for the People of God;* and this Remnant in the *Line of Time*, is here in our *Apocalypſe*, variouſly Emboſſed, Adorned, and Signalized with ſuch Diſtinguiſhing Events, if we mind them, will help us eſcape that Cenſure, *Can ye not Diſcern the Signs of the Times?*

The Apoſtle *John*, for the View of theſe Things, had laid before him, as I conceive, a *Book*, with leaves, or folds; which *Volumn* was written both on the *Backſide*, and on the *Inſide*, and Roll'd up in a Cylindriacal Form, under ſeven *Labels*, faſtned with ſo many *Seals*. The firſt *Seal* being opened, and the firſt *Label* removed, under the firſt *Label* the Apoſtle ſaw what he ſaw, of a firſt *Rider* Pourtray'd, and ſo on, till the laſt *Seal* was broken up; each of the Sculptures being enlarged with agreeable *Viſions* and *Voices*, to illuſtrate it. The Book being now Unrolled, there were *Trumpets*, with wonderful Concomitants, Exhibited ſucceſſively on the Expanding *Backſide* of it. Whereupon the Book was *Eaten*, as it were to be Hidden, from Interpretations; till afterwards, in the *Inſide* of it, the Kingdom of Anti-chriſt came to be Expoſed. Thus, the Judgments of God on the *Roman Empire*, firſt unto the Downfal of *Paganiſm*, and then, unto the Downfal of *Popery*, which is but Revived *Paganiſm*, are in theſe Diſplayes, with

Lively Colours and Features made ſenſible unto us.

[4] Accordingly, in the Twelfth Chapter of this Book, we have an Auguſt Preface, to the Deſcription of that Horrid *Kingdom*, which our Lord Chriſt refuſed, but Antichriſt accepted, from the Devils Hands; a Kingdom, which for *Twelve Hundred and Sixty* Years together, was to be a continual oppreſſion upon the People of God, and oppoſition unto his Intereſts; until the Arrival of that Illuſtrious Day, wherein, *The Kingdom ſhall be the Lords, and he ſhall be Governour among the Nations.* The Chapter is (as an Excellent Perſon calls it) an *Extravaſated Account* of the Circumſtances, which befell the *Primitive Church*, during the firſt Four or Five Hundred Years of Chriſtianity: It ſhows us the Face of the Church, firſt in *Rome* Heatheniſh, and then in *Rome* Converted, before the *Man of Sin* was yet come to *Mans Eſtate.* Our Text contains the Acclamations made upon the moſt Glorious Revolution that ever yet happened upon the Roman Empire; namely, That wherein the Travailing Church brought forth a Chriſtian Emperour. This was a moſt Eminent *Victory* over the Devil, and *Reſemblance* of the State, wherein the World, ere long ſhall ſee, *The Kingdom of our God, and the Power of his Chriſt.* It is here noted,

Firſt, As a matter of *Triumph.* 'Tis ſaid, *Rejoyce, ye Heavens, and ye that dwell in them.* The

Saints in both Worlds, took the Comfort of this Revolution; the Devout Ones that had outlived the late Perſecutions, were filled with Tranſporting Joys, when they ſaw the *Chriſtian* become the *Imperial* Religion, and when they ſaw Good Men come to give Law unto the reſt of Mankind; the Deceaſed Ones alſo, whoſe Blood had been Sacrificed in the Ten Perſecutions, doubtleſs made the Light Regions to ring with *Hallelujahs* unto God, when there were brought unto them, the Tidings of the Advances now given to the *Chriſtian* Religion, for which they had ſuffered *Martyrdom.*

Secondly, As a matter of *Horror.* 'Tis ſaid, *Wo to the Inhabiters of the Earth and of the Sea.* The *Earth* ſtill means the *Falſe Church*, the *Sea* means the *Wide World*, in Prophetical Phraſæology. There was yet left a vaſt party of Men, that were Enemies to the Chriſtian Religion, in the power of it; a vaſt party left for the Devil to work upon: Unto theſe is a *Wo* denounced; and why ſo? 'Tis added, *For the Devil is come down unto you, having great Wrath, becauſe he knows, that he has but a ſhort time.* Theſe were, it ſeems, to have ſome deſperate and peculiar Attempts of the Devil made upon them. In the mean time, we may entertain this for our Doctrine.

Great Wo proceeds from the Great WRATH, *with*

which [5] *the* DEVIL, *towards the end of his* TIME, *will make a* DESCENT *upon a miserable World.*

I have now Published a most awful and solemn Warning for our selves at this day; which has four *Propositions*, comprehended in it.

Proposition I. That there is a *Devil*, is a thing Doubted by none but such as are under the Influence of the *Devil.* For any to deny the Being of a *Devil* must be from an Ignorance or Profaneness, worse than *Diabolical. A Devil.* What is *that?* We have a Definition of the Monster, in *Eph.* 6. 12. *A Spiritual Wickedness*, that is, *A wicked Spirit.* A Devil is a *Fallen Angel*, an Angel *Fallen* from the Fear and Love of God, and from all Celestial Glories; but *Fallen* to all manner of Wretchedness and Cursedness. He was once in that Order of Heavenly Creatures, which God in the Beginning made *Ministering Spirits*, for his own peculiar Service and Honour, in the management of the Universe; but we may now write that Epitaph upon him, *How art thou fallen from Heaven! thou hast said in thine Heart, I will Exalt my Throne above the Stars of God; but thou art brought down to Hell!* A Devil is a *Spiritual* and *Rational Substance*, by his *Apostacy* from God, inclined to all that is Vicious, and for that *Apostacy* confined unto the Atmosphere of this Earth, *in Chains, under Darkness, unto the Judgment of the Great Day.* This is a *Devil;* and the *Experience* of Mankind as well as the *Testimony* of Scripture, does abundantly prove the Exiſtence of ſuch a Devil.[78]

About this *Devil,* there are many things, whereof we may reaſonably and profitably be Inquiſitive; ſuch things, I mean, as are in our Bibles Reveal'd unto us; according to which if we do not ſpeak on ſo *dark* a Subject, but according to our own uncertain, and perhaps humourſome Conjectures, *There is no Light in us.* I will carry you with me, but unto one Paragraph of the Bible, to be informed of three Things, relating to the *Devil;* 'tis the Story of the *Gadaren Energumen,* in the fifth Chapter of *Mark.*

Firſt, then, 'Tis to be granted; the *Devils* are ſo many, that ſome Thouſands, can ſometimes at once apply themſelves to vex one Child of Man. It is ſaid, in Mark 5. 15. *He that was Poſſeſſed with the Devil, had the Legion.* Dreadful to be ſpoken! A *Legion* conſiſted of Twelve Thouſand Five Hundred People: And we ſee that in one Man or two, ſo many *Devils* can be ſpared for a Garriſon. As the Prophet cryed out,

[78] To this elaborate Definition of the Devil and his Attributes it will hardly be neceſſary to add or diminiſh. But taking what Tillotſon ſays of God, not quite ſo much need be ſaid of the Devil. The Archbiſhop ſays, in his happy Manner: "We attribute nothing to God that hath any repugnancy or contradiction in it." It naturally follows then, that all elſe comes from the Devil.

The famous Iſaac Ambros ſays, "The firſt Period wherein Satan firſt begins to Aſſault the Elect, it is from their quickening in the Womb."—*War with Devils,* P. 29, 2d Ed. 1738. "So may we ſay of every Child, as ſoon as it is quickened in the Womb, that the Great Red Dragon, the Devil, ſtands ready to devour it."—*Ibid.* Our Author was not alone in remarkable Ideas.

Multitudes, Multitudes, in the Valley of Deciſion! So I ſay, *There are multitudes, multitudes, in the valley of Deſtruction, where the Devils are!* When
[6] we ſpeak of, *The Devil,* 'tis, *A name of Multitude;* it means not *One* Individual Devil, ſo Potent and Scient, as perhaps a *Manichee* would imagine; but it means a *Kind,* which a *Multitude* belongs unto. Alas, the *Devils,* they ſwarm about us, like the *Frogs of Egypt,* in the moſt Retired of our Chambers. Are we at our *Boards?* There will be Devils to Tempt us unto Senſuality: Are we in our *Beds?* There will be Devils to Tempt us unto Carnality; Are we in our *Shops?* There will be Devils to Tempt us unto Diſhoneſty. Yea, Tho' we get into the Church of God, there will be Devils to Haunt us in the very *Temple* it ſelf, and there tempt us to manifold Miſbehaviours. I am verily perſwaded, That there are very few Humane Affairs whereinto ſome Devils are not Inſinuated; There is not ſo much as a *Journey* intended, but *Satan* will have an hand in *hindering* or *furthering* of it.

Secondly, 'Tis to be ſuppoſed, That there is a ſort of Arbitrary, even Military *Government,* among the *Devils.* This is intimated, when in *Mar.* 5. 9. *The unclean Spirit ſaid, My Name is Legion:* they are under ſuch a Diſcipline as *Legions* uſe to be. Hence we read about, *The Prince of the power of the Air:* Our *Air* has a *power?* or an Army of Devils in the *High Places* of it; and theſe Devils have a *Prince* over them, who is

King over the Children of Pride. 'Tis probable, That the Devil, who was the Ringleader of that mutinous and rebellious Crew, which firſt ſhook off the Authority of God, is now the General of thoſe Helliſh Armies;[79] Our Lord, that Conquered him, has told us the Name of him; 'tis *Belzebub;* 'tis he that is *the Devil,* and the reſt are *his Angels,* or his Souldiers. Think on vaſt Regiments of cruel and bloody *French Dragoons,* with an *Intendant* over them, overrunning a pillaged Neighbourhood, and you will think a little, what the Conſtitution among the *Devils* is.

Thirdly, 'tis to be ſuppoſed, that ſome *Devils* are more peculiarly *Commiſſion'd,* and perhaps *Qualify'd,* for ſome Countries, while others are for others. This is intimated when in *Mar.* 5. 10. The Devils *beſought* our Lord much, *that he would not ſend them away out of the Countrey.* Why was that? But in all probability, becauſe *theſe Devils* were more able to *do the works of the Devil,* in ſuch a Countrey, than in another. It is not likely that every Devil does know every *Language;* or that every Devil can do every *Miſchief.*[80] 'Tis poſſible, that the *Experience,* or, if I may call it ſo, the *Education* of all Devils is not alike, and that there may be ſome difference in their *Abilities.* If one might make an Inference

[79] It does not appear how the Devil-in-chief came by his Appointment; whether his Office was by Election, or in what Manner he attained his high Station. It is not very material however.

[80] A very different Deciſion will be found elſewhere in our Pages.

from what the Devils *do,* to what they *are,* One cannot [7] forbear dreaming, that there are *degrees* of Devils. Who can allow, that fuch Trifling *Dæmons,* as that of *Mafcon,*[81] or thofe that once infefted our *New berry,* are of fo much Grandeur, as thofe *Dæmons,* whofe Games are mighty Kingdoms? Yea, 'tis certain, that all Devils do not make a like Figure in the *Invifible World.* Nor does it look agreeably, That the *Dæmons,* which were the Familiars of fuch a Man as the old *Apollonius,* differ not from thofe bafer Goblins that chufe to Neft in the filthy and loathfom Rags of a beaftly Sorcerefs. Accordingly, why may not fome Devils be more accomplifhed for what is to be done in fuch and fuch places, when others muft be *detach'd* for other Territories? Each Devil, as he fees his advantage, cries out, *Let me be in this Countrey, rather than another.* But *Enough,* if not *too much,* of thefe things.[82]

Propofition II. There is a Devilifh *Wrath* againft *Mankind,* with which the *Devil* is for *God's fake* Infpired. The Devil is himfelf broiling under the intollerable and interminable *Wrath* of God; and a fiery *Wrath* at God, is, that which the Devil is for that caufe Enflamed. Methinks I fee the pofture of the Devils in *Ifa.* 8. 21. *They fret themfelves, and Curfe their God, and look*

81 "The Devil of Mafcon" was one of the Productions following the "Glorious Reftoration," as Carlyle ironically calls it. Full Title in Bohn's Lowndes, ART. DEVIL.

82 AMEN will doubtlefs be the Refponfe of every one; but do not flatter yourfelf, Reader, that you are thus foon delivered from the Devil.

upward. The firſt and chief *Wrath* of the Devil, is at the Almighty God himſelf; he knows, *The God that made him, will not have mercy on him, and the God that formed him, will ſhew him no favour;* and ſo he can have no *Kindneſs* for that God, who has no *Mercy,* nor *Favour* for him. Hence 'tis, that he cannot bear the *Name* of God ſhould be acknowledged in the World: Every Acknowledgement paid unto *God,* is a freſh drop of the burning Brimſtone falling upon the Devil; he does make his Inſolent, tho' Impotent Batteries, even upon the *Throne* of God himſelf: and fooliſhly affects to have himſelf exalted unto that *Glorious High Throne,* by all people, as he ſometimes is, by Execrable *Witches.* This horrible Dragon does not only with his Tayl ſtrike at the *Stars of God,* but at the God himſelf, who made the *Stars,* being deſirous to outſhine them all. God and the Devil are ſworn Enemies to each other; the Terms between them, are thoſe, in *Zech.* 11. 18. *My Soul loathed them, and their Soul alſo abhorred me.* And from this Furious *wrath,* or Diſpleaſure and Prejudice at God, proceeds the Devils *wrath* at us, the poor Children of Men. Our doing the *Service* of God, is one thing that expoſes us to the *wrath* of the Devil. We are the *High Prieſts* of the World; when all Creatures are called upon, *Praiſe ye the Lord,* they bring to us thoſe demanded *Praiſes* of God, ſaying, *do you offer them for us.* Hence 'tis, that the Devil has a Quarrel with [8] us, as he had with the *High-Priest* in the Vision of Old. Our bearing the Image of God is another thing that brings the *wrath* of the Devil upon us. As a *Tyger*, thro' his Hatred at man will tear the very Picture of him, if it come in his way; such a *Tyger* the Devil is; because God said of old, *Let us make Man in our Image*, the Devil is ever saying, *Let us pull this man to pieces.* But the envious *Pride* of the Devil, is one thing more that gives an Edge unto his Furious *Wrath* against us. The Apostle has given us an hint, as if *Pride* had been the *Condemnation of the Devil.* 'Tis not unlikely, that the Devil's *Affectation* to be above that Condition which he might learn that Mankind was to be preferr'd unto, might be the occcasion of his taking up Arms against the *Immortal King.* However, the Devil now sees *Man* lying in the Bosom of God, but *himself* damned in the bottom of Hell; and this enrages him exceedingly; *O,* says he, *I cannot bear it, that man should not be as miserable as my self.*

Proposition III. The *Devil,* in the prosecution, and the execution of his *wrath* upon them, often gets a *Liberty* to make a *Descent* upon the Children of men. When the Devil *does hurt* unto us, he *comes down* unto us; for the Rendezvouze of the *Infernal Troops*, is indeed in the *supernal parts* of our Air.[83] But as 'tis said, *A sparrow of the*

[83] Perhaps it may not be irrational to conclude that the Abode of the Devil, in those *supernal* Parts is at least as far from the Earth as the fixed Stars; the nearest of these, our Author informs us, in his *Christian*

Air does not fall down without the will of God; ſo I may ſay, *Not a Devil in the Air, can come down without the leave of God.* Of this we have a famous Inſtance in that Arabian Prince, of whom the Devil was not able ſo much as to *Touch* any thing, till the moſt high God gave him a permiſſion, to *go down.*[84] The Devil ſtands with all the Inſtruments of death, aiming at us, and begging of the Lord, as that King aſk'd for the Hood-wink'd *Syrians* of old, *Shall I ſmite 'em, ſhall I ſmite 'em?* He cannot ſtrike a blow, till the Lord ſay, *Go down and ſmite,* but ſometimes he *does* obtain from the *high poſſeſſor of Heaven and Earth,* a Licenſe for the doing of it. The Devil ſometimes does make moſt rueful Havock among us; but ſtill we may ſay to him, as our Lord ſaid unto a great Servant of his, *Thou couldſt have no power againſt me, except it were given thee from above.*[85] The Devil is called in 1 *Pet.* 5. 8. *Your Adverſary.* This is a Law-term; and it notes *An Adverſary at Law.* The Devil cannot come at us, except in ſome fence according to *Law;* but ſometimes

Philoſopher, Page 18, is 2,404,520,-928,000 Miles from the Earth. Now, allowing Lucifer to be able to fly with the Velocity of Sound, he could not reach this Planet ſhort of 50,000 Years! Hence he muſt have ſet out on his Journey thouſands of Years before the World was created. But the Arabians believe that Mahomet performed that Journey ſeveral Times in the ſpace of a few Years. That Mahomet ſhould beat the Devil is not extraordinary.

[84] The Author doubtleſs viewed the Stories in the *Arabian Nights* as Realities and actual Occurrences.

[85] "Nay, though wee make Profeſſion to ſeeke GOD alone in our Troubles; yet when it comes to the Pinch, doe wee not runne vnto the Deuill?"—Cooper, *Myſtery of Witchcraft,* 18-19.

he does procure ſad things to be inflicted, according to the *Law of* the eternal King upon us. The Devil firſt *goes up* as an *Accuſer* againſt us. He is therefore ſtyled *The Accuſer;* and it is on this account, that his proper Name does belong unto him. There is a Court ſomewhere kept; a Court of Spirits, where the Devil enters all ſorts of Complaints [9] againſt us all; he charges us with manifold *ſins* againſt the Lord our God: *There* he loads us with heavy *Imputations* of Hypocryſie, Iniquity, Diſobedience; whereupon he urges, *Lord, let 'em now have the death, which is their wages, paid unto 'em!* If our *Advocate* in the Heavens do not now take off his Libel; the Devil, then, with a Conceſſion of God, *comes down*, as a *deſtroyer* upon us. Having firſt been an *Attorney*, to beſpeak that the Judgments of Heaven may be ordered for us, he then alſo pleads, that he may be the *Executioner* of thoſe Judgments; and the God of Heaven ſometimes after a ſort, ſigns a Warrant, for this *deſtroying Angel*, to do what has been *deſired* to be done for the *deſtroying of men*. But ſuch a *permiſſion* from God, for the Devil to *come down*, and *break in* upon mankind, oftentimes muſt be accompany'd with a *Commiſſion* from ſome wretches of mankind it ſelf. Every man is, as 'tis hinted in *Gen.* 4. 9. *His brother's keeper*. We are to *keep* one another from the Inroads of the Devil, by mutual and cordial Wiſhes of proſperity to one another. When ungodly people give their *Conſents* in *witchcrafts* diabolically performed, for the Devil to annoy their Neighbours, he finds a breach made in the Hedge about us, whereat he Rushes in upon us, with grievous molestations. Yea, when the impious people, that never saw the Devil, do but utter their *Curses* against their Neighbours, those are so many *watch words*, whereby the Mastives of Hell are animated presently to fall upon us. Tis thus, that the Devil gets *leave* to worry us.

Proposition IV. Most horrible *woes* come to be inflicted upon Mankind, when the *Devil* does in *great wrath*, make a *descent* upon them. The *Devil* is a *Do-Evil*, and wholly set upon mischief. When our Lord once was going to *Muzzel* him, that he might not mischief others, he cry'd out, *Art thou come to torment me?* He is, it seems, himself *Tormented*, if he be but *Restrained* from the tormenting of Men. If upon the sounding of the Three last *Apocalyptical Angels*, it was an outcry made in Heaven, *Wo, wo, wo, to the inhabitants of the Earth by reason of the voice of the Trumpet.* I am sure, a *descent* made by the Angel of *death*, would give cause for the like Exclamation: *Wo to the world, by reason of the wrath of the Devil!* what a *woful* plight, mankind would by the descent of the Devil be brought into, may be gathered from the *woful* pains, and wounds, and hideous desolations which the Devil brings upon them, with whom he has with a *bodily Possession* made a Seisure. You may both in Sacred and Profane History, read many a direful Account of the *woes*, which they that are possessed by the Devil, do undergo: And from thence conclude, *What* [10] *must the Children of Men hope from such a Devil!* Moreover, the *Tyrannical Ceremonies*, whereto the Devil uses to subjugate such *Woful* Nations or Orders of Men, as are more Entirely under his Dominion, do declare what *woful* Work the Devil would make where he comes. The very Devotions of those forlorn *Pagans*, to whom the Devil is a Leader, are most bloody *Penances;* and what *Woes* indeed must we expect from such a Devil of a *Moloch*, as relishes no Sacrifices like those of Humane Heart-blood, and unto whom there is no Musick like the bitter, dying, doleful Groans, ejaculated by the Roasting Children of Men.

Furthermore, the servile, abject, needy circumstances wherein the Devil keeps the Slaves, that are under his more sensible Vassalage, do suggest unto us, how *woful* the Devil would render all our Lives. We that live in a Province, which affords unto us all that may be necessary or comfortable for us, found the Province fill'd with vast Herds of Salvages, that never saw so much as a *Knife*, or a *Nail*, or a *Board*, or a Grain of *Salt*, in all their Days. No better would the Devil have the World provided for. Nor should we, or any else, have one convenient thing about us, but be as indigent as *usually* our most *Ragged Witches* are; if *the Devil's Malice* were not overruled by a *compassionate God*, who *preserves Man and Beaſt*. Hence 'tis, that *the Devil*, even like a *Dragon*, keeping a Guard upon ſuch *Fruits* as would *refreſh* a languiſhing World, has hindred Mankind for many Ages, from hitting upon thoſe *uſeful Inventions*, which yet *were ſo obvious* and *facil*, that it is every bodies wonder, they were no ſooner hit upon. The *bemiſted World*, muſt jog on for thouſands of Years, without the knowledg of *the Loadſtone*, till a *Neapolitan* ſtumbled upon it, about *three hundred years* ago. Nor muſt the World be *bleſt* with ſuch a *matchleſs Engine* of *Learning* and *Vertue*, as that of *Printing*, till about *the middle of the Fifteenth Century*. Nor could *One Old Man, all over the Face of the whole Earth*, have the *benefit* of ſuch a *Little*, tho' moſt *needful* thing, as a pair of *Spectacles*, till a *Dutch-Man*, a *little while* ago accommodated us.[86]

Indeed, as the Devil does begrutch us all manner of *Good*, ſo he does annoy us with all manner of *Wo*, as often as he finds himſelf capable of doing it. But ſhall we mention ſome of the *ſpecial woes* with which the Devil does uſually infeſt the World! Briefly then; *Plagues* are ſome of thoſe *woes* with which the Devil troubles us. It is ſaid of the *Iſraelites*, in 1 *Cor*. 10. 10. *They were deſtroyed of the deſtroyer*. That is, they had *the Plague* among them. 'Tis the *Deſtroyer*, or *the*

[86] If Spectacles were invented as far back as 1269, "a little while ago" would hardly have applied to the Fact; but the Author probably had Reference to Z. Janſen, a Maker of Spectacles, living in Middleburgh, in 1590. The Inventor was a Monk of Piſa, named Spina.

Devil, that scatters *Plagues* about the World. Pestilential and Contagious Diseases, 'tis the Devil who does oftentimes invade us with them. 'Tis no uneasy thing for the Devil to impreg[11]nate the Air about us, with such Malignant *Salts*, as meeting with *the Salt* of our *Microcosm*, shall immediately cast us into that Fermentation and Putrefaction, which will utterly dissolve all the Vital Tyes within us; Ev'n as an *Aqua-Fortis*, made with a conjunction of *Nitre* and *Vitriol*, Corrodes what it Seizes upon. And when the Devil has raised those *Arsenical Fumes*, which become *Venemous Quivers* full of *Terrible Arrows*, how easily can he shoot the deleterious *Miasms* into those Juices or Bowels of Mens Bodies, which will soon Enflame them with a Mortal Fire! Hence come such *Plagues*, as that *Beesom of Destruction*, which within our memory swept away such a Throng of People from one *English* City in one Visitation;[87] And hence those Infectious Fevers, which are but so many *Disguised Plagues* among us, causing Epidemical Desolations. Again, *Wars* are also some of those *Woes*, with which the Devil causes our Trouble. It is said in *Rev.* 12. 17. *The Dragon was Wrath and he went to make War;* and there is in truth scarce any *War*, but what is of the *Dragon's* kindling.[88]

[87] A great Plague in London was not then (1692) a very remote Event. That which raged in 1665 carried off 68,000 People, according to the best Estimate which could be made at the Time.

[88] This fabulous Monster was considered a Reality among a large

The Devil is that *Vulcan*, out of whose Forge come the instruments of our *Wars*, and it is he that finds us Employments for those Instruments. We read concerning *Dæmoniacks*, or People in whom the Devil was, that they would cut and wound themselves; and so, when the Devil is in Men, he puts 'em upon dealing in that barbarous fashion with one another. *Wars* do often furnish him with some Thousands of Souls in one Morning from one Acre of Ground; and for the sake of such *Thyestæan* Banquets, he will push us upon as many *Wars* as he can.

Once more, why may not *Storms* be reckoned among those *Woes*, with which the Devil does disturb us? It is not improbable that *Natural Storms* on the World are often of the Devils raising. We are told in *Job* 1. 11, 12, 19. that the Devil made a *Storm*, which hurricano'd the House of *Job*, upon the Heads of them that were Feasting in it. *Paracelsus* could have informed the Devil, if he had not been informed, as besure he was before, That if much *Aluminious* matter, with *Salt Petre* not throughly prepared, be mixed, they will send up a cloud of Smoke, which *will* come down in Rain. But undoubtedly the *Devil* understands as *well* the way to make a *Tempest* as to turn the *Winds* at the *Solicitation* of a *Laplander*;[89] whence perhaps it is, that Thunders are

Portion of the human Family. A satisfactory Account of what a Dragon is or is not, may be seen in that useful little Work entitled The *Home Cyclopedia*, compiled by Messrs. George Ripley and Bayard Taylor.

89 A very considerable Part of the learned John Scheffer's *History*

obferved oftner to break upon *Churches* than upon any other *Buildings;* and befides many a Man, yea many a Ship, yea, many a Town has mifcarried, when the Devil has been permitted from above to make an horrible Tempeft.[90] However that the Devil has raifed many *Metaphorical Storms* upon the Church, is a thing, than which there is nothing more notorious. It was faid unto Believers in *Rev.* 2. 10. *The Devil fhall caft fome of* [12] *you into Prifon.* The Devil was he that at firft fet *Cain upon Abel* to butcher him, as the Apoftle feems to fuggeft, for his Faith in God, as a *Rewarder.* And in how many *Perfecutions,* as well as *Herefies* has the Devil been ever fince Engaging all the Children of *Cain!* That Serpent the Devil has acted his curfed Seed in unwearied endeavours to have them, *Of whom the World is not worthy,* treated as thofe who are *not worthy to live in the World.* By the impulfe of the Devil, 'tis that firft the old *Heathens,* and

of Lapland is taken up in Details of Witchcraft, as obferved in that Country. He was a Native of Germany, born 1621, refided fome Time in Sweden, died 1679. For later Tranfactions of the fame Kind, and in the fame Country, the Reader may confult Dr. Horneck's *Account,* before referred to, "Done from the High-Dutch."

90 This will all be found verified (if the Reader can command fufficient Credulity) in a curious little Work entitled *England's Warning Pieces,* printed in 1642, and fully illuftrated by Engravings. Among *Prodigies* related, the Writer fays: "I remember our Brethren in New England, not long fince, made ufe of another moft prodigious and mifhapen and monftrous Birth, brought foorth by a Gentlewoman of that New Plantation, who had beene a maine Fautrix, if not originall Broacher of very many moft wicked, dangerous and damnable Opinions in their Church." Page 27. For further Particulars fee Savage's *Winthrop's Journal,* i, 261-3.

then the mad *Arians* were *pricking Briars* to the true Servants of God; and that the *Papiſts* that came after them, have out done them all for Slaughters, upon thoſe that have been *accounted as the Sheep for the Slaughters*. The late *French* Perſecution is perhaps the horribleſt that ever was in the World:[91] And as the Devil of *Maſcon* ſeems before to have meant it in his out-cries upon *the Miſeries preparing for the poor Hugonots!* Thus it has been all acted by a ſinglar Fury of the old Dragon inſpiring of his Emiſſaries.

But in reality, *Spiritual Woes* are the *principal Woes* among all thoſe that the Devil would have us undone withal. *Sins* are the worſt of *Woes*, and the Devil ſeeks nothing ſo much as to plunge us into Sins. When men do commit a Crime for which they are to be Indicted, they are uſually *mov'd by the Inſtigation of the Devil*. The Devil will put *ill men upon being worſe*. Was it not he that ſaid in 1 *King*. 22. 22. *I will go forth, and be a lying Spirit in the Mouth of all the Prophets?* Even ſo the Devil becomes an *Unclean Spirit, a Drinking Spirit, a Swearing Spirit, a Worldly Spirit, a Paſſionate Spirit, a Revengeful*

[91] This has Reference to the then late Perſecution of the Huguenots in France. They had been protected by the Edict of Henry the Fourth (Nantes, 1598), which was revoked in 1685 by Louis XIV; by which Revocation about 50,000 Proteſtants were forced to fly the Kingdom. Some fled to Germany, Holland, Switzerland, England, and ſome even took Refuge in New England, where their Poſterity are yet well known, reſpected and honored.

Spirit, and the like in the Hearts of thoſe that are already too much of ſuch a Spirit; and thus they become improv'd in Sinfulneſs. Yea, the Devil will put *good men upon doing ill.* Thus we read in 1 *Chron.* 21. 1.. *Satan provoked David to number Iſrael.* And ſo the *Devil provokes* men that are Eminent in Holineſs unto ſuch things as may become eminently Pernicious; he *provokes* them eſpecially unto *Pride*, and unto many unſuitable Emulations. There are likewiſe moſt lamentable Impreſſions which the *Devil* makes upon the *Souls of Men* by way of puniſhment upon them for their *Sins.* 'Tis thus when an Offended God puts the *Souls* of *Men* over into the Hands of that Officer *who has the power of Death, that is, the Devil.* It is the woful Miſery of Unbelievers in 2 *Cor.* 4. 4. *The god of this World has blinded their minds.* And thus it may be ſaid of thoſe woful Wretches whom the *Devil* is a God unto, *the Devil ſo muffles them that they cannot ſee the things of their peace.* And *the Devil ſo hardens them, that nothing will awaken their cares about their Souls:* How come ſo many to be *Seared* in their Sins? 'Tis the Devil that with a red hot Iron fetcht from his Hell [13] does *cauteriſe* them. Thus 'tis, till perhaps at laſt they come to have a *Wounded Conſcience* in them, and the Devil has often a ſhare in their Torturing and confounded Anguiſhes. The *Devil* who Terrified *Cain*, and *Saul*, and *Judas* into Deſperation, ſtill becomes a *King of Terrors* to many Sinners, and frights them from laying hold on the Mercy of God in the Lord Jeſus Chriſt. In theſe regards, *Wo unto us, when the Devil comes down upon us.*[92]

Propoſition V. Toward the *End* of his *Time* the *Deſcent* of the Devil in *Wrath* upon the World will produce more *woful Effects*, than what have been in *former Ages.* The dying Dragon, will bite more cruelly and ſting more bloodily than ever he did before: The Death-pangs of the Devil will make him to be more of a *Devil* than ever he was; and the Furnace of this *Nebuchadnezzar* will be heated *ſeven times* hotter, juſt before its putting out.

We are in the firſt place to apprehend, that there is a time fixed and ſtated by God for the Devil to enjoy a dominion over our ſinful and therefore woful World. The *Devil* once exclaimed in *Mat.* 8. 29. *Jeſus, thou Son of God, art thou come hither to Torment us before our Time?* It is plain, that until the ſecond coming of our Lord the *Devil* muſt have a time of plagueing the World, which he was afraid would have Expired at his firſt. The *Devil* is *by the wrath of God the Prince of this World;* and the time of his Reign is to continue until the time when our Lord himſelf ſhall *take to himſelf his great Power and*

92 If, according to our Author, there is anything good or bad, that the Devil does not do, and is not the Author of, one might not unreaſonably inquire what it is? Certainly in his Charges againſt the Devil every Accuſation imaginable is exhauſted, not one left even to father upon a Witch. Erratic Brains thus overdo themſelves.

Reign. Then 'tis that the *Devil* ſhall hear the Son of God ſwearing with loud Thunders againſt him, *Thy time ſhall now be no more!* Then ſhall the *Devil* with his Angels receive their doom, which will be, *depart into the everlaſting Fire prepared for you.*

We are alſo to apprehend, that in the *mean time,* the Devil can give a ſhrewd gueſs, when he draws near to the *End of his Time.* When he ſaw Chriſtianity enthron'd among the *Romans,* it is here ſaid, in our *Rev.* 12. 12. *He knows he hath but a ſhort time.* And how does he *know it?* Why *Reaſon* will make the Devil to *know* that God won't ſuffer him to have the *Everlaſting Dominion;* and that when God has once begun to reſcue the World out of his hands, he'll go through with it, until the *Captives of the mighty ſhall be taken away and the prey of the terrible ſhall be delivered.* But the Devil will have *Scripture* alſo, to make him *know,* that when his Antichriſtian *Vicar,* the *ſeven-headed Beaſt* on the *ſeven-hilled* City,[93] ſhall have ſpent his determined years, he with his *Vicar* muſt unavoidably go down into the *bottomleſs Pit.* It is not improbable, that the Devil often hears the *Scripture* expounded in our Congregations; yea that we never aſſemble without a *Satan* among us. As there are ſome Divines, who do with more uncertainty conjecture, from a certain place in the Epiſtle to the *Epheſians,* That the Angels

[93] Rome was built on ſeven Hills. It is to that he alludes.

X

do ſometimes come into our Churches, to gain ſome advantage from our Miniſtry. But be ſure our *Demonſtrable Interpretations* may give Repeated Notices to the Devil, *That his time is almoſt out;* and what the Preacher ſays unto the *Young Man, Know thou, that God will bring thee into Judgment!* THAT may our Sermons tell unto the *Old Wretch, Know thou, that the time of thy Judgment is at hand.*

But we muſt now, likewiſe, apprehend, that in *ſuch a time,* the *woes* of the World will be heightened, beyond what they were at *any time* yet from the foundation of the World. Hence 'tis, that the Apoſtle has forewarned us, in 2 *Tim.* 3. 1. *this know, that* [14] *in the laſt days, perillous times ſhall come.* Truly, when the Devil *knows,* that he is got into his *Laſt days,* he will make *perillous times* for us; the times will grow more full of *Devils,* and therefore more full of *Perils,* than ever they were before. Of this, if we would *know,* what cauſe is to be aſſigned; It is not only, becauſe the Devil grows more *able,* and more *eager* to vex the World; but alſo, and chiefly, becauſe the World is more *worthy* to be vexed by the Devil, than ever heretofore. The *Sins* of Men in this Generation, will be more *mighty Sins,* than thoſe of the former Ages; men will be more Accurate and Exquiſite and Refined in the arts of *Sinning,* than they uſe to be. And beſides, their own ſins, the ſins of all the former Ages will alſo lie upon the ſinners of this generation. Do we aſk why the *miſchievous powers of darkneſs* are to prevail more in our days, than they did in thofe that are paft and gone! 'Tis becaufe that men by finning over again the fins of the former days, have a *Fellowfhip with all thofe unfruitful works of darknefs.* As 'twas faid in *Matth.* 23. 36. *All thefe things fhall come upon this generation;* fo the men of the laft Generation, will find themfelves involved in the guilt of all that went before them. Of Sinners 'tis faid, *They heap up Wrath;* and the finners of the Laft Generations do not only add unto the *heap* of fin that has been pileing up ever fince the Fall of man, but they Intereft themfelves in every fin of that enormous heap. There has been a *Cry* of all former ages going up to God, *That the Devil may come down!* and the finners of the Laft Generations, do fharpen and louden that *cry,* till the thing do come to pafs, as Deftructively as Irremediably. From whence it follows, that the Thrice Holy God, with his Holy Angels, will now after a fort more *abandon* the World, than in the former ages. The roaring Impieties of the *old World,* at laft gave mankind fuch a diftaft in the Heart of the Juft God, that he came to fay, *It Repents me that I have made fuch a Creature!* And however, it may be but a witty Fancy, in a late Learned Writer, that the *Earth* before the Flood was nearer to the Sun, than it is at this Day; and that Gods Hurling down the *Earth* to a further diftance from the *Sun,* were the caufe of that Flood;[94] yet we may fitly enough fay, that men

94 Ray refers to the Subject of the Earth having been once nearer

perished by a *Rejection* from the God of Heaven. Thus the enhanc'd Impieties of this *our World*, will Exasperate the Displeasure of God, at such a rate, as that he will more *cast us off*, than heretofore; until at last, he do with a more than ordinary Indignation say, *Go Devils; do you take them, and make them beyond all former measures miserable!*

If Lastly, We are inquisitive after Instances of those aggravated *woes*, with which the Devil will towards the *End* of his *Time* assault us; let it be remembered, That all the Extremities which were foretold by the *Trumpets* and *Vials* in the Apocalyptick Schemes of these things, to come upon the World, were the *woes* to come from the *wrath* of the Devil, upon the *shortning* of his *Time*. The horrendous desolations that have come upon mankind, by the Irruptions of the old *Barbarians* upon the *Roman* World, and then of the *Saracens*, and since, of the *Turks*, were such *woes* as men had never seen before. The Infandous *Blindness* and *Vileness* which then came upon mankind, and the Monstrous *Croisadoes* which thereupon carried the *Roman* World by Millions together unto the Shambles; were also such *woes* as had never yet had a Parallel. And yet these were some of the things here intended, when it was said, *Wo! For the Devil is come down in great Wrath, having but a short time.*

the Sun than at present. See *Physico-Theological Discourses*, P. 381; also Dr. John Woodward's *Natural History of the Earth*, 245, Edition 1695, 8vo. Other Authors might be referred to.

But besides all these things, and besides the increase of *Plagues* and *Wars*, and *Storms*, and *Internal Maladies* now in our days, there are especially two most extraordinary *Woes*, one would fear, will in these days become very ordinary. One *Woe* that may be look'd for is, A frequent Repition of *Earthquakes*, and this perhaps by the energy of the Devil in the *Earth*. The Devil will be clap't up, as a Prisoner in or near the Bowels of the earth, when once that *Conflagration* shall be dispatched, which will make, *The New Earth wherein shall dwell Righteousness*; and that *Conflagration* will doubtless be much promoted by the Subterraneous *Fires*, which are a cause of the *Earthquakes* in our Dayes. Accordingly, we read, *Great Earthquakes in divers places*, enumerated among the Tokens of the *Time* approaching, when the Devil shall have no longer *Time*. I suspect, That we shall now be visited with more Usual [15] and yet more Fatal *Earthquakes* than were our Ancestors; in asmuch as the *Fires* that are shortly to *Burn unto the Lowest Hell, and set on Fire the Foundations of the Mountaions*, will now get more Head than they use to do; and it is not impossible, that the Devil, who is ere long to be punished in those *Fires*, may aforehand augment his Desert of it, by having an hand in using some of those *Fires*, for our Detriment. Learned Men have made no scruple to charge the Devil with it; *Deo permittente, Terræ motus causat.* The Devil surely, was a party in the *Earthquake*,[95] whereby the Vengeance of God, in one black Night ſunk Twelve conſiderable Cities of *Aſia*, in the Reign of *Tiberious*.[96] But there will be more ſuch *Cataſtrophe's* in our Dayes; *Italy* has lately been *Shaking*, till its *Earthquakes* have brought Ruines at once upon more than thirty Towns; but it will within a little while, *ſhake* again, and *ſhake* till the Fire of God have made an Entire *Etna* of it. And behold, This very Morning, when I was intending to utter among you ſuch Things as theſe, we are caſt into an *Heartquake* by Tidings of an *Earthquake* that has lately happened at *Jamaica:* an horrible *Earthquake*, whereby the *Tyrus* of the Engliſh *America*, was at once pull'd into the Jaws of the Gaping and Groaning Earth, and many Hundreds of the Inhabitants buried alive.[97] The Lord ſanctifie ſo diſmal a Diſpenſation of his Providence, unto all the *American* Plantations! But be aſſured, my Neighbours, the *Earthquakes* are not over yet! We have not yet ſeen *the laſt*. And then, Another *Wo* that may be Look'd for is, The Devils being now let Looſe in *preternatural*

[95] So far as the Annotator's Reading goes he has not found the Devil charged with making Earthquakes previous to our Author's Time. He certainly was in Advance of all Philoſophers, ancient and modern, as reſpects that Diſcovery.

[96] Claudius Nero Tiberius died A. D. 37, aged 78.

[97] On the 7th of June, 1692, Jamaica was partly deſtroyd. Some 1500 People periſhed. Why Jamaica or its Capitol is compared to the ancient *Tyros* or *Tyrus* it is not eaſy to underſtand, as it might be difficult to find two Places differing wider in moſt Reſpects. See Ray's *Diſcourſes*, 258, where may be ſeen a particular Account of this Earthquake.

Operations more than formerly; and perhaps in *Possessions* and *Obsessions* that shall be very marvellous. You are not Ignorant, That just before our Lords *First Coming*, there were most observable Outrages committed by the Devil upon the Children of Men: And I am suspicious, That there will again be an unusual Range of the Devil among us, a little before the *Second Coming* of our Lord, which will be, to give the last stroke, in *Destroying the works of the Devil.* The *Evening Wolves* will be much abroad, when we are near the *Evening* of the World. The Devil is going to be Dislodged of the *Air*, where his present Quarters are; God will with flashes of hot *Lightning* upon him, cause him to *fall as Lightning* from his Ancient Habitations: And the *Raised Saints* will there have a *New Heaven*, which We *expect according to the Promise of God.* Now a little before this thing, you be like to see the Devil more *sensibly* and *visibly* Busy upon *Earth* perhaps, than ever he was before. You shall oftner hear about *Apparitions* of the Devil, and about poor people strangely Bewitched, *Possessed* and *Obsessed*, by Infernal Fiends. When our Lord is going to set up His Kingdom, in the most *sensible* and *visible* manner, that ever was, and in a manner answering *the Transfiguration* in *the Mount*, it is a Thousand to One, but *the Devil* will in sundry *parts of the world*, assay *the like* for Himself, with a most Apish Imitation: and Men, at least in *some* Corners of the World, and perhaps in *ſuch* as God may have ſome ſpecial Deſigns upon, will to their Coſt, be more Familiarized *with the World of Spirits*, than they had been formerly.

So that, in fine, if juſt before *the End*, when *the times of the* Jews were to be finiſhed, a man then ran about every where, crying, *Wo to the Nation! Wo to the City! Wo to the Temple! Wo! Wo! Wo!* Much more may the deſcent of the Devil, juſt before his *End*, when alſo *the times of the Gentiles* will be finiſhed, cauſe us to cry out, *Wo! Wo! Wo! becauſe of the black things that threaten us!*

But it is now Time to make our Improvement of what has been ſaid. And, firſt, we ſhall entertain our ſelves with a few *Corollaries*, deduced from what has been thus aſſerted.

Corollary I. What cauſe have we to bleſs God, for our preſervation from the *Devils wrath*, in this which may too reaſonably be called the *Devils World!* While we are in *this preſent evil world*, We are continually ſurrounded with ſwarms of thoſe Devils, who make this *preſent world*, become ſo *evil*. What a wonder of Mercy is it, that no *Devil* could ever yet make a prey of us![98] We can ſet our foot no where but we ſhall tread in the midſt of moſt Helliſh *Rattle-Snakes;* and one of thoſe *Rattle-Snakes* once thro' the mouth of a Man, on whom he had Seized, hiſſed out

[98] The Annotator is very greatly out in his Reckoning if the Reader does not decide that the Author was of all Men the moſt "bedeviled" of any ever heard or read of by him. This is the Editor's *Corollorary.*

ſuch a Truth as this, *If God would let me looſe upon you, I ſhould find enough in the Beſt of you all, to make you all mine.*[99] What ſhall I ſay? The *Wilderneſs* thro' which we are paſſing to the *Pro-* [16]
miſed Land, is all over fill'd with *Fiery flying ſerpents.* But, bleſſed be God; None of them have hitherto ſo faſtned upon us, as to confound us utterly! All our way to Heaven, lies by the *Dens of Lions,* and the *Mounts of Leopards;* there are incredible Droves of Devils in our way. But have we ſafely got on our way thus far? O let us be thankful to our Eternal preſerver for it. It is ſaid in Pſal. 76. 10. *Surely the wrath of Man ſhall praiſe thee, and the Remainder of wrath ſhalt thou reſtrain;* But *ſurely* it becomes to praiſe God, in that we have yet ſuſtain'd no more Damage by the *wrath of the Devil,* and in that he has reſtrain'd that Overwhelming *wrath.* We are poor, Travellers in a World, which is as well the Devils *Field,* as the Devils *Gaol;*[100] a World in every Nook whereof the Devil is encamped with *Bands of Robbers,* to peſter all that have their *Face looking Zion-ward:* And are we all this while preſerved from the undoing Snares of the *Devil?* it is, *Thou, O keeper of Iſrael, that haſt hitherto been*

99 This is related by one Mr. Balſom. See Clarke's *Martyrology,* ii, 179. The Devil had Poſſeſſion of the Body of the Man, and uttered the Language italicized in the Text, making Uſe of the Man's Organs of Speech.

100 It may not be eaſy for the Reader to diſcern how the whole Earth and the infinite Realms of Space about it can be much of a *Gaol,* eſpecially with ſuch a liberal Yard. The Doctor's Imagination is ſingularly at random ſometimes.

our Keeper! And therefore, *Bleſs the Lord, O my ſoul, Bleſs his Holy Name, who has redeemed thy Life from the Deſtroyer!*

Corollary II. We may ſee the riſe of thoſe multiply'd, magnify'd, and Singularly-ſtinged Afflictions, with which *aged,* or *dying* Saints frequently have their *Death* Prefaced, and their *Age* embittered. When the Saints of God are going to leave the World, it is uſually a more *Stormy World* with them, than ever it was; and they find more *Vanity,* and more *Vexation* in the world than ever they did before. It is true, *That many are the afflictions of the Righteous;* but a little before they bid adieu to all thoſe many *Afflictions,* they often have greater, harder, Sorer, Loads thereof laid upon them, than they had yet endured. It is true, *That thro' much Tribulation we muſt enter into the Kingdom of God;* but a little before our *Entrance* thereinto, our *Tribulation* may have ſome ſharper accents of Sorrow, than ever were yet upon it. And what is the cauſe of this? It is indeed the *Faithfulneſs of our God unto us,* that we ſhould find the *Earth* more full of *Thorns* and *Briars* than ever, juſt before he fetches us from *Earth* to *Heaven;* that ſo we may go away the more willingly, the more eaſily, and with leſs Convulſion, at his calling for us. O there are *ugly Ties,* by which we are faſtned unto this world; but God will by *Thorns and Briars* tear thoſe *Ties* aſunder. But, *is not the Hand of Joab here?* Sure, There is the *wrath* of the *Devil* alſo in it. A little before we ſtep into Heaven, the *Devil* thinks with himſelf, *My time to abuſe that Saint is now but ſhort; what Miſchief I am to do that Saint, muſt be done quickly, if at all; he'l ſhortly be out of my Reach for ever.* And for this cauſe he will now fly upon us with the Fierceſt Efforts and Furies of his *Wrath.* It was allowed unto the *Serpent,* in Gen. 2. 15. *To Bruiſe the Heel.* Why, at the *Heel,* or at the *Cloſe,* of our Lives, the *Serpent* will be nibbling, more than ever in our Lives before: and it is *Becauſe now he has but a ſhort time.* He knows, That we ſhall very ſhortly be, *Where the wicked ceaſe from Troubling, and where the Weary are at Reſt;* wherefore that *Wicked* one will now *Trouble* us, more than ever he did, and we ſhall have ſo much *Diſreſt,* as will make us more *weary* than ever we were, of things here below.

Corollary III. What a Reaſonable Thing then is it, that they whoſe *Time* is but *ſhort,* ſhould make as great *Uſe* of their *Time,* as ever they can! I pray, let us learn ſome *good,* even from the *wicked One* himſelf. It has been adviſed, *Be wiſe as Serpents:* why, there is a piece of *Wiſdom,* whereto that old *Serpent,* the Devil himſelf, may be our Moniter. When the Devil perceives his *Time* is but *ſhort,* it puts him upon *Great Wrath.* But how ſhould it be with *us,* when we perceive that our *Time* is but *ſhort?* why, it ſhould put us upon *Great Work.* The motive which makes the Devil to be more full of *wrath;* ſhould make us more full of *warmth*, more full of *watch*, and more full of *All Diligence to make our Vocation, and Election ſure.* Our *Pace* in our Journey *Heaven-ward*, muſt be Quickened, if our *ſpace* for that Journey be ſhortned, even as *Iſrael* went further the *two laſt* years of their Journey *Canaan-ward*, than they did in 38 years before. The Apoſtle brings this, as a *ſpur* to the Devotions of Chriſtians, in 1 *Cor.* 7. 29. *This I ſay, Brethren, the time is ſhort.* Even ſo, I *ſay* this; ſome things I lay before you, which I do only *think*, or *gueſs*, but here is a thing which I venture to *ſay* with all the [33] freedom imaginable. You have now a *Time* to *Get* good, even a *Time* to make ſure of *Grace and Glory, and every good thing*, by true Repentance: But, *This I ſay, the time is but ſhort.* You have now *Time* to *Do* good, even to *ſerve out your generation*, as by the *Will*, ſo for the *Praiſe* of God; but, *This I ſay, the time is but ſhort.* And what I ſay thus to *All* People, I ſay to *Old* People, with a peculiar Vehemency: Sirs, It cannot be long before your *Time* is out; there are but a few ſands left in the glaſs of your *Time:* And it is of all things the ſaddeſt, for a man to ſay, *My time is done, but my work undone!* O then, *To work* as faſt as you can; and of Soul-work, and Church-work, diſpatch as much as ever you can. Say to all *Hindrances*, as the gracious *Jeremiah Burroughs*[101] would ſometimes to *Viſitants: You'll*

[101] A noted Puritan of the Time of Cromwell. In ſuch of his Books as have come under my Notice, his Name is uniformly *Burroughs*. His

excuse me if I ask you to be short with me, for my work is great, and my time is but short. Methinks every *time* we hear a Clock, or see a Watch, we have an admonition given us, that our *Time* is upon the *wing*, and it will all be gone within a little while. I remember I have read of a famous man, who having a *Clock-watch* long lying by him, out of Kilture in his Trunk, it unaccountably struck Eleven just before he died. Why, there are many of you, for whom I am to do that office this day: I am to tell you *You are come to your* Eleventh *hour;* there is no more than a *twelfth part* at most, of your life yet behind. But if we neglect our business, till our *short Time* shall be reduced into *none*, then, *woe to us, for the great wrath of God will send us down from whence there is no Redemption.*

Corollary IV.

How welcome should a *Death in the Lord* be unto them that belong not unto the Devil, but unto the Lord! While we are sojourning in this World, we are in what may upon too many accounts be called *The Devils Country:* We are where the Devil may come upon us in *great wrath* continually. The day when God shall take us out of this World, will be, *The day when the Lord will deliver us from the hand of all our Enemies, and from the hand of Satan.* In such a day, why should not our song

Rare Jewell, 4to, 1648, was formerly very popular, and there is a handsome Edition of it as late as 1845.

be that of the Pſalmiſt, *Bleſſed be my Rock, and let the God of my Salvation be exalted!* While we are here, we are in *the valley of the ſhadow of death;* and what is it that makes it ſo? 'Tis becauſe the *wild Beaſts of Hell* are lurking on every ſide of us, and every minute ready to ſalley forth upon us. But our *Death* will fetch us out of that *Valley,* and carry us where we ſhall be *for ever with the Lord.* We are now under the daily *Buffetings* of the Devil, and he does moleſt us with ſuch *Fiery Darts,* as cauſe us even to cry out, *I am weary of my Life.* Yea, but are we as *willing to die,* as, *weary of Life?* Our Death will then ſoon ſet us where we cannot be reach'd by the *Fiſt of Wickedneſs;* and where the *Perfect cannot be ſhotten at.* It is ſaid in *Rev.* 14. 13. *Bleſſed are the* [34] *Dead which die in the Lord, they reſt from their labours.* But we may ſay, *Bleſſed are the Dead in the Lord, inaſmuch as they reſt from the Devils!* Our *dying* will be but our *taking wing:* When attended with a Convoy of winged Angels, we ſhall be convey'd into that Heaven, from whence the Devil having been thrown he ſhall never more come thither after us. What if God ſhould now ſay to us, as to *Moſes, Go up and die!* As long as we *go up,* when we *die,* let us receive the Meſſage with a joyful Soul; we ſhall ſoon be there, where the Devil can't *come down* upon us. If the *God of our Life* ſhould now ſend that Order to us, which he gave to *Hezekiah, Set thy houſe in order, for thou ſhalt die, and not live*; we need not be caſt into ſuch deadly Agonies thereupon, as *Hezekiah* was: We are but going to that *Houſe*, the Golden Doors whereof, cannot be entred by the Devil that here did uſe to perſecute us. Methinks I ſee the Departed *Spirit* of a Believer, triumphantly carried thro' the Devils *Territories*, in ſuch a ſtately and Fiery Chariot, as the *Spiritualizing Body* of *Elias* had; methink I ſee the Devil, with whole Flocks of *Harpies*, grinning at this Child of God, but unable to faſten any of their griping Talons upon him: And then, upon the utmoſt edge of our *Atmoſphære*, methinks I overhear the holy Soul, with a moſt heavenly Gallantry, deriding the defeated Fiend, and ſaying, *Ah! Satan! Return to thy Dungeons again; I am going where thou canſt not come for ever!* O 'tis a brave thing ſo to die! and eſpecially ſo to die, in *our time*. For, tho' when we call to mind, *That the Devils time is now but ſhort*, it may almoſt make us wiſh to *live* unto the *end* of it; and to ſay with the Pſalmiſt, *Becauſe the Lord will ſhortly appear in his Glory to build up* Zion. *O my God! Take me not away in the midſt of my days.* Yet when we bear in mind, *that the Devils Wrath is now moſt great*, it would make one willing to be *out of the way*. Inaſmuch as now is the time for the doing of thoſe things in the proſpect whereof *Balaam* long ago cry'd out *Who ſhall live when ſuch things are done!* We ſhould not be inordinatly loth to *die* at ſuch a time. In a word, the *Times* are ſo *bad*, that we may well count it, as *good* a *time* to die in, as ever we ſaw.

Corollary V.

Good News for the *Iſrael* of God, and particularly for his *New-Engliſh Iſrael.* If the Devils *Time* were above a *thouſand years ago*, pronounced *ſhort*, what may we ſuppoſe it now in *our* Time? Surely *we* are not a *thouſand years* diſtant from thoſe happy *thouſand years* of reſt and peace, and [which is better] *Holineſs* reſerved for the People of God in the latter days; and if we are not a *thouſand years* yet ſhort of that Golden Age, there is cauſe to think, that we are not an *hundred.* That the bleſſed *Thouſand years* are not yet begun, is abundantly clear [35] from this, *We do not ſee the Devil bound;* No, the Devil was never more let *looſe* than in our Days; and it is very much that any ſhould imagine otherwiſe: But the ſame thing that proves the *Thouſand Years* of proſperity for the Church of God, under the whole Heaven, to be not yet *begun*, does alſo prove, that it is not very *far off;* and that is the prodigious *wrath* with which the Devil does in our days Perſecute, yea, deſolate the World. Let us caſt our Eyes almoſt where we will, and we ſhall ſee the *Devils* domineering at ſuch a rate as may juſtly fill us with aſtoniſhment; it is queſtionable whether *Iniquity* ever were ſo rampant, or whether *Calamity* were ever ſo pungent, as in this Lamentable *time;* We may truly ſay, *'Tis the Hour and the Power of*

Darkneſs. But, tho' the *wrath* be ſo *great*, the *time* is but *ſhort:* when we are perplexed with the *wrath* of the Devil, the *Word* of our God at the ſame time unto us, is that in Rom. 16. 20. *The God of Peace ſhall bruiſe Satan under your feet Shortly.* Shortly, didſt thou ſay, deareſt Lord! O gladſome word! Amen, *Even ſo, come Lord! Lord Jeſus, come quickly! We ſhall never be rid of this troubleſome Devil, till thou do come to Chain him up!*

But becauſe the people of God, would willingly be told *whereabouts* we are, with reference to the *wrath and the time* of the Devil, you ſhall give me leave humbly to ſet before you a few *Conjectures.*

The firſt Conjecture.

The Devils *Eldeſt Son* ſeems to be towards the *End* of his laſt *Half-time;* and if it be ſo, the Devils Whole-time, cannot but be very near its *End.* It is a very ſcandalous thing that any *Proteſtant,* ſhould be at a loſs where to find *the Anti-Chriſt.* But, we have a ſufficient aſſurance, that the Duration of *Anti-Chriſt,* is to be but for a *Time,* and for *Times,* and for *Half a time;* that is for *Twelve Hundred and Sixty Years.* And indeed, thoſe *Twelve Hundred and Sixty Years,* were the very Spott of *Time* left for the *Devil,* and meant when 'tis here ſaid, *He has but a ſhort time.* Now, I ſhould have an *eaſie time* of it, if I were never put upon an *Harder Taſk,* than to produce what might render it extreamly probable, that Antichrift entred his laft *Half-time*, or the laft *Hundred* and *Fourfcore* years of his Reign, *at* or foon *after* the celebrated *Reformation* which began at the year 1517 in the former Century.[102] Indeed, it is very agreeable to fee how Antichrift then loft *Half* of his Empire; and how that *half* which then became *Reformed*, have been upon many accounts little more than *Half-reformed*. But by this computation, we muft needs be within a very few years of fuch a *Mortification* to befal the See of *Rome*, as that Antichrift, who has lately been planting (what proves no more lafting than) a *Tabernacle in the Glorious Holy Mountain between the Seas*, muft quickly, *Come to his End and none fhall help him.* [36] So then, within a very little while, we fhall fee the Devil ftript of the grand, yea, the laft, *Vehicle*, wherein he will be capable to abufe our World. The *Fires*, with which, *That Beaft* is to be confumed, will fo finge the Wings of the *Devil* too, that he fhall no more fet the Affairs of *this* world on *Fire*. Yea, they fhall both go into the fame *Fire*, to be *tormented for ever and ever*.

The Second Conjecture.

That which is, perhaps, the greateft Effect of the *Devils Wrath*, feems to be in a manner at an

[102] One has indeed a very "*eafie Time* of it" in prophecying, and it is quite as eafy to be laughed at for fuch Folly by thofe who come after fuch fhallow-pated Soothfayers. The Author felt very fure that by

end: and this would make one hope that the *Devils time* cannot be far from its *end.* It is in Persecution, that the *wrath* of the Devil uses to break forth, with its greatest fury. Now there want not probabilities, that the *last Persecution* intended for the Church of God, before the Advent of our Lord, has been upon it. When we see the *second Woe passing away*, we have a fair signal given unto us, *That the last slaughter of our Lord's Witnesses is over;* and then what Quickly follows? The next thing is, *The Kingdoms of this World, are become the Kingdoms of Our Lord, and of His Christ:* and then *down* goes the Kingdom of the Devil, so that he cannot any more *come down* upon us. Now, the Irrecoverable and Irretrievable Humiliations that have lately befallen the *Turkish Power*, are but so many Declarations of the *second Woe passing away.*[103] And the dealings of God with the *European* parts of the world, at this day do further strengthen this our expectation. We *do* see, *at this hour a great Earth-quake all Europe over:* and *we shall* see, that this *great Earth-quake*, and these great Commotions, will but contribute unto the advancement of our Lords hitherto de-

the Year 1697, only five Years from the Time he was writing, that the Devil would have "his Wings so singed that he should no more set the Affairs of this World on Fire." That is to say—the Millenium would then begin!

[103] The Turks had not received their greatest Check until after our Author wrote. Mahomet IV commenced with renewed Vigor the War against Germany in 1663. It was continued with alternate Success and Disaster, until 1683, when John Sobieski, King of Poland, raised the Siege of Vienna; but it was not till 1699 that the Turks were driven out of Transylvania.

preſſed Intereſts. 'Tis alſo to be remark'd that, a diſpoſition to recognize the *Empire* of God over the *Conſcience* of man, does now prevail more in the world than formerly; and God from on High more touches the Hearts of Princes and Rulers with an averſeneſs to Perſecution. 'Tis particularly the unſpeakable happineſs of the Engliſh Nation, to be under the Influences of that excellent Queen, who could ſay, *In as much as a man cannot make himſelf believe what he will, why ſhould we Perſecute men for not believing as we do! I wiſh I could ſee all good men of one mind; but in the mean time I pray, let them however love one another.*[104] Words worthy to be written in Letters of Gold! and by *us* the more to be conſidered, becauſe to one of *Ours* did that royal Perſon expreſs Her ſelf ſo excellently, ſo obligingly. When the late King *James* publiſhed his Declaration for *Liberty of Conſcience,* a worthy Divine in the Church of *England,* then ſtudying the *Revelation,* ſaw cauſe upon *Revelational* Grounds, to declare himſelf in ſuch words as theſe, *Whatſoever others may intend or deſign by this Liberty of Conſcience, I cannot believe, that it will ever be recalled in* England, *as long as the World ſtands.* And you know how miraculouſly [37] the *Earth-quake*[105] which then immediately came upon the Kingdom, has

[104] The reported Utterance of Queen Mary (Consort of William the Third) at an Interview between her and the Author's Father, at Whitehall, April 9th, 1691. See *Parentator,* p. 130.

[105] This refers to the coming in of the Prince of Orange, and the Overthrow of James the Second's Government.

eſtabliſhed that *Liberty!* But that which exceeds all the tendencies this way, is, the diſpenſation of God at this Day, towards the bleſſed *Vaudois.* Thoſe renowned *Waldenſes,* which were a ſort of *Root* unto all Proteſtant Churches, were never diſſipated, by all the Perſecutions of many Ages, till within theſe few years, the *French* King and the Duke of *Savoy* leagued for their diſſipation.[106] But juſt *Three years and a half after* the *ſcattering* of that holy people, to the ſurpriſe of all the World, *Spirit of life from God* is come into them; and having with a thouſand Miracles repoſſeſſed themſelves of their antient Seats, their hot *Perſecutor* is become their great *Protector.* Whereupon the reflection of the worthy perſon, that writes the ſtory is, *The Churches of* Piemont, *being the Root of the Proteſtant Churches, they have been the firſt eſtabliſhed; the Churches of other places, being but the Branches, ſhall be eſtabliſhed in due time, God will deliver them ſpeedily, He has already delivered the Mother, and He will not long leave the Daughter behind: He will finiſh what he has gloriouſly begun!*

The Third Conjecture.

There is *little room* for hope, that the *great wrath* of the Devil, will not prove the preſent

106 On the 15th of March, 1691, Louis the XIV captured Nice in Piedmont, defended by the Duke of Savoy. But in the following Year the French loſt the Supremacy of the Sea in the terrible Battle off La Hogue. That Supremacy they have never yet obtained.

ruine of our poor *New-England* in particular. I believe, there never was a poor Plantation, more purſued by the *wrath* of the *Devil,* than our poor *New-England;* and that which makes our condition very much the more deplorable is, that the *wrath* of the *great God* Himſelf, at the ſame time alſo preſſes hard upon us. It was a rouſing *alarm* to the Devil, when a great Company of Engliſh *Proteſtants* and *Puritans,* came to erect Evangelical Churches, in a corner of the World, where he had reign'd without any controul for many Ages; and it is a vexing *Eye-ſore* to the Devil, that our Lord Chriſt ſhould be known, and own'd and preached in this *howling Wilderneſs.* Wherefor he has left no *Stone unturned,* that ſo he might undermine his Plantation, and force us out of our Country.

Firſt, The Indian *Powawes,* uſed all their Sorceries to moleſt the firſt Planters here;[107] but God ſaid unto them, *Touch them not!* Then, *Seducing Spirits* came to *root* in this Vineyard, but God ſo rated them off, that they have not prevail'd much farther than the Edges of our Land.[108] After this, we have had a continual *blaſt* upon ſome of our principal Grain, annually diminiſhing a vaſt part of our *ordinary Food.* Herewithal, waſting *Sickneſses,* eſpecially Burning and Mortal Agues, have Shot the Arrows of Death in at our

107 See *Morton's Memorial,* P. 38, Edition 16°. *Edition* 1721. Mather's *Relation,* 110, Ed. 4°, 1864. Johnſon's *Wonderworking Providence,* 51.

108 Having Reference, probably, to the Antinomians, as the more liberal Chriſtians were called.

Windows. Next, we have had many Adversaries of our own Language, who have been perpetually assaying to deprive us of those *English Liberties*, in the encouragement whereof these Territories have been settled.[109] As if this had not been [38] enough; The *Tawnies* among whom we came, have watered our Soil with the Blood of many Hundreds of our Inhabitants. Desolating *Fires* also have many times laid the chief Treasure of the whole Province in Ashes. As for *Losses* by Sea, *they* have been multiply'd upon us: and particularly in the present *French War*, the whole English Nation have observ'd that no part of the Nation has proportionably had so many Vessels taken, as our poor *New-England*. Besides all which, now at last the Devils are (if I may so speak) *in Person* come down upon us with such a *Wrath*, as is justly *much*, and will quickly be *more*, the Astonishment of the World. Alas, I may sigh over *this* Wilderness, as *Moses* did over *his*, in Psal. 90. 7. 9. *We are consumed by thine Anger, and by thy Wrath we are troubled: All our days are passed away in thy Wrath.* And I may add this unto it, *The Wrath of the Devil too has been troubling and spending of us, all our days.*

But what will become of this poor *New-England* after all? Shall we sink, expire, perish, before the *short time* of the Devil shall be finished?[110] I must confess, That when I consider

109 The Difficulties with the Episcopalians.

110 The absurd Notion that the Devil's *Time was very short* in

the lamentable *Unfruitfulneſs* of men, among us, under as powerful and perſpicuous Diſpenſations of the Goſpel, as are in the World; and when I conſider the declining ſtate of the *Power of Godlineſs* in our Churches, with the moſt horrible Indiſpoſition that perhaps ever was, to recover out of this declenſion; I cannot but *Fear* leſt it comes to this, and leſt an *Aſiatic* Removal of Candleſticks come upon us. But upon ſome other Accounts, I would fain *hope* otherwiſe; and I will give *you* therefore the opportunity to try what Inferences may be drawn from theſe probable Prognoſtications.

I ſay, *Firſt*, That ſurely, *America's* Fate muſt at the long run include *New-Englands* in it. What was the deſign of our God, in bringing over ſo many *Europæans* hither of late Years? Of what uſe or ſtate will *America* be, when the *Kingdom of God* ſhall come? If it muſt all be the Devils propriety, while the *ſaved Nations* of the other Hæmiſphere ſhall be *Walking in the Light of the New Jeruſalem*, Our *New-England* has then, 'tis likely, done all that it was erected for. But if God have a purpoſe to make here a ſeat for any of *thoſe glorious things which are ſpoken of thee, O thou City of God;* then even thou, O *New-England*, art within a very little while of better days than ever yet have dawn'd upon thee.

1693, was generally entertained by Chriſtians. This Matter has already been referred to. When the World and its Affairs can go on without antagoniſtic Forces it is pretty certain the Devil's *Time* will be about out.

I ſay, *Secondly*, That tho' there be very *Threatning* Symptoms on *America*, yet there are ſome *hopeful* ones. I confeſs, when one thinks upon the crying Barbarities with which the moſt of thoſe *Europeans* that have Peopled this New world, became the Maſters of it; it looks but *Ominouſly*. When one alſo thinks how much the way of living in many parts of *America*, is utterly inconſiſtent with the very Eſſentials of *Chriſtianity;* yea, how much Injury and Violence is there-
[39]in done to *Humanity* it ſelf; it is enough to damp the Hopes of the moſt Sanguine Complexion. And the *Frown* of Heaven which has hitherto been upon Attempts of better Goſpellizing the Plantations, conſidered, will but increaſe the *Damp*. Neverthelеſs, on the other ſide, what ſhall be ſaid of all the *Promiſes*, That *our Lord Jeſus Chriſt ſhall have the uttermoſt parts of the Earth for his Poſſeſſion?* and of all the *Prophecies*, That *All the ends of the Earth ſhall remember and turn unto the Lord?* Or does it look *agreeably*, That ſuch a rich quarter of the World, equal in ſome regards to all the reſt, ſhould never be out of the *Devils* hands, from the firſt Inhabitation unto the laſt Diſſolution of it? No ſure; why may not the *laſt* be the *firſt?* and the *Sun of Righteouſneſs* come to ſhine *brighteſt*, in Climates which it roſe *lateſt* upon!

I ſay, *Thirdly*, That *as* it fares with *Old England*, ſo it will be moſt likely to fare with *New-England*. For which cauſe, by the way, there may be more of the Divine Favour in the preſent Circumſtances of our dependence on *England*, than we are well aware of. This is very ſure, if matters *go ill* with our *Mother*, her poor American *Daughter* here, muſt feel it; nor could our former Happy Settlement have hindred our ſympathy in that Unhappineſs. But if matters *go Well* in the Three Kingdoms; as long as God ſhall bleſs the Engliſh Nation, with Rulers that ſhall encourage *Piety*, *Honeſty*, *Induſtry*, in their Subjects, and that ſhall caſt a Benign Aſpect upon the Intereſts of our Glorious Goſpel, *Abroad* as well as at *Home;* ſo long, *New-England* will at leaſt keep its head above water: and ſo much the more, for our comfortable Settlement in ſuch a Form as we are now caſt into. Unleſs there ſhould be any ſingular, deſtroying, *Topical Plagues*, whereby an offended God ſhould at laſt make us *Riſe;* But, *Alas, O Lord, what other Hive haſt thou provided for us!*

I ſay, *Fourthly*, That the *Elder England* will certainly and ſpeedily be Viſited with the *ancient loving kindneſs* of God. When one ſees, how ſtrangely the Curſe of our *Joſhua*, has fallen upon the Perſons and Houſes of them that have attempted the Rebuilding of the *Old* Romiſh *Jericho*, which has there been ſo far demoliſhed, they cannot but ſay, That the *Reformation* there, ſhall not only be maintained, but alſo purſued, proceeded, perfected; and that God will ſhortly there have a *New Jeruſalem*. Or, Let a Man in his thoughts run over but the ſeries of amazing Providences towards the Engliſh Nation for the laſt *Thirty Years:* Let him reflect, how many *Plots* for the ruine of the Nation have been ſtrangely diſcovered? yea, how very unaccountably thoſe very *Perſons,* yea, I may alſo ſay, and thoſe very *Methods* which were intended for the tools of that ruine, have become the inſtruments or occaſions of Deliverances? A man cannot but ſay upon theſe Reflec[40]tions, as the Wife of *Manoah* once prudently expreſſed her ſelf, *If the Lord were pleaſed to have Deſtroyed us, He would not have ſhew'd us all theſe things.* Indeed, It is not unlikely, that the Enemies of the Engliſh Nation, may yet provoke ſuch a *Shake* unto it, as may perhaps exceed any that has hitherto been undergone: the Lord prevent the Machinations of his Adverſaries! But that *ſhake* will uſher in the moſt *glorious Times* that ever aroſe upon the Engliſh *Horizon.* As for the *French* Cloud which hangs over *England,* tho' it be like to Rain ſhowers of *Blood* upon a Nation, where the *Blood* of the Bleſſed Jeſus has been too much treated as an *Unholy Thing;* yet I believe God will ſhortly ſcatter it: and my belief is grounded upon a bottom that will bear it. If that overgrown *French Leviathan*[111] ſhould accompliſh any thing like a

[111] Although the Affairs of the French King had begun to decline when the Author wrote the above, his Opponents were not without great Fear from him, as he achieved ſeveral conſiderable Victories on the Land after the ſignal Defeat of his Fleet mentioned in a previous Note.

Conqueſt of *England*, what could there be to hinder him from the Univerſal Empire of the *Weſt?* But the *Viſions* of the Weſtern World, in the *Views* both of *Daniel* and of *John*, do aſſure us, that whatever Monarch, ſhall while the *Papacy* continues go to ſwallow up the *Ten Kings* which received *their Power* upon the Fall of the Weſtern Empire, he muſt miſcarry in the Attempt. The *French Phaetons* Epitaph ſeems written in that, *Sure Word of Prophecy.*

[Since the making of this Conjecture, there are arriv'd unto us, the News of a Victory obtain'd by the *Engliſh* over the *French*, which further confirms our Conjecture; and cauſes us to ſing, *Pharaohs Chariots, and his Hoſts, has the Lord caſt down into the Sea; Thy right-hand has daſhed in pieces the Enemy!*][112]

Now, *In the Salvation of* England, the Plantations cannot but *Rejoyce*, and *New-England* alſo will *be Glad.*

But ſo much for our *Corollaries*, I haſten to the main thing deſigned for your entertainment. And that is,

[112] This Paragraph, though bracketed, is in the original Edition, *Page* 47.

AN HORTATORY AND NECESSARY ADDRESS, TO A COUNTRY NOW EXTRAORDINARILY ALARUM'D BY THE WRATH OF THE DEVIL. *TIS THIS,*

LET us now make a good and a right ufe of the prodigious *defcent* which the *Devil* in *Great Wrath* is at this day making upon our Land. Upon the Death of a Great Man once, an Orator call'd the Town together, crying out, *Concurrite Cives, Dilapfa funt veftra Mœnia!* that is, *Come together, Neighbours, your Town-Walls are fallen down!* But fuch is the defcent of the Devil at this day upon our felves, that I may truly tell you, *The Walls of the whole World are broken down!* The ufual *Walls* of defence about mankind have fuch a Gap made in them, that the very *Devils* are broke in upon us, to feduce the *Souls,* torment the *Bodies,* fully the *Credits,* and confume the *Eftates* of our Neighbours, [41] with Impreffions both as *real* and as *furious,* as if the *Invifible* World were becoming *Incarnate,* on purpofe for the vexing of us. And what ufe ought now to be made of fo tremendous a difpenfation? We are engaged in a *Faft* this day;[113] but fhall we try to fetch *Meat out of the*

[113] Written in 1692.

Eater, and make the *Lion* to afford ſome *Hony* for our *Souls?*

That the Devil is *come down unto us with great Wrath*, we find, we feel, we now deplore.[114] In many ways, for many years hath the Devil been aſſaying to Extirpate the Kingdom of our Lord Jeſus here. *New-England* may complain of the Devil, as in Pſal. 129. 1, 2. *Many a time have they afflicted me, from my Youth, may* New-England *now ſay; many a time have they afflicted me from my Youth; yet they have not prevailed againſt me.* But now there is a more than ordinary *affliction*, with which the *Devil* is Galling of us: and ſuch an one as is indeed Unparallelable. The things confeſſed by *Witches*, and the things endured by *Others*, laid together, amount unto this account of our Affliction. The *Devil*, Exhibiting himſelf ordinarily as a ſmall *Black man*, has decoy'd a fearful knot of proud, froward, ignorant, envious and malicious creatures, to liſt themſelves in his horrid Service, by entring their Names in a *Book* by him tendred unto them.[115] Theſe *Witches*,

[114] Notwithſtanding the extraordinary Familiarity of our Author with the Devil, he does not as yet pretend to have ſeen him, although he muſt have been in Everybody's Way. About twenty Years later, according to De Foe, he had become quite ſcarce, inſomuch that few could pretend to have ſeen him; and hence People became ſomewhat credulous about the Exiſtence of his Majeſty, "as if nothing but ſeeing the Devil could ſatisfie them there was ſuch a Perſon; and nothing is more wonderful to me, in the whole Syſtem of Spirits, than that Satan does not think fit to juſtify the Reality of his Being, by appearing to ſuch in ſome of his worſt Figures, and tell them in full Grimace who he is."—*Eſſay on Apparitions.*

[115] The appearing of the Devil in the Shape of a black Man, or a

whereof above a Score have now *Confessed and shown their Deeds*, and some are now tormented by the Devils, for *Confessing*, have met in Hellish *Randezvouzes*, wherein the Confessors do say, they have had their diabolical Sacraments, imitating the *Baptism* and the *Supper* of our Lord. In these hellish meetings, these Monsters have associated themselves to do no less a thing than, *To destroy the Kingdom of our Lord Jesus Christ, in these parts of the World;* and in order hereunto, First they each of them have their *Spectres*, or Devils, commission'd by them, & representing of them, to be the Engines of their Malice. By these wicked *Spectres*, they seize poor people about the Country, with various & bloudy *Torments;* and of those evidently Preternatural torments there are some have dy'd. They have bewitched some, even so far as to make *Self-destroyers:*[116] and others are in many Towns here and there languishing under their *Evil hands.* The people thus afflicted, are miserably scratched and bitten, so that the Marks are most visible to all the World, but the causes utterly invisible; and the same Invisible Furies do most visibly stick Pins into the bodies of the afflicted, and *scald* them, and hideously distort, and disjoint all their mem-

Man in black is the old Story imported from England. See *Examination and Confession of* Christian Green, Wife of Robert Green *of Brewham, Co. Somerset,* printed in *Sadducismus Triumphatus,* ed. 1726, P. 306.

[116] It is not so remarkable that some should have destroyed themselves under such Circumstances, as that the greater Part of them did not so perish.

bers, besides a thousand other sorts of Plagues beyond these of any natural diseases which they give unto them. Yea, they sometimes drag the poor people out of their chambers, and carry them over Trees and Hills, for divers miles together. A large part of the persons tortured by these Diabolical *Spectres*, are horribly tempted by them, sometimes with fair [42] promises, and sometimes with hard threatnings, but always with felt miseries, to sign the *Devils Laws* in a Spectral Book laid before them; which two or three of these poor Sufferers, being by their tiresome sufferings overcome to do, they have immediately been released from all their miseries and they appear'd in *Spectre* then to Torture those that were before their Fellow-Sufferers. The *Witches* which by their covenant with the Devil, are become Owners of *Spectres*, are oftentimes by their own *Spectres* required and compelled to give their consent, for the molestation of some, which they had no mind otherwise to fall upon; and cruel Depredations are then made upon the Vicinage. In the Prosecution of these Witchcrafts, among a thousand other unaccountable things, the *Spectres* have an odd faculty of cloathing the most substantial and corporeal Instruments of Torture, with Invisibility, while the wounds thereby given have been the most palpable things in the World; so that the Sufferers assaulted with Instruments of Iron, wholly unseen to the standers by, though, to their cost, seen by themselves, have, upon snatching, wrested the Instruments out of the *Spectres* hands, and every one has then immediately not only *beheld*, but *handled*, an Iron Instrument taken by a Devil from a Neighbour. These wicked *Spectres* have proceeded so far, as to steal several quantities of Mony from divers people, part of which Money, has, before sufficient Spectators, been dropt out of the Air into the Hands of the Sufferers, while the *Spectres* have been urging them to subscribe their *Covenant with Death.*[117] In such extravagant ways have these Wretches propounded, the *Dragooning* of as many as they can, in their own Combination, and the *Destroying* of others, with lingring, spreading, deadly diseases; till our Countrey should at last become too hot for us. Among the Ghastly Instances of the *success* which those Bloody Witches have had, we have seen even some of their own Children, so dedicated unto the Devil, that in their Infancy, it is found, the *Imps* have sucked them, and rendred them Venemous to a Prodigy. We have also seen the Devils first batteries upon the Town, where the first Church of our Lord in this Colony was gathered, producing those distractions, which have almost ruin'd the Town.[118] We have seen likewise the *Plague* reaching afterwards into other Towns far and near,

117 This is not a Whit behind the far-famed Story of "The Devil and Dr. Faustus."

118 Church Difficulties were so common, that it is not quite certain to which the Author has Reference; though it seems likely he refers to the Troubles in the Time of Mr. Nicholet. — See Felt, *History of Salem*, ii, 587-8.

where the Houſes of good Men have the Devils filling of them with terrible Vexations!

This is the Deſcent, which, it ſeems, the Devil has now made upon us. But that which makes this Deſcent the more formidable, is; the *multitude* and *quality* of Perſons accuſed of an intereſt in this *Witchcraft*, by the Efficacy of the *Spectres* which take their Name and ſhape upon them; cauſing very many good and wiſe Men to fear, [43] That many *innocent*, yea, and ſome *vertuous* perſons, are by the Devils in this matter, impoſed upon; That the Devils have obtain'd the power, to take on them the likeneſs of harmleſs people, and in that likeneſs afflict other people, and be ſo abuſed by Præſtigious *Dæmons*, that upon their look or touch, the afflicted ſhall be oddly affected. Arguments from the *Providence of God*, on the one ſide, and from our *Charity* towards *Man* on the other ſide, have made this now to become a moſt agitated Controverſie among us. There is an *Agony* produced in the Minds of Men, leſt the Devil ſhould ſham us with *Devices*, of perhaps a finer Thred, than was ever yet practiſed upon the World. The whole buſineſs is become hereupon ſo *Snarled*, and the determination of the Queſtion one way or another, ſo *diſmal*, that our Honourable Judges have a Room for *Jehoſhaphat's* Exclamation, *We know not what to do!*[119] They have

[119] This was indeed a Dilemma; but it may now ſeem exceeding ſtrange that learned Judges had not adopted the only ſafe Courſe at ſuch a Time, and ſimply *to have done nothing*. They appear to have been

used, as Judges have heretofore done, the *Spectral Evidences*, to introduce their further Enquiries into the *Lives* of the persons accused; and they have thereupon, by the wonderful Providence of God, been so strengthened with *other evidences*, that some of the *Witch Gang* have been fairly Executed. But what shall be done, as to those against whom the *evidence* is chiefly founded in the *dark world?* Here they do solemnly demand our Addresses to the *Father of Lights*, on their behalf. But in the mean time, the Devil improves the *Darkness* of this Affair, to push us into a *Blind Mans Buffet*, and we are even ready to be *sinfully*, yea, hotly, and madly, mauling one another in the *dark*.[120]

The consequence of these things, every *considerate* Man trembles at; and the more, because the frequent cheats of Passion, and Rumour, do precipitate so many, that I wish I could say, The most were *considerate*.

But that which carries on the formidableness of our Trials, unto that which may be called, *A wrath unto the uttermost*, is this: It is not without the *wrath* of the Almighty *God* himself, that the *Devil* is permitted thus to come down upon us in

as much amazed and out of their Wits as the poor Sufferers; and to find Relief proceeded to shed their Blood, and to shout thereupon that they "*had been fairly executed!*"

120 How the Judges could have read these Admissions of a "snarled Business" into which no one could pretend to see, and to "declare their singular Approbation thereof," it is difficult to comprehend, upon any other Grounds than as expressed in the last Note. They were indeed as blind as any in the "*Buffet.*"

wrath. It was ſaid, in *Iſa.* 9. 19. *Through the wrath of the Lord of Hoſts, the Land is darkned.* Our Land is *darkned* indeed; ſince the *Powers of Darkneſs* are turned in upon us: 'tis a *dark time,* yea a black night indeed, now the *Ty-dogs*[121] of the Pit are abroad among us: but, *It is through the wrath of the Lord of Hoſts!* Inaſmuch as the *Fire-brands* of *Hell* it ſelf are uſed for the ſcorching of us, with cauſe enough may we cry out, *What means the heat of this Anger?* Bleſſed Lord! Are all the other Inſtruments of thy Vengeance, too good for the chaſtiſement of ſuch tranſgreſſors as we are? Muſt the very *Devils* be ſent out of *Their own place,* to be our Troublers: Muſt we be laſh'd with *Scorpions,* fetch'd from the *Place of* [44]
Torment? Muſt this *Wilderneſs* be made a Receptacle for the *Dragons of the Wilderneſs?* If a *Lapland* ſhould nouriſh in it vaſt numbers, the ſucceſſors of the old *Biarmi,*[122] who can with looks or words bewitch other people, or ſell Winds to Mariners, and have their *Familiar Spirits* which they bequeath to their Children when they die, and by their Enchanted Kettle-Drums can learn things done a Thouſand Leagues off; If a *Swedeland* ſhould afford a Village, where ſome ſcores of Haggs, may not only have their Meetings with *Familiar Spirits,* but alſo by their Enchantments

121 By theſe "Ty-dogs" the Author probably had Reference to *Cerberus.* Writers on Mythology do not mention, as I remember, that their Monſter was ever turned looſe to worry Mankind.

122 There was a Line of Swediſh Monarchs of the Name of Biorn. The firſt of the Name began to reign about 829 of the preſent era.

drag many scores of poor children out of their Bed-chambers, to be spoiled at those Meetings; This, were not altogether a matter of so much wonder! But that *New-England* should this way be harrassed! They are not *Chaldeans*, that *Bitter and Hasty Nation*, but they are, *Bitter and Burning Devils;* They are not *Swarthy Indians*, but they are *Sooty Devils;* that are let loose upon us. Ah, Poor *New-England!* Must the plague of *Old Ægypt* come upon thee? Whereof we read in *Psal.* 78. 49. *He cast upon them the fierceness of his Anger, Wrath, and Indignation, and Trouble, by sending Evil Angels among them.* What, O what must next be looked for? Must that which is there next mentioned, be next encountered? *He spared not their soul from death, but gave their life over to the Pestilence.* For my part, when I consider what *Melancthon* says, in one of his Epistles, *That these Diabolical Spectacles are often Prodigies;* and when I consider, how often people have been by *Spectres* called upon, just before their Deaths; I am verily afraid, lest some wasting *Mortality* be among the things, which this Plague is the *Forerunner* of. I pray God prevent it!

But now, *What shall we do?*

I. Let the Devils *coming down* in *great wrath* upon us, cause us to *come down* in *great grief* before the Lord. We may truly and sadly say, *We are brought very low! Low* indeed, when the Serpents of the dust, are crawling and coyling about us, and Insulting over us. May we not say,

We are in the very Belly of Hell, when *Hell* it ſelf is feeding upon us? But how *Low* is that! O let us then moſt penitently lay our ſelves very *Low* before the God of Heaven, who has thus Abaſed us.[123] When a Truculent *Nero* a *Devil* of a Man, was turned in upon the World, it was ſaid, in 1 Pet. 5. 6. *Humble your ſelves under the mighty hand of God.* How much more now ought we to *humble our ſelves* under that *Mighty Hand* of that God who indeed has the *Devil* in a *Chain,* but has horribly lengthened on the *Chain!*[124] When the old people of God heard any *Blaſphemies,* tearing of his Ever-Bleſſed Name to pieces, they were to *Rend their Cloaths* at what they heard. I am ſure that we have cauſe to *Rend our Hearts* this Day, when we ſee [45] what an High Treaſon has been committed againſt the moſt high God, by the Witchcrafts in our Neighbourhood. We may ſay; and ſhall we not be *humbled* when we ſay it? *We have ſeen an horrible thing done in our Land!* O 'tis a moſt humbling thing, to think, that ever there ſhould be ſuch an abomination among us, as for a crue of humane race to renounce their *Maker,* and to unite with the *Devil,* for the troubling of mankind, and for People to

123 When theſe *Wonders* were written, the *Paradiſe Loſt* had been publiſhed twenty-five Years. The Author muſt have been very familiar with it, yet I have not met with any Reference to Milton in any of his Writings.

124 It may be Difficult for ſome to comprehend wherein the Devil was blamed; for, according to the Text he goes no further than he is commanded or permitted to go by a Power whereby he was fully and completely controlled.

be, (as is by some confess'd) *Baptized* by a *Fiend* using this form upon them, *Thou art mine and I have a full power over thee!* afterwards communicating in an Hellish *Bread* and *Wine*, by that Fiend administred unto them. It was said in Deut. 18. 10, 11, 12. *There shall not be found among you an Inchanter, or a Witch, or a Charmer, or a Consulter with Familiar Spirits, or a Wizzard, or a Necromancer; For all that do these things are an Abomination to the Lord, and because of these Abominations, the Lord thy God doth drive them out before thee.* That *New-England* now should have these *Abominations* in it, yea, that some of no mean *Profession*, should be found guilty of them: Alas, what *Humiliations* are we all hereby oblig'd unto? O 'tis a *Defiled Land*, wherein we live; Let us be humbled for these *Defiling Abominations*, lest we be driven out of our Land. It's a very *humbling* thing to think, what reproaches will be cast upon us, for this matter, among *The Daughters of the Philistines.* Indeed, enough might easily be said for the vindication of *this* Country from the *Singularity* of this matter, by ripping up, what has been discovered in *others. Great Britain* alone, and this also in our days of *Greatest Light*, has had that in it, which may divert the Calumnies of an ill-natured World, from centring here. They are words of the Devout Bishop *Hall*,[125]

[125] "The pious Bishop of Norwich." He was a Cotemporary of the weak King James, and his Companion on one of his Excursions into Scotland. He was mild and temperate compared with Laud and

Satans prevalency in this Age, is most clear in the marvellous Number of Witches abounding in all places. Now Hundreds are discovered in one Shire; and, if Fame Deceives us not, in a Village of Fourteen Houses in the North, are found so many of this Damned Brood. Yea, and those of both Sexes, who have Professed much Knowledge, Holiness, and Devotion, are drawn into this Damnable Practice. I suppose the Doctor in the first of those Passages, may refer to what happened in the Year 1645. When so many Vassals of the Devil were Detected, that there were *Thirty* try'd at one time, whereas about *fourteen* were Hang'd, and an Hundred more detained in the Prisons of *Suffolk* and *Essex*. Among other things which many of these Acknowledged, one was, That they were to undergo certain *Punishments*, if they did not such and such *Hurts*, as were appointed them. And, among the rest that were then Executed, there was an Old Parson, called *Lowis*, who confessed, That he had a couple of *Imps*, whereof *one* was always putting him upon the doing of Mischief; Once particularly, that *Imp* calling for his Consent so to do, went immediately and Sunk a *Ship*, then under Sail.[126] I pray, let not *New-*

others of his Time. He was born in Leicester about 1574, and died in Norfolk in 1656, in the 82d Year of his Age. He appears not to have been much behind Dr. Mather in speaking of the "damned Brood" of Witches. His Works are even now held in much Repute by many, and were collected and published in three heavy Folios, 1647-62.

[126] The Reader may perhaps find all he will care to know respecting the Suffolk Witches in Hutchinson's

England become of an Unsavoury and a Sulphurous Resentment in the Opinion of the World abroad, for the Doleful things which are now fallen out among us, while there are such *Histories* of other places abroad in the World.[127] Neverthelesss, I am sure that *we*, the People of *New-England*, have cause enough to *Humble* our selves under our most *Humbling* Circumstances. We must no more be *Haughty, because of the Lords Holy Mountain among us;* No it becomes us rather to be, *Humble, because we have been such an Habitation of Unholy Devils!*

II. Since the Devil is *come down in great wrath* upon us, let not us in our *great wrath* against one another provide a *Lodging* for him. It was a most wholesome caution, in *Eph.* 4. 26, 27. *Let not the Sun go down upon your wrath: Neither give place to the Devil.* The Devil is come down to see what *Quarter* he shall find among us:[128] And if his coming down, do now fill us with *wrath* against one another, and if between the cause of the *Sufferers* on one hand, and the cause of the *Suspected* on t'other, we carry things to such extreams of *Passion* as are now gaining upon us, the

Historical Essay, 79, *et sequen.* second Edition. But Suffolk furnishes but a small Portion of England infected by Witchcraft, and Mr. Hutchinson's Work has not the hundredth Part of them.

[127] Witchcraft may be said to have been on the Wane in Old England when this of 1692-3 began in New England. Indeed there is no Comparison, as to the Extent of the Delusion between the two Countries.

[128] If he *is* such a knowing Devil as was generally supposed, he certainly must have known to a certainty the Success he was to meet with before setting out.

Devil will Bleſs himſelf, to find ſuch a convenient *Lodging* as we ſhall therein afford unto him.[129] And it may be that the *wrath* which we have had againſt one another has had more than a little influence upon the coming down of the Devil in that *wrath* which now amazes us. Have not many of us been *Devils* one unto another for Slanderings, for Backbitings, for Animoſities? For *this*, among other cauſes, perhaps, God has permitted the Devils to be worrying, as they now are, among us. But it is high time to leave off all *Deviliſm*, when the *Devil* himſelf is falling upon us: And it is *no time* for us to be Cenſuring and Reviling one another, with a *Deviliſh wrath*, when the *wrath* of the *Devil* is annoying of us. The way for us to out-wit the Devil, in the *Wiles* with which he now *Vexes* [46] us, would be for us to joyn as one man in our cries to God, for the Directing, and Iſſuing of this Thorny Buſineſs; but if we do not *Lift up* our Hands to Heaven, *without Wrath*, we cannot then do it *without Doubt*, of ſpeeding in it. I am aſhamed when I read French Authors giving this Character of Engliſhmen [*Ils ſe haiſſent Les uns les autres, et ſont en Diviſion Continuelle.*] *They hate one another, and are always Quarelling one with another.*[130] And

[129] It is hardly to be inferred from the Sentiments here expreſſed, that the Author was among the moſt earneſt of his blind Advocates for extreme Meaſures againſt thoſe accuſed.

[130] Not a good Tranſlation, but the Senſe is ſufficiently apparent. Voltaire has the ſame in Subſtance in one of his "Letters concerning the Engliſh Nation." A Condition not peculiar to any Country.

I shall be much more ashamed, if it become the Character of *New-Englanders;* which is indeed what the Devil would have. *Satan* would make us *bruise* one another, by breaking of the *Peace* among us; but O let us disappoint him. We read of a thing that sometimes happens to the *Devil,* when he is foaming with his *Wrath,* in Mat. 12. 43. *The unclean Spirit seeks rest, and finds none.* But we give *rest* unto the Devil, by *wrath* one against another. If we would lay aside all fierceness, and keenness, in the disputes which the Devil has raised among us; and if we would use to one another none but the *soft Answers, which turn away wrath:* I should hope that we might light upon such Counsels, as would quickly Extricate us out of our *Labyrinths.* But the old *Incendiary* of the world, is come from Hell, with *Sparks* of Hell-Fire flashing on every side of him; and we make ourselves *Tynder* to the Sparks. When the Emperour *Henry* III.[131] kept the Feast of *Pentecost,* at the City *Mentz,* there arose a dissension among some of the people there, which came from words to blows, and at last it passed on to the shedding of Blood. After the Tumult was over, when they came to that clause in their Devotions, *Thou hast made this day Glorious;* the Devil to the unexpressible Terrour of that vast Assembly, made the Temple Ring with that Outcry *But I have made this Day Quarrelsome!* We are truly come into a day, which by being

[131] The Time of Henry III was from 1574 to 1589.

well managed might be very *Glorious*, for the exterminating of thoſe *Accurſed things*, which have hitherto been the Clogs of our Proſperity; but if we make this day *Quarrelſome*, thro' any *Raging Confidences*, Alas, *O Lord, my Fleſh Trembles for Fear of thee, and I am afraid of thy Judgments*. *Eraſmus*, among other Hiſtorians, tells us, that at a Town in *Germany*, a Witch or Devil, appeared on the Top of a Chimney, Threatning to ſet the Town on *Fire*: And at length, Scattering a Pot of Aſhes abroad, the Town was preſently and horribly Burnt unto the Ground.[132] Methinks, I ſee the *Spectres*, from the Top of the Chimneys to the Northward, threatning to ſcatter *Fire*, about the Countrey; but let us quench that *Fire*, by the moſt amicable Correſpondencies: Leſt, as the *Spectres*, have, they ſay, already moſt Literally burnt ſome of our Dwellings there do come forth a further *Fire* from the *Brambles* of Hell, which may more terribly *Devour* us. Let us not be like a *Troubled Houſe*, altho' we are ſo much haunted by the *Devils*. Let our *Long ſuffering* be a well-placed piece of *Armour*, about us, againſt the *Fiery Darts* of the wicked ones. Hiſtory informs us, That ſo long ago, as the year, 858, a certain

132 Thoſe who are familiar with the Works of Eraſmus may verify the Story. He may have been, and probably was, like the Reſt of the learned World, a Believer in ſuch Nonſenſe. The great Poet who has contributed to his Immortality in the following Lines may not have heard of the above Story:

"At length Eraſmus, that great injured Name,
(The Glory of the Prieſthood and the Shame!)
Stem'd the wild Torrent of a bar'brous Age,
And drove thoſe holy Vandals off the Stage."

Pestilent and Malignant sort of *Dæmon*, molested *Caumont* in *Germany* with all sorts of methods to stir up strife among the Citizens. He uttered Prophecies, he detected Villanies, he branded people with all kind of Infamies. He incensed the Neighbourhood against one Man particularly, as the cause of all the mischiefs: who yet proved himself innocent. He threw stones at the Inhabitants, and at length burnt their Habitations, till the Commission of the *Dæmon* could go no further. I say, let us be well aware lest such *Dæmons* do *Come hither also*.

III. Inasmuch as the Devil is come down in *Great Wrath*, we had need Labour, with all the Care and Speed we can to Divert the *Great Wrath* of Heaven from coming at the same time upon us. The God of Heaven has with long and loud Admonitions, been calling us to *a Reformation of our Provoking Evils*, as the only way to avoid that *Wrath* of His, which does not only *Threaten* but *Consume* us. 'Tis because we have been Deaf to those *Calls* that we are now by a provoked God, laid open to the *Wrath* of the Devil himself. It is said in Pr. 16. 7. *When a mans ways please the Lord, he maketh even his Enemies to be at peace with him.* The Devil is our grand *Enemy;* and tho' we would not be at peace *with* him, yet we would be at peace from him, that is, we would have him unable to disquiet our *peace*. But inasmuch as the *wrath* which we endure from this *Enemy*, will allow us no *peace*, we may be sure, *our ways have not pleaſed the Lord.* It is becauſe we have *broken the hedge* of Gods *Precepts*, that the hedge of Gods *Providence* is not ſo entire as it uſes to be about us; but *Serpents* are *biting* of us. O let us then ſet [47] our ſelves to make our *peace* with our God, whom we have *diſpleaſed* by our iniquities: and let us not imagine that we can encounter the *Wrath* of the Devil, while there is the *Wrath* of God Almighty to ſet that Maſtiff upon us. REFORMATION! REFORMATION! has been the repeated *Cry* of all the Judgments that have hitherto been upon us; becauſe we have been as *deaf Adders* thereunto, the *Adders* of the Infernal Pit are now hiſſing about us. At length, as it was of old ſaid, *Luke* 16. 30. *If one went unto them from the dead, they will repent;* even ſo, there are ſome come unto us from the *Damned.* The great God has looſed the Bars of the Pit, ſo that many *damned Spirits* are come in among us, to make us *repent* of our Miſdemeanours. The means which the Lord had formerly employ'd for our *awakening*, were ſuch, that he might well have ſaid, *What could I have done more?* and yet after all, he has done *more*, in ſome regards, than was ever done for the awakening of any People in the World. The things now done to awaken our Enquiries after our *provoking Evils*, and our endeavours to Reform thoſe evils, are moſt *extraordinary* things; for which cauſe I would freely ſpeak it, if we now do not ſome *extraordinary* things in returning to God; we are the moſt *incurable*, and I wiſh it be not quickly ſaid, the most *miserable* People under the Sun. Believe me, 'tis a time for all people to do something *extraordinary, in searching and trying of their ways, and in turning to the Lord.* It is at an *extraordinary* rate of *Circumspection* and *Spiritual mindedness,* that we should all now maintain a *walk with God.* At such a time as this ought *Magistrates* to do something *extraordinary* in promoting of what is laudable, and in restraining and chastising of *Evil Doers.* At such a time as this ought *Ministers* to do something *extraordinary* in pulling the Souls of Men out of the *Snares* of the Devil, not only by publick Preaching, but by personal Visits and Counsels, *from house to house.* At such a time as this ought *Churches* to do something *extraordinary,* in *renewing* of their Covenants, and in *remembring,* and *reviving* the Obligations of what they have renewed. Some admirable Designs about the *Reformation* of Manners, have lately been on foot in the English Nation, in pursuance of the most excellent Admonitions which have been given for it, by the Letters of Their Majesties.[133] Besides the vigorous Agreements of the *Justices* here and there in the Kingdom, assisted by godly Gentlemen and Informers, to execute the *Laws* upon prophane Offenders: there has been started a *Proposal* for the well-affected people in every Parish, to enter into orderly *Societies,* whereof every

[133] There was about this Time a Society established in England expressly for the "Reformation of Manners," and a small octavo Volume was issued under its Auspices, setting forth the Objects and Necessity for such a Society. In it the Plantations are remembered.

Member ſhall bind himſelf, not only to *avoid* Prophaneneſs in himſelf, but alſo according unto to their Place, to do their utmoſt in firſt *Reproving;* and, if it muſt be ſo, then *Expoſing*, and ſo *Puniſhing*, as the Law directs, for others that ſhall be guilty. It has been obſerved, that the Engliſh Nation has had ſome of its greateſt Succeſſes, upon ſome ſpecial and ſignal *Actions* this way; and a diſcouragement given under Legal Proceedings of this kind, muſt needs be very exerciſing to the *Wiſe that obſerve theſe things.* But O why ſhould not *New-England* be the moſt forward part of the Engliſh Nation in ſuch *Reformations?* Methinks I hear the Lord from Heaven ſaying over us, *O that my People had hearkened unto me; then I ſhould ſoon have ſubdued the Devils, as well as their other Enemies!* There have been ſome feeble Eſſays towards *Reformation* of late in our *Churches;* but, I pray what comes of them? Do we ſtay till the *Storm* of his *Wrath* be over? Nay, let us be doing what we can, as faſt as we can, to divert the *Storm.* The Devils having broke in upon our World,[134] there is great aſking, *Who is it that has brought them in?* And many do by *Spectral* Exhibitions come to be *cry'd out* upon. I hope in Gods time it will be found, that among thoſe that are thus *cry'd out* upon, there are perſons yet *Clear from the great Tranſ-*

[134] The Author does not ſeem to remember that he has elſewhere ſaid with much Emphaſis, that "this remote Part of the Earth" was the Devil's own Territory, that he was undiſturbed here before the white People came and that he did not expect to be diſturbed here.

grefsion; but indeed, all the *Unreformed* among us, may juftly be *cry'd out* upon, as having too much of an hand in letting of the Devils into our Borders; 'tis *our* Worldlinefs, *our* Formality, *our* Senfuality, and *our* Iniquity that has help'd this letting of the Devils in. O let us then at laft, *confider our ways.* 'Tis a ftrange paffage recorded by Mr. *Clark*[135] in the Life of his Father That the People of his Parifh, refufing to be Reclaimed from their *Sabbath breaking*, by all the zealous Teftimonies which that good Man bore againft it; at laft, on a night after the people had retired home from a Revelling Prophanation of the *Lords Day*, there was heard a great Noife, with rattling of Chains up and down the Town, and an horrid Scent of Brimftone fill'd the Neighbourhood. Upon which the *guilty Confciences* of the Wretches told [48] them, the Devil was come to fetch them away; and it fo terrifi'd them, that an Eminent *Reformation* follow'd the Sermons which that Man of God Preached thereupon. Behold, Sinners, behold and *wonder*, left you *perifh*: the very *Devils* are walking about our Streets, with lengthened *Chains*, making a dreadful Noife in our Ears,

[135] This was Mr. Samuel Clarke or Clark (as he indifferently wrote his own Surname), and his Father's Name was Hugh Clark. The Life fpoken of is in the *Martyrology* by the Son, a Work not now often referred to, but one abounding with interefting and curious biographical and hiftorical Information, having intimate Connection with the Founders of New England, and containing a good deal concerning many of them. See his *Lives*, appended to the *Martyrology*, Page 127, *et feq.* Folio, 1677. I have often had Occafion to refer to his various Works.

and *Brimſtone* even without a Metaphor, is making an helliſh and horrid ſtench in our Noſtrils.[136] I pray leave off all thoſe things whereof your *guilty Conſciences* may now accuſe you, leſt theſe Devils do yet more direfully fall upon you. *Reformation* is at this time our only *Preſervation*.

IV. When the Devil is come down in *great Wrath*, let every *great Vice* which may have a more particular tendency to make us a Prey unto that *Wrath*, come into a due diſcredit with us. It is the general Conceſſion of all men, who are not become too *Unreaſonable* for common Converſation, that the Invitation of *Witchcrafts* is the thing that has now introduced the Devil into the midſt of us. I ſay then, let not only all *Witchcrafts* be duly abominated with us, but alſo let us be duly watchful againſt all the *Steps* leading thereunto. There are leſſer *Sorceries* which they ſay, are too frequent in our Land. As it was ſaid in 2 *King*. 17. 9. *The Children of* Iſrael *did ſecretly thoſe things that were not right, againſt the Lord their God.* So 'tis to be feared, the Children of *New-England* have *ſecretly* done many things that have been pleaſing to the Devil.

136 There appears to have been ſome Myſtery about that Perfume of Brimſtone, if indeed "Metaphor" be left out of the Account, as the Author ſays it is to be. One might be led to ſuppoſe that the Circumſtance which happened at Oxford in 1577, was of the Character of that in the Text, as alluded to by Hutchinſon, in his *Hiſtorical Eſſay concerning Witchcraft*, Page 38, but on Reference to his Authority, a Parallel is hardly warranted. The Story will be found fully related in Camden's *Reign of Elizabeth*, 237, Ed. 1675.

They say, that in some Towns it has been an usual thing for People to cure Hurts with *Spells*, or to use detestable Conjurations, with *Sieves*, *Keys*, and *Pease*, and *Nails*, and *Horse-shoes*, and I know not what other Implements, to learn the things for which they have a forbidden, and an impious *Curiosity*.[137] 'Tis in the Devils Name, that such things are done; and in Gods Name I do this day charge them, as vile Impieties. By these Courses 'tis, that People play upon *The Hole of the Asp*, till that cruelly venemous *Asp* has pull'd many of them into the deep *Hole* of *Witch-craft* it self. It has been acknowledged by some who have sunk the deepest into this *horrible Pit*, that they began at these little *Witchcrafts*; on which 'tis pity but the Laws of the English Nation, whereby the incorrigible repetition of those *Tricks*, is made *Felony*, were severally Executed. From the like sinful *Curiosity* it is, that the Prognostications of *Judicial Astrology*, are so injudiciously regarded by multitudes among us; and altho' the Jugling *Astrologers* do scarce ever hit right, except it be in such *Weighty Judgments*, forsooth, as that many *Old Men* will die such a

137 In that curious Poem entitled *The Sorceress*, are the following Lines, among others, on "The Spell:"

"Rust of the Gibbet, and Bone of the Dead,
I mingle and into the Teakettle throw,
Root of Skunk-cabbage and Rattlesnakes Head,
And Leaves pluck'd at Midnight from Juniper bough,
Charm break the Rest
Of the Parson distrest,
From his Eyes let the Blessing of Slumber depart;
Lucifer aid me
And Night overshade me,
Spirit of Beelzebub, lend me thine Art."
&c.

year, and that there will be many *Loſſes* felt by ſome that venture to Sea, and that there will be much *Lying* and *Cheating* in the World; yet their fooliſh Admirers will not be perſwaded but that the Innocent *Stars* have been concern'd in theſe Events. It is a diſgrace to the Engliſh Nation, that the Pamphlets of ſuch idle, futil, trifling *Stargazers* are ſo much conſidered; and the Countenance hereby given to a Study, wherin at laſt, all is done by *Impulſe*, if any thing be done to any purpoſe at all, is not a little perillous to the Souls of Men. It is (*a Science*, I dare not call it, but) a *Juggle*, whereof the Learned *Hall* well ſays, *It is preſumptious and unwarrantable, and cry'd ever down by Councils and Fathers, as unlawful, as that which lies in the mid-way between Magick and Impoſture, and partakes not a little of both.*[138] Men conſult the Aſpects of Planets, whoſe Northern or Southern motions receive denominations from a *Cæleſtial Dragon*, till the *Infernal Dragon* at length inſinuate into them, with a *Poiſon* of *Witchcraft* that can't be cured. Has there not alſo been a world of *diſcontent* in our Borders? 'Tis no wonder, that the *fiery Serpents* are ſo Stinging of us; We have been a *Murmuring Generation*. It is not Irrational, to aſcribe the late Stupendious growth of *Witches* among us, partly to the bitter *diſcontents*, which Affliction and

[138] A vaſt Number of Books had been publiſhed previous to our Author's Time upon Magic, and Aſtrology. A principal Writer on theſe Subjects was Dr. John Dee. His Diary was publiſhed by the *Camden Society* in 1842. See alſo William Lilley's *Hiſt. of his Life and Times.*

Poverty has fill'd us with: it is inconceivable, what advantage the Devil gains over men, by *difcontent.* Moreover, the Sin of *Unbelief* may be reckoned as perhaps the chief *Crime* of our Land. We are told, *God fwears in wrath, againft them that believe not;* and what follows then but this, *That the Devil comes unto them in wrath!* Never were the offers of the *Gofpel,* more freely tendered, or more bafely defpifed, among any People under the whole Cope of Heaven, than in this *N. E.*[139] Seems it all marvellous unto us, that the *Devil* fhould get fuch a footing in our Country? Why, 'tis becaufe the *Saviour* has been flighted here, perhaps more than any where. The Bleffed Lord Jefus Chrift [49] has been profering to us, *Grace, and Glory, and every good thing,* and been alluring of us to Accept of Him, with fuch Terms as thefe, *Undone Sinner, I am All; Art thou willing that I fhould be thy All?* But, as a proof of that Contempt which this Unbelief has caft upon thefe proffers, I would ferioufly afk of the fo many Hundreds above a Thoufand People within thefe Walls; which of you all, O how few of you, can indeed fay, *Chrift is mine, and I am his, and he is the Beloved of my Soul?* I would only fay thus much: When the precious and

139 This moft uncharitable Affertion is a complete Contradiction of what has before been afferted. He had already made poor New England bad enough, but this feems to place her in a perfectly hopelefs Condition. Not many Pages back the Author cautioned the World left it fhould not do Juftice to New England, by believing her worfe than Old England. A difordered Brain will always drive a Pen at random.

glorious Jeſus, is Entreating of us to Receive *Him*, in all His *Offices*, with all His *Benifits*; the Devil minds what Reſpect we pay unto that Heavenly Lord; if we *Refuſe Him that ſpeaks from Heaven*, then he that, *Comes from Hell*, does with a ſort of claim ſet in, and cry out, *Lord, ſince this Wretch is not willing that thou ſhouldſt have him, I pray, let me have him.* And thus, by the juſt vengeance of Heaven, the Devil becomes a *Maſter*, a *Prince*, a *God*, unto the miſerable Unbelievers: but O what are many of them then hurried unto! All of theſe Evil Things, do I now ſet before you, as *Branded* with the Mark of the Devil upon them.

V. With *Great Regard*, with *Great Pity*, ſhould we Lay to Heart the Condition of thoſe, who are caſt into Affliction, by the *Great Wrath* of the Devil. There is a Number of our Good Neighbours, and ſome of them very particularly noted for Goodneſs and Vertue, of whom we may ſay, *Lord, They are vexed with Devils.* Their Tortures being primarily Inflicted on their *Spirits*, may indeed cauſe the Impreſſions thereof upon their Bodies to be the leſs *Durable*, tho' rather the more *Senſible*: but they Endure Horrible Things, and many have been actually Murdered. Hard *Cenſures* now beſtow'd upon theſe poor Sufferers, cannot but be very Diſpleaſing unto our Lord, who, as He ſaid, about ſome that had been Butchered by a *Pilate*, in Luc. 13. 2, 3. *Think ye that theſe were Sinners above others, becauſe they ſuffered ſuch Things? I tell you No, But except ye*

Repent, ye ſhall all likewiſe Periſh: Even ſo, he now ſays, *Think ye that they who now ſuffer by the Devil, have been greater Sinners than their Neighbours?* No, Do you Repent of your *own Sins,* Leſt the Devil come to fall foul of *you,* as he has done to *them.* And if this be ſo, How *Raſh* a thing would it be, if ſuch of the poor Sufferers, as carry it with a Becoming Piety, Serioufneſs, and Humiliation under their preſent Suffering, ſhould be unjuſtly *Cenſured;* or have their very *Calamity* imputed unto them as a *Crime?* It is an eaſie thing, for us to fall into the Fault of, *Adding Affliction to the Afflicted,* and of, *Talking to the Grief of thoſe that are already wounded.* Nor can it be wiſdom to ſlight the Dangers of ſuch a Fault. In the mean time, We have no Bowels in us, if we do not Compaſſionate the Diſtreſſed County of *Eſſex,* now crying to all theſe Colonies, *Have pity on me, O ye my Friends, Have pity on me, for the Hand of the Lord has Touched me, and the Wrath of the Devil has been therewithal turned upon me.* But indeed, if an hearty *pity* be due to any, I am ſure, the Difficulties which attend our Honourable *Judges,* do demand no Inconſiderable ſhare in that *Pity.* What a Difficult, what [50] an Arduous Taſk, have thoſe Worthy Perſonages now upon their Hands? To carry the *Knife* ſo exactly, that on the one ſide, there may be no Innocent Blood Shed,[140] by too unſeeing a *Zeal*

140 An Idea reminding one of the Caſe of the Jew in the *Merchant of Venice.* Unfortunately for the poor accuſed Wretches, there was no

for the Children of Iſrael; and that on the other ſide, there may be no Shelter given to thoſe Diabolical *Works of Darkneſs*, without the Removal whereof we never ſhall have *Peace;* or to thoſe *Furies* whereof ſeveral have kill'd *more people* perhaps than would ſerve to make a Village: *Hic Labor, Hoc Opus eſt!* O what need have we, to be concerned, that the Sins of our *Iſrael*, may not provoke the God of Heaven to leave his *Davids*, unto a wrong Step, in a matter of ſuch Conſequence, as is now before them! Our Diſingenuous, Uncharitable, Unchriſtian Reproaching of ſuch *Faithful Men*, after all, *The Prayers and Supplications, with ſtrong Crying and Tears*, with which we are daily plying the Throne of Grace, that they may be kept, from what *They Fear*, is none of the way for our preventing of what We *Fear*. Nor all this while, ought our *Pity* to forget ſuch *Accuſed* ones, as call for indeed our moſt Compaſſionate *Pity*, till there be fuller Evidences that they are leſs worthy of it.[141] If *Satan* have any where maliciouſly brought upon the *Stage*, thoſe that have hitherto had a juſt and good ſtock of Reputation for their juſt and good Living, among us; If the *Evil One* have obtained a permiſſion to *Appear*, in the Figure of ſuch as we have cauſe to think, have

Daniel to ſit in Judgment, and to ſee that no Blood was taken with the Pound of Fleſh.

141 This certainly does not exhibit the Author as a "principal Ringleader" in thoſe Perſecutions. A Remark ſimilar has been made to a previous Paſſage in the Text, of a like Purport. And frequent parallel Paſſages may be found.

hitherto *Abstained*, even from the *Appearance of Evil:* It is in Truth, such an Invasion upon *Mankind*, as may well Raise an Horror in us all: But, O what Compassions are due to such as may come under such Misrepresentations, of the *Great Accuser!* Who of us can say, what may be shewn in the *Glasses* of the Great *Lying Spirit?* Altho' the *Usual Providence* of God [we praise Him!] keeps us from such a Mishap; yet where have we an *Absolute Promise*, that we shall every one always be kept from it? As long as *Charity* is bound to Think *no Evil*, it will not Hurt us that are *Private Persons*, to forbear the *Judgment* which belongs not unto us. Let it rather be our Wish, May the Lord help them to Learn the *Lessons*, for which they are now put unto so hard a School.

VI. With a *Great Zeal*, we should lay hold on the *Covenant* of God, that we may secure *Us* and *Ours*, from the *Great Wrath*, with which the Devil Rages. Let us come into the *Covenant of Grace*, and then we shall not be hook'd into a *Covenant with the Devil*, nor be altogether unfurnished with Armour against the Wretches that are in that *Covenant*. The way to come under the Saving Influences of the *New Covenant*, is, to close with the Lord Jesus Christ, who is the All-sufficient *Mediator* of it: Let us therefore do, *that*, by Resigning up our selves unto the Saving, Teaching, and Ruling Hands of this Blessed *Mediator*. Then we shall be, what we read in

Jude 1. *Preſerved in Chriſt Jeſus:* That is, as the *Deſtroying Angel,* could not meddle with ſuch as had been diſtinguiſhed, by the Blood of the *Paſſeover* on their Houſes: Thus the Blood of the Lord Jeſus Chriſt, Sprinkled on our Souls, will *Preſerve* us from the Devil. The *Birds of prey* (and indeed the *Devils* [51] moſt literally in the ſhape of great *Birds!*) are flying about. Would we find a Covert from theſe *Vultures?* Let us then Hear our Lord Jeſus from Heaven Clocquing[142] unto us, *O that you would be gathered under my wings!* Well; when this is done, Then let us own the *Covenant,* which we are now come into, by joining ourſelves to a Particular *Church,* walking in the Order of the Goſpel; at the doing whereof, according to that *Covenant* of God, We give up Our ſelves unto the Lord, and in Him unto One Another. While others have had their Names Entred in the *Devils Book;* let our Names be found in the *Church Book,* and let us be *Written among the Living in Jeruſalem.* By no means let, *Church work* ſink and fail in the midſt of us; but let the Tragical Accidents which now happen, exceedingly Quicken that *work.* So many of the *Riſing Generation,* utterly forgetting the Errand of our Fathers to build Churches in this Wilderneſs, and ſo many of our *Cottages* being allow'd to Live, where they do not, and perhaps

142 This is the French Form of what we now write *Clucking.* The Verb *to cluck* is well known, and in frequent Uſe where Hens are raiſed, but to employ it as the Doctor does cannot but excite Ridicule.

cannot, wait upon God with the Churches of His People; 'tis as likely as any one thing to procure the ſwarmings of *Witch crafts* among us.[143] But it becomes us, with a like Ardour, to bring our poor *Children* with us, as we ſhall do, when we come our ſelves, into the *Covenant* of God. It would break an heart of Stone, to have ſeen, what I have lately ſeen; Even poor Children of ſeveral Ages, even from ſeven to twenty, more or leſs, *Confeſſing* their Familiarity with Devils; but at the ſame time, in Doleful bitter Lamentations, that made a little Pourtraiture of *Hell* it ſelf, Expoſtulating with their execrable Parents, for *Devoting* them to the Devil in their Infancy, and ſo *Entailing* of Devilliſm upon them! Now, as the Pſalmiſt could ſay, *My Zeal hath conſumed me, becauſe my Enemies have forgotten thy words:* Even ſo, let the Nefarious wickedneſs of thoſe that have Explicitly dedicated their Children to the Devil, even with Deviliſh Symbols, of ſuch a Dedication, Provoke our *Zeal* to have our Children, Sincerely, Signally, and openly *Conſecrated* unto God; with an *Education* afterwards aſſuring and confirming that Conſecration.

VII. Let our *Prayer* go up with great Faith, againſt the Devil, that comes down in great

143 Allowing this to be a juſt Concluſion it is remarkable that the Devil did not ſet his Witches at Work in the Beginning in the Colony of Plymouth; there were repeated Complaints to the Commiſſioners of the United Colonies, that various Towns in that Colony had neglected Miniſters and Churches altogether; while from the County of Eſſex we hear of no ſuch Complaints.

Wrath. Such is the Antipathy of the Devil to our *Prayer*, that he cannot bear to ſtay long where much of it is: Indeed it is *Diaboli Flagellum*, as well as *Miſeriæ Remedium;* the Devil will ſoon be Scourg'd out of the Lord's Temple, by a *Whip*, made and uſed, with the *effectual fervent Prayer of Righteous Men.* When the Devil by Afflicting of us, drives us to our Prayers, he is *The Fool making a Whip for his own Back.* Our Lord ſaid of the Devil in *Matt.* 17. 21. *This Kind goes not out, but by Prayer and Faſting.* But, *Prayer and Faſting* will ſoon make the Devil be gone. Here are *Charms* indeed! Sacred and bleſſed *Charms*, which the Devil cannot ſtand before. A Promiſe of God, being well managed in the *Hands* of them that are much upon their Knees, will ſo reſiſt the Devil, that he will *Flee from us.* At every other Weapon the Devils will be too hard for us; the *Spiritual Wickedneſſes in High Places*, have manifeſtly the Upper hand of
[52] us; that *Old Serpent* will be too old for us, too cunning, too ſubtil; they will ſoon *out wit* us, if we think to Encounter them with any *Wit* of our own. But when we come to *Prayers*, Inceſſant and Vehement *Prayers* before the Lord, there we ſhall be too hard for them. When well-directed *Prayers*, that great Artillery of Heaven, are brought into the Field, *There* methinks I ſee, *There are theſe workers of Iniquity fallen, all of them!* And who can tell, how much the moſt *Obſcure Chriſtian* among you all, may do towards the Deliverance of our Land from the Moleſta-

tions which the Devil is now giving to us. I have Read, That on a day of Prayer kept by ſome good People for and with a Poſſeſſed Perſon, the Devil at laſt flew out of the Window, and referring to a Devout, plain, mean Woman then in the Room, he cry'd out, *O the Woman behind the Door!*[144] *'Tis that Woman that forces me away!* Thus the Devil that now troubles us, may be forced within a while to forſake us; and it ſhall be ſaid, *He was driven away by the Prayers of ſome Obſcure and Retired Souls, which the World has taken but little notice of!* The Great God is about a *Great Work* at this day among us: Now, there is extream Hazard, leſt the Devil who by Compulſion muſt ſubmit unto that *Great Work*, may alſo by *Permiſſion*, come to Confound that *Work;* both in the Detections of ſome, and in the Confeſſions of others, whoſe Ungodly deeds may be brought forth, by a *Great Work* of God; there is Hazard leſt the Devil intertwiſt ſome of his Deluſions. 'Tis PRAYER, I ſay, 'tis PRAYER, that muſt carry us well through the ſtrange things that are now upon us. Only that Prayer muſt then be the Prayer of Faith: O where is our Faith in him, Who *hath ſpoiled theſe Principalities and Powers, on his Croſs, Triumphing over them!*

VIII. Laſtly, Shake off, every Soul, ſhake off the *hard Yoak* of the Devil. Where 'tis ſaid, *The*

144 Additional Particulars reſpecting this Woman may be ſeen in Dr. I. Mather's *Prevalency of Prayer*, publiſhed in Connection with his *Relation*. See *Early Hiſt. New England*, 275.

whole World lyes in Wickedneſs; 'tis by ſome of the Ancients rendred, *The whole World lyes in the Devil.* The Devil is a Prince, yea, the Devil is a God unto all the Unregenerate; and alas, there is *A whole World of them.*[145] Deſolate Sinners, conſider what an horrid Lord it is that you are Enſlav'd unto; and Oh ſhake off your Slavery to ſuch a Lord. Inſtead of *him,* now make your Choice of the Eternal God in Jeſus Chriſt; Chuſe him with a moſt unalterable Reſolution, and unto him ſay, with *Thomas, My Lord, and my God!* Say with the Church, *Lord, other Lords have had the Dominion over us, but now thou alone ſhalt be our Lord for ever.* Then inſtead of your Periſhing under the wrath of the Devils, God will fetch you to a place among thoſe that fill up the Room of the Devils, left by their Fall from the Ethereal Regions. It was a moſt awful Speech made by the Devil, Poſſeſſing a young Woman, at a Village in *Germany, By the command of God, I am come to Torment the Body of this young Woman, tho I cannot hurt her Soul; and it is that I may warn Men, to take heed of ſinning againſt God. Indeed* (ſaid he) *'tis very ſore againſt my will that I do it; but the command of God forces me to declare what I do; however I know that at the Laſt Day, I ſhall have more Souls than God himſelf.* So ſpoke that horrible Devil! But O that none [53] of our Souls

[145] Many, no Doubt, will think it ſtrange that the Author did not count himſelf in. Had he done ſo he aſſuredly would have loſt no Credit with his Readers now, nor probably by thoſe in future.

may be found among the Prizes of the Devil, in the Day of God! O that what the Devil has been forced to declare, of his Kingdom among us, may prejudice our Hearts againft him for ever!

My Text fays, *The Devil is come down in great Wrath, for he has but a fhort time.* Yea, but if you do not by a fpeedy and through Converfion to God, efcape the Wrath of the Devil, you will your felves go down, where the Devil is to be, and you will there be fweltring under the Devils Wrath, not for a *fhort Time*, but *World without end;* not for a *Short Time* but for *Infinite Millions of Ages.* The fmoke of your Torment under that Wrath, will *Afcend for ever and ever!* Indeed, the Devil's time for his Wrath upon you in this World, can be but fhort, but his time for you to do his Work, or, which is all one, to delay your turning to God, that is a *Long Time.* When the Devil was going to be Difpoffeffed of a Man, he Roar'd out, *Am I to be Tormented before my time?* You will *Torment* the Devil, if you Refcue your Souls out of his hands, by true Repentance: If once you begin to look that way, he'll Cry out, *O this is before my Time, I muft have more Time, yet in the Service of fuch a guilty Soul.* But, I befeech you, let us join thus to torment the Devil, in an holy Revenge upon him, for all the Injuries which he has done unto us; let us tell him, *Satan, thy time with me is but fhort, Nay, thy time with me fhall be no more; I am unutterably forry that it has been fo much; Depart from me thou*

Evil-Doer, that would'ſt have me an Evil-Doer like thy ſelf; I will now for ever keep the Commandments of that God, in whom I Live and Move, and have my Being! The Devil has plaid a fine Game for himſelf indeed, if by his troubling of our Land, the Souls of many People ſhould come to *think upon their ways, till even they turn their Feet into the Teſtimonies of the Lord.* Now that the Devil may be thus outſhot in his own Bow, is the deſire of all that love the Salvation of God among us, as well as of him, who has thus Addreſſed you. *Amen.*

HAVING thus diſcourſed on the *Wonders of the Inviſible World,* I ſhall now, with God's help, go on to relate ſome Remarkable and Memorable Inſtances of *Wonders* which that *World* has given to ourſelves. And altho the chief Entertainment which my Readers do expect, and ſhall receive, will be a true Hiſtory of what has occurred, reſpecting the WITCHCRAFTS wherewith we are at this day Perſecuted; yet I ſhall chooſe to uſher in the mention of thoſe things, with

A Narrative of an APPARITION *which a Gentleman in* BOSTON, *had of his Brother, juſt then murthered in* LONDON.

IT was on the Second of *May* in the Year 1687, that a moſt ingenious, accompliſhed and well-diſpoſed young Gentleman, Mr. *Joſeph Beacon,* by about Five a Clock in the Morning, as he lay, whether Sleeping or [54] Waking he could not say, (but judged the latter of them) had a View of his Brother then at *London*, altho he was now himself at our *Boston*, distanced from him a thousand Leagues.[146] This his Brother appear'd unto him, in the Morning about Five a Clock at *Boston*, having on him a *Bengal* Gown, which he usually wore, with a Napkin tyed about his Head; his Countenance was very Pale, Gastly, Deadly, and he had a bloody Wound on one side of his Fore-head. *Brother!* says the Affrighted *Joseph*. *Brother!* Answered the Apparition. Said *Joseph*, *What's the matter Brother? How came you here!* The Apparition replied, *Brother, I have been most barbarously and injuriously Butchered, by a Debauched Drunken Fellow, to whom I never did any wrong in my Life.* Whereupon he gave a particular Description of the Murderer; adding, *Brother, This Fellow changing his Name, is attempting to come over unto* New-England, *in* Foy, *or* Wild; *I would pray you on the first Arrival of either of these, to get an Order from the Governor, to Seize the Person, whom I have now described; and then do you Indict him for the Murder of me your Brother: I'll stand by you and prove the Indictment.* And so he Vanished. Mr. *Beacon* was extreamly astonished at what he had seen and hear'd; and the

[146] This Mr. Beacon does not appear to have belonged to Boston. He was probably a casual Resident at that Time.

People of the Family not only obſerved an extraordinary Alteration upon him, for the Week following, but have alſo given me under their Hands a full Teſtimony, that he then gave them an Account of this Apparition.

All this while, Mr. *Beacon* had no advice of any thing amiſs attending his Brother then in *England;* but about the latter end of *June* following, he underſtood by the common ways of Communication, that the *April* before, his Brother going in haſte by Night to call a Coach for a Lady, met a Fellow then in Drink, with his *Doxy* in his Hand: Some way or other the Fellow thought himſelf Affronted with the haſty paſſage of this *Beacon,* and immediately ran into the Fire-ſide of a Neighbouring Tavern, from whence he fetched out a Fire-fork, wherewith he grievouſly wounded *Beacon* in the Skull; even in that very part where the Apparition ſhow'd his Wound. Of this Wound he Languiſhed until he Dyed on the Second of *May,* about five of the Clock in the Morning at *London.* The Murderer it ſeems was endeavouring an Eſcape, as the Apparition affirm'd, but the Friends of the Deceaſed *Beacon,* Seized him; and Proſecuting him at Law, he found the help of ſuch Friends as brought him off without the loſs of his Life; ſince which, there has no more been heard of the Buſineſs.

This Hiſtory I received of Mr. *Joſeph Beacon* himſelf; who a little before his own Pious and hopeful Death, which follow'd not long after, gave me the Story written and figned with his own Hand, and attefted with the Circumftances I have already mentioned.

BUT I fhall no longer detain my Reader, from his expected Entertainment, in a brief account of the Tryals which have paffed upon fome of the Malefactors lately Executed at *Salem*, for the *Witchcrafts* whereof they ftood Convicted. For my own part, I was not prefent at any of them; [55] nor ever had I any Perfonal prejudice at the Perfons thus brought upon the Stage; much lefs at the Surviving Relations of thofe Perfons, with and for whom I would be as hearty a Mourner as any Man living in the World: *The Lord Comfort them!* But having received a Command fo to do, I can do no other than fhortly relate the chief *Matters of Fact*, which occur'd in the Tryals of fome that were Executed, in an Abridgment Collected out of the *Court-Papers*, on this occafion put into my hands. You are to take the *Truth*, juft as it was; and the Truth will hurt no good Man. There might have been more of thefe, if my Book would not thereby have fwollen too big; and if fome other worthy hands did not perhaps intend fomething further in thefe *Collections;* for which caufe I have only fingled out Four or Five, which may ferve to illuftrate the way of Dealing, wherein *Witchcrafts* ufe to be concerned; and I report matters not as an *Advocate*, but as an *Hiftorian*.

They were ſome of the Gracious Words inſerted in the Advice, which many of the Neighbouring Miniſters, did this Summer humbly lay before our Honorable Judges, *We cannot but with all thankfulneſs, acknowledge the ſucceſs which the Merciful God has given unto the Sedulous and Aſſiduous endeavours of Our Honourable Rulers, to detect the abominable Witchcrafts which have been committed in the Country; Humbly Praying, that the diſcovery of thoſe myſterious and miſchievous wickedneſſes, may be Perfected.* If in the midſt of the many Diſſatisfactions among us, the Publication of theſe Tryals may promote ſuch a Pious Thankfulneſs unto God, for Juſtice being ſo far executed among us, I ſhall Rejoice that God is Glorified; and pray, that no wrong ſteps of ours may ever ſully any of his Glorious Works. But we will begin with,

A Modern Inſtance of Witches, Diſcovered and Condemned in a Tryal, before that celebrated Judge, Sir Matthew Hale.[147]

IT may caſt ſome Light upon the Dark things now in *America*, if we juſt give a glance upon the *like things* lately happening in *Europe*. We

147 We are told by Biſhop Burnet (the Father of our Governor Burnet), that Judge Hale was born at Alderly in Glouceſterſhire, the firſt of November, 1609, and died on the 25th of December, 1676. In the Life of Sir Matthew, appended to his *Contemplations*, is given one of the moſt intereſting Pieces of Biography extant. In Accordance with one of his Sayings he was buried in the Church-yard of Alderly, and not in the Church, as was in his Time the prevailing Cuſtom—that

may see the *Witchcrafts* here most exactly resemble the *Witchcrafts* there; and we may learn what sort of Devils do trouble the World.

The Venerable *Baxter* very truly says, *Judge* Hale *was a Person, than whom, no Man was more Backward to Condemn a Witch, without full Evidence.*

Now, one of the latest Printed Accounts about a *Tryal of Witches*, is of what was before him, and it ran on this wise. [Printed in the Year 1682.] And it is here the rather mentioned, because it was a Tryal, much considered by the Judges of *New England.*

Saying was: "The Churches were for the Living, and the Churchyards for the Dead." In the Bishop's Life of him will be found a particular Account of his Family. After the great Fire of London he was one of the principal Judges that sat in Clifford's Inn, to regulate the Affairs between Landlord and Tenant, growing out of that Desolation. And with Sir Orlando Bridgman he rendered great Service in accommodating Differences which otherwise would long have retarded the rebuilding of the City. Whereas its "sudden and quiet building is justly reconed one of the Wonders of the Age." He was made "Lord Chief Justice of England," May 18th, 1671, which Office he resigned but a few Months previous to his Death, owing to his Infirmity. He lamented the rigorous Proceedings against the Nonconformists, though the adherent to the established Church; and used to say, "Those of the Separation were good Men, but they had *narrow Souls*, who would break the Peace of the Church, about such *inconsiderable Matters*, as the Points in Difference were." There does not appear to be taken any Notice of the Trials of Witches by Burnet in his Life of the Judge. It may be sufficient to say, that, like our Judges, Sewall and Stoughton, he was a Believer in Witchcraft, because there was Evidence of its Existence in the Bible! He was a timid Man, and this Timidity would not allow him so much as "to sum up the Evidence" in the Trial above given, and thus was the Case submitted to the Jury, who speedily gave in their Verdict of Guilty. There can be no Doubt but if Sir Matthew Hale had lived until the End of the New England Trials, he would, like Judge Sewall, have repented of his Course.

I. Roſe Cullender and *Amy Duny*, were ſeverally Indicted, for Bewitching *Elizabeth Durent, Ann Durent, Jane Bocking, Suſan Chandler, William Durent, Elizabeth* and *Deborah Pacy.* And the Evidence whereon they were Convicted, ſtood upon divers particular Circumſtances.

[56] *II. Ann Durent, Suſan Chandler*, and *Elizabeth Pacy*, when they came into the Hall, to give Inſtructions for the drawing the Bills of Indictments, they fell into ſtrange and violent Fits, ſo that they were unable to give in their Depoſitions, not only then, but alſo during the whole Aſſizes. *William Durent* being an Infant, his Mother Swore, that *Amy Duny* looking after her Child one Day in her abſence, did at her return confeſs, that ſhe had *given ſuck to the Child:* (tho' ſhe were an Old Woman:) Whereat, when *Durent* expreſſed her diſpleaſure, *Duny* went away with Diſcontents and Menaces.

The Night after, the Child fell into ſtrange and ſad Fits, wherein it continued for Divers Weeks. One Doctor *Jacob* adviſed her to hang up the Childs Blanket, in the Chimney Corner all Day, and at Night when ſhe went to put the Child into it, if ſhe found any Thing in it then to throw it without fear into the Fire. Accordingly, at Night, there fell a great Toad out of the Blanket, which ran up and down the Hearth. A Boy catch't it, and held it in the Fire with the Tongs: where it made an horrible Noiſe, and Flaſh'd like to Gun-Powder, with a report like that of a Piſtol: Whereupon the Toad was no more to be ſeen. The next Day a Kinſwoman of *Duny's*, told the Deponent, that her Aunt was all grievouſly ſcorch'd with the Fire, and the Deponent going to her Houſe, found her in ſuch a Condition. *Duny* told her, ſhe might thank her for it; but ſhe ſhould live to ſee ſome of her Children Dead, and herſelf upon Crutches. But after the Burning of the Toad, this Child Recovered.

This Deponent further Teſtifi'd, That Her Daughter *Elizabeth*, being about the Age of Ten Years, was taken in like manner, as her firſt Child was, and in her Fits complained much of *Amy Duny*, and ſaid, that ſhe did appear to Her, and afflict her in ſuch a manner as the former. One Day ſhe found *Amy Duny* in her Houſe, and thruſting her out of Doors, *Duny* ſaid, *You need not be ſo Angry, your Child won't live long*. And within three Days the Child died. The Deponent added, that ſhe was Her ſelf, not long after taken with ſuch a Lameneſs in both her Legs, that ſhe was forced to go upon Crutches; and ſhe was now in Court upon them. [It was Remarkable, that immediately upon the Juries bringing in *Duny* Guilty, *Durent* was reſtored unto the uſe of her Limbs, and went home without her Crutches.]

III. As for *Elizabeth* and *Deborah Pacy*, one Aged Eleven Years, the other Nine; the elder, being in Court, was made utterly ſenſeleſs, during all the time of the Trial: or at leaſt ſpeechleſs. By the direction of the Judge *Duny* was privately brought to *Elizabeth Pacy*, and ſhe touched her Hand: whereupon the Child, without ſo much as ſeeing her, ſuddenly leap'd up and flew upon the Priſoner; the younger was too ill, to be brought unto the Aſſizes. But *Samuel Pacy*, their Father, teſtifi'd, that his Daughter *Deborah* was taken with a ſudden Lameneſs; and upon the grumbling of *Amy Duny*, for being denied ſomething, where this Child was then [57] ſitting, the Child was taken with an extream pain in her ſtomach, like the pricking of Pins; and ſhrieking at a dreadful manner, like a Whelp, rather than a Rational Creature. The Phyſicians could not conjecture the cauſe of the Diſtemper; but *Amy Duny* being a Woman of ill Fame, and the Child in Fits crying out of *Amy Duny*, as affrighting her with the Apparition of her Perſon, the Deponent ſuſpected her, and procured her to be ſet in the ſtocks. While ſhe was there, ſhe ſaid in the hearing of Two Witneſſes, *Mr.* Pacy *keeps a great ſtir about his Child, but let him ſtay till he has done as much by his Children, as I have done by mine:* And being Aſked, What ſhe had done to her Children, ſhe Anſwered, *She had been fain to open her Childs Mouth with a Tap to give it Victuals.* The Deponent added, that within Two Days, the Fits of his Daughters were ſuch, that they could not preſerve either Life or Breath, without the help of a Tap. And that the Children Cry'd out of *Amy Duny*, and of *Rose Cullender*, as afflicting them with their Apparitions.

IV. The Fits of the Children were various. They would sometimes be Lame on one side; sometimes on t'other. Sometimes very sore; sometimes restored unto their Limbs, and then Deaf, or Blind, or Dumb, for a long while together. Upon the Recovery of their Speech, they would Cough extreamly; and with much Flegm, they would bring up Crooked Pins; and one time, a Two-penny Nail, with a very broad Head. Commonly at the end of every Fit, they would cast up a Pin. When the Children Read, they could not pronounce the Name of, *Lord*, or *Jesus*, or *Christ*, but would fall into Fits; and say, Amy Duny *says, I must not use that Name.* When they came to the Name of *Satan*, or *Devil*, they would clap their Fingers on the Book, crying out, *This bites, but it makes me speak right well!* The Children in their Fits would often Cry out, *There stands* Amy Duny, or *Rose Cullender;* and they would afterwards relate, *That these Witches appearing before them, threatned them, that if they told what they saw or heard, they would Torment them ten times more than ever they did before.*

V. Margaret Arnold, the Sister of Mr. *Pacy*, Testifi'd unto the like Sufferings being upon the Children, at her House, whither her Brother had Removed them. And that sometimes, the Children (*only*) would see things like Mice, run about the Houſe; and one of them ſuddenly ſnap'd one with the Tongs, and threw it into the Fire, where it ſcreeched out like a Rat. At another time, a thing like a Bee, flew at the Face of the younger Child; the Child fell into a Fit; and at laſt Vomited up a *Two-penny Nail,* with a Broad Head; affirming, *That the Bee brought this Nail, and forced it into her Mouth.* The Child would in like manner be aſſaulted with Flies, which brought Crooked Pins, unto her, and made her firſt ſwallow them, and then Vomit them. She one Day caught an Inviſible *Mouſe,* and throwing it into the Fire, it Flaſh'd like to Gun-Powder. None beſides the Child ſaw the *Mouſe,* but every one ſaw the *Flaſh.* She alſo de[58]clared, out of her Fits, that in them, *Amy Duny* much tempted her to deſtroy her ſelf.

VI. As for *Ann Durent,* her Father Teſtified, That upon a Diſcontent of *Roſe Cullender,* his Daughter was taken with much Illneſs in her Stomach and great and ſore Pains, like the Pricking of Pins: and then Swooning Fits, from which Recovering, ſhe declared, *She had ſeen the Apparition* of Roſe Cullender, *Threatning to Torment her.* She likewiſe Vomited up diverſe Pins. The Maid was Preſent at Court, but when *Cullender* look'd upon her, ſhe fell into ſuch Fits, as made her utterly unable to declare any thing.

Ann Baldwin depoſed the ſame.

VII. Jane Bocking, was too weak to be at the Aſſizes. But her Mother Teſtifi'd, that her

Daughter having formerly been Afflicted with Swooning Fits, and Recovered of them; was now taken with a great Pain in her Stomach; and New Swooning Fits. That ſhe took little Food, but every Day Vomited Crooked Pins. In her firſt Fits, ſhe would Extend her Arms, and uſe Poſtures, as if ſhe catched at ſomething, and when her Clutched Hands were forced open, they would find ſeveral Pins diverſely Crooked, unaccountably lodged there. She would alſo maintain a Diſcourſe with ſome that were Inviſibly preſent, when caſting abroad her Arms, ſhe would often ſay, *I will not have it!* but at laſt ſay, *Then I will have it!* and cloſing her Hand, which when they preſently after opened, a Lath-Nail was found in it. But her great Complaints were of being Viſited by the ſhapes of *Amy Duny*, and *Roſe Cullender*.

VIII. As for *Suſan Chandler*, her Mother Teſtified, That being at the ſearch of *Roſe Cullender*, they found on her Belly a thing like a Teat, of an Inch long; which the *ſaid Roſe* aſcribed to a ſtrain. But near her Privy-parts, they found Three more, that were ſmaller than the former. At the end of the long Teat, there was a little Hole, which appeared, as if newly Sucked; and upon ſtraining it, a white Milky matter iſſued out. The Deponent further ſaid, That her Daughter being one Day concerned at *Roſe Cullenders* taking her by the Hand, ſhe fell very ſick, and at Night cry'd out, *That* Roſe Cullender *would come to Bed unto her*. Her Fits grew violent, and in the Intervals of them, ſhe declared, *That ſhe ſaw* Roſe Cullender *in them, and once having of a great Dog with her.* She alſo Vomited up Crooked Pins; and when ſhe was brought into Court, ſhe fell into her Fits. She Recovered her ſelf in ſome Time, and was aſked by the Court, whether ſhe was in a Condition to take an Oath, and give Evidence. She ſaid, ſhe could; but having been Sworn, ſhe fell into her Fits again, and, *Burn her! Burn her!* were all the words that ſhe could obtain power to ſpeak. Her Father likewiſe gave the ſame Teſtimony with her Mother; as to all but the Search.

IX. Here was the Sum of the Evidence: Which Mr. Serjeant *Keeling*,[148] thought not ſufficient to Convict the Priſoners. For admitting the Chil[59]dren were Bewitched, yet, ſaid he, it can never be Apply'd unto the Priſoners, upon the Imagination only of the Parties Afflicted; inaſmuch as no perſon whatſoever could then be in Safety.

Dr. *Brown*, a very Learned Perſon then preſent, gave his Opinion, that theſe Perſons were Bewitched. He added, That in *Denmark*, there had been lately a great Diſcovery of Witches; who uſed the very ſame way of Afflicting people, by Conveying Pins and Nails into them. His Opinion was, that the Devil in Witchcrafts, did Work upon the Bodies of Men and Women, upon

[148] Spelt Keyling in the *Life of Hale*, whom he (Hale) ſucceeded as Lord Chief Juſtice, without taking his good Senſe with him.

a *Natural Foundation;* and that he did Extraordinarily afflict them, with such Distempers as their Bodies were most subject unto.

X. The Experiment about the *Usefulness*, yea, or *Lawfulness* whereof Good Men have sometimes disputed, was divers Times made, That tho' the Afflicted were utterly deprived of all sense in their Fits, yet upon the *Touch* of the Accused, they would so screech out, and fly up, as not upon any other persons. And yet it was also found that once upon the touch of an innocent person, the like effect follow'd, which put the whole Court unto a stand: altho' a small Reason was at length attempted to be given for it.

XI. However, to strengthen the Credit of what had been already produced against the Prisoners, One *John Soam* Testifi'd, That bringing home his Hay in Three Carts, one of the Carts wrenched the Window of *Rose Cullenders* House, whereupon she flew out, with violent Threatenings against the Deponent. The other Two Carts, passed by Twice, Loaded, that Day afterwards; but the Cart which touched *Cullenders* House, was Twice or Thrice that Day overturned. Having again Loaded it, as they brought it thro' the Gate which Leads out of the Field, the Cart stuck so fast in the Gates Head, that they could not possibly get it thro', but were forced to cut down the Post of the Gate, to make the Cart pass thro', altho' they could not perceive that the Cart did of either side touch the Gate-Post. They afterwards, did with much Difficulty get it home to the Yard; but could not for their Lives get the Cart near the place, where they ſhould unload. They were fain to unload at a great Diſtance; and when they were Tired, the Noſes of them that came to Aſſiſt them, would burſt forth a Bleeding; ſo they were fain to give over till next morning; and then they unloaded without any difficulty.

XII. Robert Sherringham alſo Teſtifi'd, That the Axle-Tree of his Cart, happening in paſſing, to break ſome part of *Roſe Cullenders* Houſe, in her Anger at it, ſhe vehemently threatned him, *His Horſes ſhould ſuffer for it.* And within a ſhort time, all his Four Horſes dy'd; after which he ſuſtained many other Loſſes in the ſudden Dying of his Cattle. He was alſo taken with a Lameneſs in his Limbs; and ſo vexed with Lice of an extraordinary Number and Bigneſs, that no Art could hinder the Swarming of them, till he burnt up two Suits of Apparel.

[60] *XIII.* As for *Amy Duny*, 'twas Teſtifi'd by one *Richard Spencer* that he heard her ſay, *The Devil would not let her Reſt; until ſhe were Revenged on the Wife of* Cornelius Sandſwel. And that *Sandſwel* teſtifi'd, that her Poultry dy'd ſuddenly, upon *Amy Dunys* threatning of them; and that her Huſbands Chimney fell, quickly after *Duny* had ſpoken of ſuch a diſaſter. And a Firkin of Fiſh could not be kept from falling into the Water, upon ſuſpicious words of *Duny's.*

XIV. The Judge told the Jury, they were to

inquire now, firft, whether thefe Children were Bewitched; and fecondly, Whether the Prifoners at the Bar were guilty of it. He made no doubt, there were fuch Creatures as Witches; for the Scriptures affirmed it; and the Wifdom of all Nations had provided Laws againft fuch perfons. He pray'd the God of Heaven to direct their Hearts in the weighty thing they had in hand; for, *To Condemn the Innocent, and let the Guilty go free, were both an Abomination to the Lord.*

The Jury in half an hour brought them in *Guilty* upon their feveral Indictments, which were Nineteen in Number.

The next Morning, the Children with their Parents, came to the Lodgings of the Lord Chief Juftice, and were in as good health as ever in their Lives; being Reftored within half an Hour after the Witches were Convicted.

The Witches were Executed; and *Confeffed* nothing; which indeed will not be wondred by them, who Confider and Entertain the Judgment of a Judicious Writer, *That the Unpardonable Sin, is moft ufually Committed by Profeffors of the Christian Religion, falling into Witchcraft.*

We will now proceed unto feveral of the like Tryals among our felves.[149]

[149] There is different, and fomewhat more of a common Senfe Account of this Trial in Hutchinfon's *Effay*, Pp. 139-157, Chap. viii.

I.

THE TRYAL OF G. B.

At a Court of OYER *and* TERMINER, HELD IN SALEM, 1692.

GLAD ſhould I have been, if I had never known the Name of this Man; or never had this occaſion to mention ſo much as the firſt Letters of his Name. But the Government requiring ſome Account of his [61] Trial to be inſerted in this Book, it becomes me with all Obedience to ſubmit unto the Order.

I. This *G. B.*[150] was Indicted for Witch-craft, and in the proſecution of the Charge againſt him, he was Accuſed by five or ſix of the Bewitched, as the Author of their Miſeries; he was Accuſed by Eight of the Confeſſing Witches, as being an head

150 George Burroughs. Why the Author merely gave the Initials of the Name of Mr. Burroughs is left to Conjecture. Perhaps he conſidered him deeper in the Devil's Arts than the Reſt of the accuſed, and perhaps he (the Author) had been more uncharitable towards him than towards others. See the Rev. Mr. Upham's highly intereſting *Lectures on Witchcraft*, 101, *et ſeq.* He was "the moſt prominent Victim of the diabolical Fanaticiſm of 1692. He was Son of that 'Mrs. Rebecca Burrows, who came from Virginia when her Son was quite young.' He was admitted a Member of Mr. Eliot's Church, Roxbury, 12 Apl., 1674. Probably his Father had died in Virginia, and we may hope, that the Mother alſo had gone to another World before the ſad Proof of Perverſeneſs of God's Ordinances in her choſen Refuge by the horrible Proceedings againſt her only Child." —*Savage.* His Wife, as will appear preſently, was a Siſter of "Mr. Ruck" of Salem. See Mr. Willis's *Hiſt. Portland,*

Actor at some of their Hellish Randezvouzes, and one who had the promise of being a King in Satan's Kingdom, now going to be Erected: He was accused by Nine Persons for extraordinary Lifting, and such feats of Strength, as could not be done without a Diabolical Assistance. And for other such things he was Accused, until about thirty Testimonies were brought in against him; nor were these judg'd the half of what might have been considered for his Conviction: However they were enough to fix the Character of a Witch upon him according to the Rules of Reasoning, by the Judicious *Gaule*, in that Case directed.

II. The Court being sensible, that the Testimonies of the Parties Bewitched, use to have a Room among the *Suspicions* or *Presumptions*, brought in against one Indicted for Witchcraft; there were now heard the Testimonies of several Persons, who were most notoriously Bewitched, and every day Tortured by Invisible Hands, and these now all charged the Spectres of *G. B.* to have a share in their Torments. At the Examination of this *G. B.* the Bewitched People were grievously harassed with Preternatural Mischiefs, which could not possibly be dissembled; and they still ascribed it unto the endeavours of *G. B.* to Kill them. And now upon his Tryal of one of the Bewitched Persons, testified, that in her Agonies, a little black Hair'd Man came to her, saying his Name was *B.* and bidding her set her hand unto a Book which he shewed unto her; and bragging that he was a *Conjurer*, above the ordinary Rank of Witches; That he often Perſecuted her with the offer of that Book, ſaying, *She ſhould be well, and need fear nobody, if ſhe would but Sign it;* But he inflicted cruel Pains and Hurts upon her, becauſe of her denying ſo to do. The Teſtimonies of the other Sufferers concurred with theſe; and it was remarkable, that whereas *Biting* was one of the ways which the Witches uſed for the vexing of the Sufferers; when they cry'd out of *G. B.* Biting them, the print of the Teeth would be ſeen on the Fleſh of the Complainers, and juſt ſuch a Set of Teeth as *G. B's* would then appear upon them, which could be diſtinguiſhed from thoſe of ſome other Mens. Others of them teſtified, That in their Torments, *G. B.* tempted them to go unto a Sacrament, unto which they perceived him with a Sound of Trumpet, Summoning of other Witches, who quickly after the Sound, would come from all Quarters unto the Rendezvouz. One of them falling into a kind of Trance, afterwards affirmed, that *G. B.* had carried her into a very high Mountain, where he ſhewed her mighty and glorious Kingdoms, and ſaid, *He would give them all to her, if ſhe would* [62] *write in his Book;* but ſhe told him, *They were none of his to give;* and refuſed the Motions; enduring of much Miſery for that refuſal.

It coſt the Court a wonderful deal of Trouble, to hear the Teſtimonies of the Sufferers; for when they were going to give in their Depoſitions, they would for a long time be taken with Fits, that made them uncapable of ſaying anything. The Chief Judg aſked the Priſoner, who he thought hindred theſe Witneſſes from giving their *Teſtimonies?* And he anſwered, *He ſuppoſed it was the Devil.* That Honourable Perſon, then repli'd, *How comes the Devil ſo loathe to have any Teſtimony born againſt you?* Which caſt him into very great Confuſion.[151]

III. It has been a frequent thing for the Bewitched People to be entertained with Apparitions of *Ghoſts* of Murdered People, at the ſame time that the *Spectres* of the Witches trouble them. Theſe Ghoſts do always affright the Beholders more than all the other ſpectral Repreſentations; and when they exhibit themſelves, they cry out, of being Murdered by the Witchcrafts or other Violences of the Perſons who are then in Spectre preſent. It is further conſiderable, that once or twice, theſe *Apparitions* have been ſeen by others, at the very ſame time that they have ſhewn themſelves to the Bewitched; and ſeldom have there been theſe *Apparitions*, but when ſomething unuſual or ſuſpected, have attended the Death of the Party thus Appearing. Some that have been accuſed by theſe *Apparitions* accoſting of the Bewitched People, who had never heard a word of any ſuch Perſons ever being in the World, have upon a fair Examination, freely and fully

[151] It is not difficult to underſtand how a Perſon, believing, as all then believed, would be "caſt into very great Confuſion" at ſuch Queſtions.

confeſſed the Murthers of thoſe very Perſons, altho theſe alſo did not know how the Apparitions had complained of them. Accordingly ſeveral of the Bewitched, had given in their Teſtimony, that they had been troubled with the Apparitions of two Women, who ſaid, that they were *G. B's* two Wives, and that he had been the Death of them; and that the Magiſtrates muſt be told of it, before whom if *B.* upon his Tryal denied it, they did not know but that they ſhould appear again in the Court. Now, *G. B.* had been Infamous for the Barbarous uſage of his two late Wifes, all the Country over. Moreover, it was teſtified, the Spectre of *G. B.* threatning of the Sufferers, told them, he had Killed (beſides others) Mrs. *Lawſon* and her Daughter *Ann.*[152] And it was noted, that theſe were the Vertuous Wife and Daughter of one at whom this *G. B.* might have a prejudice for his being ſerviceable at *Salem Village*, from whence himſelf had in ill Terms removed ſome Years before: And that when they

[152] Deodat Lawſon, who had preached at Salem Village; and on the 24th of March, 1692, he there preached a Sermon, entitled *Chriſt's Fidelity the only Shield againſt Satan's Malignity;* being Lecture Day, and a Time of Publick Examination, of ſome Suſpected for Witchcraft." The ſecond Edition of this Sermon was reprinted in London is 1704, in 12mo. Mr. Lawſon was a ſincere Believer in Witchcraft, and in his dedicatory Remarks, hopes "that it may pleaſe the ALMIGHTY GOD, to manifeſt his Power, in putting an End to your Sorrows of this Nature, by bruiſing *Satan* under your Feet ſhortly."—What is at preſent known of him and his Family will be found in Savage, under the appropriate Head. Reſpecting his Wife and Daughter, he ſays they had been dead above three Years. *Appendix* to the above *Sermon*, P. 99. He does accuſe Mr. Burroughs.

dy'd, which was long since, there were some odd Circumstances about them, which made some of the Attendents there suspect something of Witchcraft, tho none Imagined from what Quarter it should come.

Well, *G. B.* being now upon his Tryal, one of the Bewitched Persons was cast into Horror at the Ghost of *B's* two Deceased Wives then appearing before him, and crying for *Vengeance* against him. Hereupon seve[63]ral of the Bewitched Persons were successively called in, who all not knowing what the former had seen and said, concurred in their Horror of the Apparition, which they affirmed that he had before him. But he, tho much appalled, utterly deny'd that he discerned any thing of it; nor was it any part of his *Conviction.*

IV. Iudicious Writers have assigned it a great place in the Conviction of *Witches, when Persons are Impeached by other notorious Witches, to be as ill as themselves; especially, if the Persons have been much noted for neglecting the Worship of God.* Now, as there might have been Testimonies enough of *G. B's* Antipathy to *Prayer*, and the other Ordinances of God, tho by his Profession, singularly Obliged thereunto; so, there now came in against the Prisoner, the Testimonies of several Persons, who confessed their own having been horrible *Witches*, and ever since their Confessions, had been themselves terribly Tortured by the Devils and other Witches, even like the other Sufferers; and therein undergone the Pains of many *Deaths* for their Confeſſions.

Theſe now teſtified, that *G. B.* had been at Witch-meetings with them; and that he was the Perſon who had Seduc'd, and Compell'd them into the ſnares of Witchcraft: That he promiſed them *Fine Cloaths*, for doing it; that he brought Poppets to them, and Thorns to ſtick into thoſe Poppets, for the Afflicting of other People; and that he exhorted them with the reſt of the Crew, to Bewitch all *Salem Village*, but beſure to do it Gradually, if they would prevail in what they did.

When the *Lancaſhire Witches* were Condemn'd I don't remember that there was any conſiderable further Evidence, than that of the Bewitched, and than that of ſome that confeſſed. We ſee ſo much already againſt *G. B.* But this being indeed not enough, there were other things to render what had already been produced *credible*.

V. A famous Divine recites this among the Convictions of a Witch; *The Teſtimony of the party Bewitched, whether Pining or Dying; together with the joint Oaths of ſufficient Perſons that have ſeen certain Prodigious Pranks or Feats wrought by the Party Accuſed.* Now, God had been pleaſed ſo to leave this *G. B.* that he had enſnared himſelf by ſeveral Inſtances, which he had formerly given of a Preternatural Strength, and which were now produced againſt him. He was a very Puny Man, yet he had often done things beyond

the ſtrength of a Giant. A Gun of about ſeven foot Barrel, and ſo heavy that ſtrong Men could not ſteadily hold it out with both hands; there were ſeveral Teſtimonies, given in by Perſons of Credit and Honor, that he made nothing of taking up ſuch a Gun behind the Lock, with but one hand, and holding it out like a Piſtol, at Arms-end. *G. B.* in his Vindication, was ſo fooliſh as to ſay, That *an* Indian *was there, and held it out at the ſame time:* Whereas none of the Spectators ever ſaw any ſuch *Indian;* but they ſuppoſed the *Black Man,* (as the Witches call the Devil; and they generally ſay he reſembles an *Indian*) might
[64] give him that Aſſiſtance. There was Evidence likewiſe brought in, that he made nothing of taking up whole Barrels fill'd with *Malaſſes* or *Cider,* in very diſadvantageous Poſtures, and Carrying of them through the difficulteſt Places out of a Canoo to the Shore.

[Yea, there were two Teſtimonies that *G. B.* with only putting the Fore Finger of his Right hand into the Muzzle of an heavy Gun, a Fowling-piece of about ſix or ſeven foot Barrel, did lift up the Gun, and hold it out at Arms-end; a Gun which the Deponents though ſtrong Men could not with both hands lift up, and hold out at the But-end, as is uſual. Indeed, one of theſe Witneſſes was over-perſwaded by ſome Perſons to be out of the way upon *G. B's* Tryal; but he came afterwards with Sorrow for his withdraw, and gave in his Teſtimony: Nor were either of theſe Witneſſes made uſe of as Evidences in the Trial.]

VI. There came in ſeveral Teſtimonies relating to the Domeſtick Affairs of *G. B.* which had a very hard Aſpect upon him; and not only prov'd him a very ill Man; but alſo confirmed the belief of the Character, which had been already faſtned on him.

'Twas teſtified, that keeping his two Succeſſive Wives in a ſtrange kind of Slavery, he would when he came home from abroad, pretend to tell the Talk which any had with them; That he has brought them to the point of Death, by his harſh Dealings with his Wives, and then made the People about him, to promiſe that in caſe Death ſhould happen, they would ſay nothing of it; That he uſed all means to make his Wives Write, Sign, Seal, and Swear a Covenant, never to reveal any of his Secrets; That his Wives had privately complained unto the Neighbours about frightful Apparitions of Evil Spirits, with which their Houſe was ſometimes infeſted; and that many ſuch things have been whiſpered among the Neighbourhood. There were alſo ſome other Teſtmonies relating to the Death of People whereby the Conſciences of an Impartial Jury were convinced that *G. B.* had Bewitched the Perſons mentioned in the Complaints. But I am forced to omit ſeveral paſſages, in this, as well as in all the ſucceeding Tryals, becauſe the Scribes who took notice of them, have not ſupplyed me.

VII. One Mr. *Ruck*, Brother-in-Law to this *G. B.* teſtified, that *G. B.* and he himſelf, and his Siſter, who was *G. B's* Wife, going out for two or three Miles to gather Straw-berries, *Ruck* with his Siſter, the Wife of *G. B.* Rode home very Softly, with *G. B.* on Foot in their Company, *G. B.* ſtept aſide a little into the Buſhes; whereupon they halted and Halloo'd for him. He not anſwering, they went away homewards, with a quickened pace, without expectation of ſeeing him in a conſiderable while; and yet when they were got near home, to their Aſtoniſhment, they found him on foot with them, having a Baſket of Straw-berries. *G. B.* immediately then fell to Chiding his Wife, on the account of what ſhe had been ſpeaking to her [65] Brother, of him, on the Road: which when they wondred at, he ſaid, *He knew their thoughts.* *Ruck* being ſtartled at that, made ſome Reply, intimating, that the Devil himſelf did not know ſo far; but *G. B.* anſwered, *My God makes known your Thoughts unto me.* The Priſoner now at the Bar had nothing to anſwer, unto what was thus witneſſed againſt him, that was worth conſidering. Only he ſaid, *Ruck, and his Wife left a Man with him, when they left him.* Which *Ruck* now affirm'd to be falſe; and when the Court aſked *G. B. What the Man's Name was?* his Countenance was much altered; nor could he ſay, who 'twas. But the Court began to think, that he then ſtep'd aſide, only that by the aſſiſtance of the *Black Man*, he might put on his *Inviſibility*, and in that *Faſcinating Miſt*, gratifie his own Jealous Humour, to hear what they ſaid of him. Which trick of rendring themſelves *Inviſible*, our Witches do in their Confeſſions pretend, that they ſometimes are Maſters of; and it is the more credible, becauſe there is Demonſtration, that they often render many other things utterly *Inviſible*.

VIII. *Faltring, faulty, unconſtant, and contrary Anſwers upon judicial and deliberate Examination*, are counted ſome unlucky Symptoms of Guilt, in all Crimes, eſpecially in Witchcrafts. Now there never was a Priſoner more eminent for them, than *G. B.* both at his Examination and on his Trial. His *Tergiverſations, Contradictions*, and *Falſhoods*, were very ſenſible: he had little to ſay, but that he had heard ſome things that he could not prove, Reflecting upon the Reputation of ſome of the Witneſſes. Only he gave in a Paper to the Jury; wherein, altho' he had many times before, granted, not only that there are *Witches*, but alſo, that the preſent Sufferings of the Country are the effects of *horrible Witchcrafts*, yet he now goes to evince it, *That there neither are, nor ever were Witches, that having made a Compact with the Devil, can ſend a Devil to Torment other people at a diſtance*. This Paper was Tranſcribed out of *Ady;* which the Court preſently knew, as ſoon as they heard it. But he ſaid, he had taken none of it out of any Book; for which, his Evaſion afterwards, was, That a

Gentleman gave him the Discourse in a Manuscript, from whence he Transcribed it.

IX. The Jury brought him in *Guilty:* But when he came to Dy, he utterly deni'd the Fact, whereof he had been thus convicted.[153]

II. *The Tryal of* Bridget Bishop,[154] *alias Oliver, at the Court of Oyer and Terminer, held at Salem, June* 2. 1692.

I. SHE was Indicted for Bewitching of several Persons in the Neighbourhood, the Indictment being drawn up, according to the *Form* in [66] such Cases as usual. And pleading, *Not Guilty*, there were brought in several persons, who

153 It is refreshing, after reading this Case of Mr. Burroughs, as related by our Author, and to which we are at a Loss to find Words denunciatory enough to apply, to read the Conclusion to which my learned and judicious Friend, Mr. Willis comes, after a full View of all the Circumstances: "There has nothing survived Mr. Burroughs, either in his Living or Dying, that casts any Reproach upon his Character; and although he died the Victim of Fanaticism as wicked and stupid as any which has ever been countenanced in civilized Society, and which for a Time prejudiced his Memory, yet his Reputation stands redeemed in a more enlightened Age from any Blemish."—*History of Portland*, 246, Ed. 1865.

154 In 1680 poor Bridget Bishop appears to have been simply Bridget Oliver, and in that Year she was accused of being a Witch. "Feb. 22, the Negro of John Ingersol testified, before the Court of Commissioners, that he saw the Shape of said Bridget on a Beam of the Barn, with an Egg in its Hand, and that while he looked for a Rake or Pitchfork to strike it with, it vanished." She was ordered to give Bonds or go to Prison. See Felt, *Annals of Salem*, 265. She was the Wife of Edward Bishop, as will be seen further on. Her Husband was probably the Son of the first Edward Bishop of Salem. The Paternity of Bridget is uncertain. She may have been of the Family of Thomas Oliver, whose coming to Salem is recorded in the *Founders of New England.*

had long undergone many kinds of Miſeries, which were preternaturally inflicted, and generally aſcribed unto an *horrible Witchcraft.* There was little occaſion to prove the *Witchcraft,* it being evident and notorious to all beholders. Now to fix the *Witchcraft* on the Priſoner at the Bar, the firſt thing uſed, was the Teſtimony of the *Bewitched;* whereof ſeveral teſtifi'd, That the *Shape* of the Priſoner did oftentimes very grivouſly Pinch them, Choak them, Bite them, and Afflict them; urging them to write their Names in a *Book,* which the ſaid Spectre called, *Ours.* One of them did further teſtifie, that it was the *Shape* of this Priſoner, with another, which one day took her from her Wheel, and carrying her to the River-ſide, threatned there to Drown her, if ſhe did not Sign to the *Book* mentioned: which yet ſhe refuſed. Others of them did alſo teſtifie, that the ſaid *Shape* did in her Threats brag to them that ſhe had been the Death of ſundry Perſons, then by her named; that ſhe had *Ridden* a Man then likewiſe named. Another teſtifi'd, the Apparition of *Ghoſts* unto the Spectre of *Biſhop,* crying out, *You Murdered us!* About the Truth whereof, there was in the Matter of Fact but too much ſuſpicion.

II. It was teſtifi'd, That at the Examination of the Priſoner before the Magiſtrates, the Bewitched were extreamly tortured. If ſhe did but caſt her Eyes on them, they were preſently ſtruck down; and this in ſuch a manner as there could be no Collufion in the Bufinefs. But upon the Touch of her Hand upon them, when they lay in their Swoons, they would immediately Revive; and not upon the Touch of any ones elfe. Moreover, Upon fome Special Actions of her Body, as the fhaking of her Head, or the turning of her Eyes, they prefently and painfully fell into the like poftures. And many of the like Accidents now fell out, while fhe was at the Bar. One at the fame time teftifying, That fhe faid, *She could not be troubled to fee the afflicted thus tormented.*

III. There was Teftimony likewife brought in, that a Man ftriking once at the place, where a bewitched perfon faid, the *Shape* of this *Bifhop* ftood, the bewitched cried out, *That he had tore her Coat,* in the place then particularly fpecifi'd; and the Woman's Coat was found to be Torn in that very place.

IV. One *Deliverance Hobbs,*[155] who had confeffed her being a Witch, was now tormented by the Spectres, for her Confeffion. And fhe now teftifi'd, That this *Bifhop* tempted her to Sign the *Book* again, and to deny what fhe had confeff'd. She affirm'd, That it was the Shape of this Prifoner, which whipped her with Iron Rods, to compel her thereunto. And fhe affirmed, that this *Bifhop* was at a General Meeting of the

[155] There was a Family of Hobbs at Topsfield. On May 13th, 1692, William Hobbs of that Place was taken and fent to the Jail in Bofton. On the 23d of the fame Month Deliverance and Abigail, probably of the Family of William before named, were alfo fent to Bofton and imprifoned. See Felt's *Annals*, 304, alfo *Hift. Colls. Effex Inft.*, 141.

Witches, in a Field at *Salem*-Village, and there partook of a Diabolical Sacrament in Bread and Wine then adminiſtred.

[67] V. To render it further unqueſtionable, that the Priſoner at the Bar, was the Perſon truly charged in THIS *Witchcraft*, there were produced many Evidences of OTHER *Witchcrafts*, by her perpetrated. For Inſtance, *John Cook* teſtifi'd, That about five or ſix Years ago, one Morning, about Sun-Riſe, he was in his Chamber aſſaulted by the *Shape* of this Priſoner: which look'd on him, grinn'd at him, and very much hurt him with a Blow on the ſide of the Head: and that on the ſame day, about Noon, the ſame *Shape* walked in the Room where he was, and an Apple ſtrangely flew out of his Hand, into the Lap of his Mother, ſix or eight Foot from him.

VI. *Samuel Gray*[156] teſtifi'd, That about fourteen Years ago, he wak'd on a Night, and ſaw the Room where he lay full of Light; and that he then ſaw plainly a Woman between the Cradle, and the Bed-ſide, which look'd upon him. He roſe, and it vaniſhed; tho' he found the Doors all faſt. Looking out at the Entry-door, he ſaw the ſame Woman, in the ſame Garb again; and ſaid, *In God's Name, what do you come for?* He went to Bed, and had the ſame Woman again aſſaulting

156 Mr. Felt does not ſeem to have met with this Perſon in the *Salem Records*. He is mentioned in Savage's *Dictionary*, as marrying, at Salem, 28 Dec. 1671, Abigail Lord. More will be found of him when we come to the *More Wonders*. See alſo *Colls. Eſſex Inſt.* ii, 140. There are alſo numerous other References to Perſons of the Name.

him. The Child in the Cradle gave a great Screech, and the Woman disappeared. It was long before the Child could be quieted; and tho' it were a very likely thriving Child, yet from this time it pined away, and after divers Months, died in a sad Conditon. He knew not *Bishop*, nor her Name; but when he saw her after this, he knew by her Countenance, and Apparel, and all Circumstances, that it was the Apparition of this *Bishop*, which had thus troubled him.

VII. *John Bly*[157] and his Wife testifi'd, That he bought a Sow of *Edward Bishop*, the Husband of the Prisoner; and was to pay the Price agreed, unto another person. This Prisoner being angry that she was thus hindred from fingring the Mony, quarrell'd with *Bly*. Soon after which, the Sow was taken with strange Fits; Jumping, Leaping, and Knocking her Head against the Fence; she seem'd Blind and Deaf, and would neither Eat nor be Suck'd. Whereupon a Neighbour said, she believed the Creature was *Over-looked;* and sundry other Circumstances concurred, which made the Deponents believe that *Bishop* had bewitched it.

VIII. *Richard Coman*[158] testifi'd, That eight Years ago, as he lay awake in his Bed, with a

[157] Often spelt *Bligh.* A Brickmaker of Salem. His Wife was Rebecca, Daughter, probably, of Deac. Charles Gott, by whom he had a large Family. The Names of his Children are given by Savage.

[158] The Man who had the following extraordinary Experience was unknown to both Felt and Savage, although he appears to have been an old Inhabitant of Salem. His Name was probably *Cumin, Cuming*, or *Cummings*, and may have been the Freeman of 1669.

Light burning in the Room, he was annoy'd with the Apparition of this *Bishop*, and of two more that were ſtrangers to him, who came and oppreſſed him ſo, that he could neither ſtir himſelf, nor wake any one elſe, and that he was the Night after, moleſted again in the like manner; the ſaid *Biſhop*, taking him by the Throat, and pulling him almoſt out of the Bed. His Kinſman offered for this Cauſe to lodge with him; and that Night, as they were awake, diſcourſing together, this *Coman* was once more viſited by the Gueſts which had formerly been ſo troubleſom; his Kinſman being at the ſame time ſtrook ſpeechleſs, and unable to move Hand or [68] Foot. He had laid his Sword by him, which theſe unhappy Spectres did ſtrive much to wreſt from him; only he held too faſt for them. He then grew able to call the People of his Houſe; but altho' they heard him, yet they had not power to ſpeak or ſtir; until at laſt, one of the People crying out, *What's the matter?* The Spectres all vaniſhed.

IX. *Samuel Shattock*[159] teſtifi'd, That in the Year, 1680, this *Bridget Biſhop*, often came to his Houſe upon ſuch frivolous and fooliſh Errands, that they ſuſpected ſhe came indeed with a purpoſe of miſchief. Preſently, whereupon, his eldeſt Child, which was of as promiſing Health

159 Suppoſed to be the Quaker, over a Tranſaction of which Mr. Savage with great Eagerneſs "exults." That Tranſaction will be found detailed in the *Hiſt. and Antiqs. of Boſton*, 357. Were Quakers allowed to teſtify in thoſe Days? Mr. Lemuel Shattuck has given an Account of the Family in the Appendix to his *Memorials*, 361, *et ſeq.*

and Senſe, as any Child of its Age, began to droop exceedingly; and the oftner that *Biſhop* came to the Houſe, the worſe grew the Child. As the Child would be ſtanding at the Door, he would be thrown and bruiſed againſt the Stones, by an Inviſible Hand, and in like ſort knock his Face againſt the ſides of the Houſe, and bruiſe it after a miſerable manner. After this *Biſhop* would bring him things to Dy, whereof he could not imagin any uſe; and when ſhe paid him a piece of Mony, the Purſe and Mony were unaccountably conveyed out of a lock'd Box, and never ſeen more. The Child was immediately, hereupon, taken with terrible Fits, whereof his Friends thought he would have dyed: Indeed he did almoſt nothing but Cry and Sleep for ſeveral Months together; and at length his Underſtanding was utterly taken away. Among other Symptoms of an Inchantment upon him, one was, That there was a Board in the Garden, whereon he would walk; and all the Invitations in the World could never fetch him off. About 17 or 18 years after,[160] there came a Stranger to *Shattock's* Houſe, who ſeeing the Child, ſaid, *This poor Child is Bewitched; and you have a Neighbour living not far off, who is a Witch.* He added, *Your Neighbour has had a falling out with your Wife; and ſhe ſaid, in her Heart, your Wife is a proud Woman, and ſhe would bring down her Pride in this Child.* He then

160 Hence it ſeems Shattuck was living at Salem as early as 1663.

remembred, that *Biſhop* had parted from his Wife in muttering and menacing Terms, a little before the Child was taken Ill. The aboveſaid Stranger would needs carry the bewitched Boy with him, to *Biſhop's* Houſe, on pretence of buying a Pot of Cyder. The Woman entertained him in a furious manner; and flew alſo upon the Boy, ſcratching his Face till the Blood came; and ſaying, *Thou Rogue, what doſt thou bring this Fellow here to plague me?* Now it ſeems the Man had ſaid, before he went, That he would fetch Blood of *her*. Ever after the Boy was follow'd with grievous Fits, which the Doctors themſelves generally aſcribed unto *Witchcraft;* and wherein he would be thrown ſtill into the *Fire* or the *Water*, if he were not conſtantly look'd after; and it was verily believed that *Biſhop* was the cauſe of it.

X. *John Louder*[160] teſtifi'd, That upon ſome little Controverſy with *Biſhop* about her Fowls, going well to Bed, he did awake in the Night by Moon[69]light, and did ſee clearly the likeneſs of this Woman grievouſly oppreſſing him; in which miſerable condition ſhe held him, unable to help himſelf, till near Day. He told *Biſhop* of this;

[161] This Name has probably undergone ſome orthographic Changes, as *Lowder*, *Lodder*, &c. There was a Lodder's Lane in Salem, ſo called becauſe "the old Man, George *Lowder* lived on the weſtern Corner where the Weſt Houſe is."—*Hiſt. Colls. Salem Inſt.* vi, 109. John Louder had a Wife "Eliz'a," and by her Sons, William, born 10 Feb. 1691; Nicholas, 31ſt 6mo., 1693; a Daughter Elizabeth, born 1 Oct. 1695, and a Son Jared, born 1 Nov. 1697.—*Ibid.* ii, 257.

but ſhe deny'd it, and threatned him very much. Quickly after this, being at home on a Lords day, with the doors ſhut about him, he ſaw a black Pig approach him; at which, he going to kick, it vaniſhed away. Immediately after, ſitting down, he ſaw a black Thing jump in at the Window, and come and ſtand before him. The Body was like that of a Monkey, the Feet like a Cocks, but the Face much like a Mans. He being ſo extreamly affrighted, that he could not ſpeak; this Monſter ſpoke to him, and ſaid, *I am a Meſſenger ſent unto you, for I underſtand that you are in ſome Trouble of Mind, and if you will be ruled by me, you ſhall want for nothing in this World.* Whereupon he endeavoured to clap his Hands upon it; but he could feel no ſubſtance; and it jumped out of the Window again; but immediately came in by the Porch, tho' the Doors were ſhut, and ſaid, *You had better take my Counſel!* He then ſtruck at it with a Stick, but ſtruck only the Ground-ſel, and broke the Stick: The Arm with which he ſtruck was preſently Diſenabled, and it vaniſhed away. He preſently went out at the Back-door, and ſpied this *Biſhop*, in her Orchard, going toward her Houſe; but he had not power to ſet one foot forward unto her. Whereupon, returning into the Houſe, he was immediately accoſted by the Monſter he had ſeen before; which Goblin was now going to fly at him; whereat he cry'd out, *The whole Armour of God be between me and you!* So it ſprang back, and flew over the Apple-tree;

ſhaking many Apples off the Tree, in its flying over. At its leap, it flung Dirt with its Feet againſt the Stomack of the Man; whereon he was then ſtruck Dumb, and ſo continued for three Days together. Upon the producing of this Teſtimony, *Biſhop* deny'd that ſhe knew this Deponent: Yet their two Orchards joined; and they had often had their little Quarrels for ſome years together.

XI. *William Stacy*[162] teſtify'd, That receiving Mony of this *Biſhop*, for work done by him; he was gone but a matter of three Rods from her, and looking for his Mony, found it unaccountably gone from him. Some time after, *Biſhop* aſked him, whether her Father would grind her Griſt for her? He demanded why? She reply'd, *Becauſe Folks count me a Witch.* He anſwered, *No queſtion but he will grind it for you.* Being then gone about ſix Rods from her, with a ſmall Load in his Cart, ſuddenly the Off-wheel ſlump't; and ſunk down into an hole, upon plain Ground; ſo that the Deponent was forced to get help for the recovering of the Wheel: But ſtepping back to look for the hole, which might give him this Diſaſter, there was none at all to be found. Some time after, he was waked in the Night; but it ſeem'd as light as day; and he perfectly ſaw the

162 Doubtleſs the ſame William, Son of Thomas Stacy of Salem, who married Priſcilla Buckley, 28th 9 mo, 1677. He had a Daughter Priſcilla, the ſame whoſe Death is mentioned in the Text, without Doubt. The Family Record is quite extenſive, and may be ſeen in *Hiſt. Colls. Salem Inſt.*, iii, 193. See alſo, Felt, *Annals of Salem*, Vol. 2, *Index.*

ſhape of this *Biſhop* [70] in the Room, troubling of him; but upon her going out, all was dark again. He charg'd *Biſhop* afterwards with it, and ſhe deny'd it not; but was very angry. Quickly after, this Deponent having been threatned by *Biſhop*, as he was in a dark Night going to the Barn, he was very ſuddenly taken or lifted from the Ground, and thrown againſt a Stone-wall: After that, he was again hoiſted up and thrown down a Bank, at the end of his Houſe. After this again, paſſing by this *Biſhop*, his Horſe with a ſmall Load, ſtriving to draw, all his Gears flew to pieces, and the Cart fell down; and this Deponent going then to lift a Bag of Corn, of about two Buſhels, could not budge it with all his Might.

Many other Pranks of this *Biſhop's* this Deponent was ready to teſtify. He alſo teſtify'd, That he verily believ'd, the ſaid *Biſhop* was the Inſtrument of his Daughter *Priſcilla's* Death; of which ſuſpicion, pregnant Reaſons were aſſigned.

XII. To crown all, *John Bly* and *William Bly* teſtify'd, That being employ'd by *Bridget Biſhop*, to help take down the Cellar-wall of the old Houſe wherein ſhe formerly lived, they did in holes of the ſaid old Wall, find ſeveral *Poppets*, made up of Rags and Hogs-bruſſels, with headleſs Pins in them, the Points being outward; whereof ſhe could give no Account to the Court, that was reaſonable or tolerable.[163]

163 That a Child's *Rag-baby*, or *Doll*, ſhould be found in an out-of-

XIII. One thing that made againſt the Priſoner was, her being evidently convicted of *groſs Lying* in the Court, ſeveral times, while ſhe was making her Plea; but beſides this, a Jury of Women found a preternatural Teat upon her Body: But upon a ſecond ſearch, within 3 or 4 hours, there was no ſuch thing to be ſeen. There was alſo an Account of other People whom this Woman had Afflicted; and there might have been many more, if they had been enquired for; but there was no need of them.

XIV. There was one very ſtrange thing more, with which the Court was newly entertained. As this Woman was under a Guard, paſſing by the great and ſpacious Meeting-houſe of *Salem*, ſhe gave a look towards the Houſe: and immediately a *Dæmon* inviſibly entring the Meeting-houſe, tore down a part of it; ſo that tho' there was no Perſon to be ſeen there, yet the People, at the noiſe, running in, found a Board, which was ſtrongly faſtned with ſeveral Nails, tranſported unto another quarter of the Houſe.

the-way Place, put there by little Girls in their Play, did certainly "crown all" the Stupidity and Folly yet exhibited among People of mature Years. It proves, as Mr. Chever ſays, in his Notes on theſe Affairs, that "the Reaſon and Wiſdom of the Magiſtrates had, for the Time, departed."—*Hiſt. Colls. Salem Inſt.*, ii, 78.

III. *The Tryal of* Susanna Martin,[164] *at the Court of Oyer and Terminer, held by Adjournment at Salem, June* 29. 1692.

I. SUSANNA MARTIN, pleading *Not Guilty* to the Indictment of *Witchcraft*, brought in againſt her, there were produced the Evidences of ma[71]ny Perſons very ſenſibly and grievouſly Bewitched; who all complained of the Priſoner at the Bar, as the Perſon whom they believed the cauſe of their Miſeries. And now, as well as in the other Trials, there was an extraordinary Endeavour by *Witchcrafts*, with Cruel and frequent Fits, to hinder the poor Sufferers from giving in their Complaints, which the Court was forced with much Patience to obtain, by much waiting and watching for it.

II. There was now alſo an account given of what paſſed at he firſt Examination before the Magiſtrates. The Caſt of her *Eye*, then ſtriking the afflicted People to the Ground, whether they ſaw that Caſt or no; there were theſe among other Paſſages between the Magiſtrates and the Examinate.

Magiſtrate. Pray, what ails theſe People?

Martin. I don't know.

164 Suſannah Martin belonged to Ameſbury. She appears to have been a Woman of ſuperior Mind, judging by her ſenſible Replies to the benighted Magiſtrate. She was a Widow, and one of thoſe ſent to Boſton and impriſoned on the 2d of May, and on the 19th of July was hanged. She was probably the ſecond Wife of George Martin of Saliſbury, a Daughter of Richard North.

Magiſtrate. But what do you think ails them?

Martin. I don't deſire to ſpend my Judgment upon it.

Magiſtrate. Don't you think they are bewitch'd?

Martin. No, I do not think they are.

Magiſtrate. Tell us your Thoughts about them then.

Martin. No, my thoughts are my own, when they are in, but when they are out they are anothers. Their Maſter.——

Magiſtrate. Their Maſter? who do you think is their Maſter?

Martin. If they be dealing in the Black Art, you may know as well as I.

Magiſtrate. Well, what have you done towards this?

Martin. Nothing at all.

Magiſtrate. Why, 'tis you or your Appearance.

Martin. I cannot help it.

Magiſtrate. Is it not *your* Maſter? How comes your Appearance to hurt theſe?

Martin. How do I know? He that appeared in the Shape of *Samuel*, a glorified Saint, may appear in any ones Shape.

It was then alſo noted in her, as in others like her, that if the Afflicted went to approach her, they were flung down to the Ground. And, when ſhe was aſked the reaſon of it, ſhe ſaid, *I cannot tell; it may be the Devil bears me more Malice than another.*

III. The Court accounted themſelves, alarum'd by theſe Things, to enquire further into the Converſation of the Priſoner; and ſee what there might occur, to render theſe Accuſations further credible. Whereupon, *John Allen* of *Saliſbury*, teſtify'd, That he refuſing, becauſe of the weakneſs of his Oxen, to Cart ſome Staves at the requeſt of this *Martin*, ſhe was diſpleaſed at it; and ſaid, *It had been as good that he had; for his Oxen ſhould never do him much more Service.* Whereupon this Deponent ſaid, *Doſt thou threaten me, thou old Witch? I'l throw thee into the Brook:* Which [72] to avoid, ſhe flew over the Bridge, and eſcaped. But, as he was going home, one of his Oxen tired, ſo that he was forced to Unyoke him, that he might get him home. He then put his Oxen, with many more, upon *Saliſbury* Beach, where Cattle did uſe to get *Fleſh.* In a few days, all the Oxen upon the Beach were found by their Tracks, to have run unto the Mouth of *Merrimack-River*, and not returned; but the next day they were found come aſhore upon *Plum-Iſland.* They that ſought them, uſed all imaginable gentleneſs, but they would ſtill run away with a violence, that ſeemed wholly Diabolical, till they came near the mouth of *Merrimack-River;* when they ran right into the Sea, ſwimming as far as they could be ſeen. One of them then ſwam back again, with a ſwiftneſs, amazing to the Beholders, who ſtood ready to receive him, and help up his tired Carcaſs: But the Beaſt ran furiouſly up into the Iſland, and from thence, through the Marſhes, up into *Newbury* Town, and ſo up into the Woods; and there after a while found near *Amesbury*. So that, of fourteen good Oxen, there was only this ſaved: The reſt were all caſt up, ſome in one place, and ſome in another, Drowned.

IV. *John Atkinſon*[165] teſtifi'd, That he exchanged a Cow with a Son of *Suſanna Martin's* whereat ſhe muttered, and was unwilling he ſhould have it. Going to receive this Cow, tho' he Hamſtring'd her, and Halter'd her, ſhe, of a Tame Creature, grew ſo mad, that they could ſcarce get her along. She broke all the Ropes that were faſtned unto her, and though ſhe were ty'd faſt unto a Tree, yet ſhe made her eſcape, and gave them ſuch further trouble, as they could aſcribe to no cauſe but Witchcraft.

V. *Bernard Peache*[166] teſtifi'd, That being in Bed, on the Lord's-day Night, he heard a ſcrabbling at the Window, whereat he then ſaw *Suſanna Martin* come in, and jump down upon the Floor. She took hold of this Deponent's Feet, and drawing his Body up into an Heap, ſhe lay upon him near Two Hours; in all which time he could neither ſpeak nor ſtir. At length, when he could begin to move, he laid hold on

[165] Probably Son of Theodore Atkinſon well known among the early prominent Men of New England; yet he finds no Place in Eliot's *Biographical Dictionary*. John was a Hatter, and his Wife was Sarah Myrick, whom he married in 1664. See Savage's *Dictionary*, i, 74.

[166] There was a Family of Peaches in the County of Eſſex. In 1668 there was John and John Jr., often mentioned in various Records.

her Hand, and pulling it up to his Mouth, he bit three of her Fingers, as he judged, unto the Bone. Whereupon ſhe went from the Chamber, down the Stairs, out at the Door. This Deponent thereupon called unto the People of the Houſe, to adviſe them of what paſſed; and he himſelf did follow her. The People ſaw her not; but there being a Bucket at the Left-hand of the Door, there was a drop of Blood found upon it; and ſeveral more drops of Blood upon the Snow newly fallen abroad: There was likewiſe the print of her 2 Feet juſt without the Threſhold; but no more ſign of any Footing further off.

At another time this Deponent was deſired by the Priſoner, to come unto an Huſking of Corn, at her Houſe; and ſhe ſaid, *If he did not come, it were better that he did!* He went not; but the Night. following, *Suſanna* [73] *Martin,* as he judged, and another came towards him. One of them ſaid, *Here he is!* but he having a Quarter-ſtaff, made a Blow at them. The Roof of the Barn, broke his Blow; but following them to the Window, he made another Blow at them, and ſtruck them down; yet they got up, and got out, and he ſaw no more of them.

About this time, there was a Rumour about the Town, that *Martin* had a Broken Head; but the Deponent could ſay nothing to that.

The ſaid *Peache* alſo teſtifi'd the Bewitching the Cattle to Death, upon *Martin's* Diſcontents.

VI. *Robert Downer*[167] teſtifi'd, That this Priſoner being ſome Years ago proſecuted at Court for a Witch, he then ſaid unto her, *He believed ſhe was a Witch.* Whereat ſhe being diſſatisfied, ſaid, *That ſome She-Devil would ſhortly fetch him away!* Which words were heard by others, as well as himſelf. The Night following, as he lay in his Bed, there came in at the Window, the likeneſs of a *Cat*, which flew upon him, took faſt hold of his Throat, lay on him a conſiderable while and almoſt killed him. At length he remembered what *Suſanna Martin* had threatned the Day before; and with much ſtriving he cried out, *Avoid, thou She-Devil! In the Name of God the Father, the Son, and the Holy Ghoſt, Avoid!* Whereupon it left him, leap'd on the Floor, and flew out at the Window.

And there alſo came in ſeveral Teſtimonies, that before ever *Downer* ſpoke a word of this Accident, *Suſanna Martin* and her Family had related, *How this* Downer *had been handled!*

VII. *John Kembal*[168] teſtified, that *Suſanna Martin*, upon a Cauſeleſs Diſguſt, had threatned him, about a certain Cow of his, *That ſhe ſhould never do him any more Good:* and it came to paſs accordingly. For ſoon after the Cow was found

[167] He was of Saliſbury, 1665, had been of Newbury. His Wife was Sarah, Daughter of John Eaton. He had ſeveral Children, whoſe Births and Names will be found in Savage.

[168] There were ſeveral contemporaneous John *Kimbals* about Eſſex or Old Norfolk County, but I meet with nothing to fix upon any one of them as this John *Kembal.* The Name is ſince *Kimball.*

ſtark dead on the dry Ground, without any Diſtemper to be diſcerned upon her. Upon which he was followed with a ſtrange Death upon more of his Cattle, whereof he loſt in one Spring to the Value of Thirty Pounds. But the ſaid *John Kembal* had a further Teſtimony to give in againſt the Priſoner which was truly admirable.

Being deſirous to furniſh himſelf with a Dog, he applied himſelf to buy one of this *Martin,* who had a Bitch with Whelps in her Houſe. But ſhe not letting him have his choice, he ſaid, he would ſupply himſelf then at one *Blezdels.* Having mark'd a Puppy, which he lik'd at *Blezdels,* he met *George Martin,* the Huſband of the Priſoner, going by, who aſked him, *Whether he would not have one of his Wife's Puppies?* and he anſwered, *No.* The ſame Day, one *Edmond Eliot,* being at *Martin's* Houſe, heard *George Martin* relate, where this *Kembal* had been, and what he had ſaid. Whereupon *Suſanna Martin* replied, *If I live, I'll give him Puppies enough!* Within a few days after, this *Kembal,* coming out of the Woods, there aroſe a little Black [74] Cloud in the N.W. and *Kembal* immediately felt a force upon him, which made him not able to avoid running upon the ſtumps of Trees, that were before him, albeit he had a broad, plain Cart-way, before him; but tho' he had his Ax alſo on his Shoulder, to endanger him in his Falls, he could not forbear going out of his way to tumble over them. When he came below the Meeting Houſe, there appeared unto him, a little thing like a *Puppy*, of a Darkiſh Colour; and it ſhot backwards and forwards between his Legs. He had the Courage to uſe all poſſible Endeavours of Cutting it with his Ax; but he could not Hit it: the Puppy gave a jump from him, and went, as to him it ſeem'd to him into the Ground. Going a little further, there appeared unto him a Black Puppy, ſomewhat bigger than the firſt, but as Black as a Cole. Its Motions were quicker than thoſe of his Ax; it flew at his Belly, and away; then at his Throat; ſo, over his Shoulder one way, and then over his Shoulder another way. His Heart now began to fail him, and he thought the Dog would have tore his Throat out. But he recovered himſelf, and called upon God in his Diſtreſs; and naming the Name of JESUS CHRIST, it vaniſhed away at once. The Deponent ſpoke not one Word of theſe Accidents, for fear of affrighting his Wife. But the next Morning, *Edmond Eliot*, going into *Martin's* Houſe, this Woman aſked him where *Kembal* was? He replied, *At home, a Bed, for ought he knew*. She returned, *They ſay, he was frighted laſt Night*. *Eliot* aſked, *With what?* She anſwered, *With Puppies*. *Eliot* aſked, *Where ſhe heard of it, for he had heard nothing of it?* She rejoined, *About the Town*. Altho' *Kembal* had mentioned the Matter to no Creature living.

VIII. *William Brown*[169] teſtifi'd, That Heaven

169 Probably Son of the Hon. William Brown of Salem, who married Hannah, Daughter of George Curwen. We have no

having blessed him with a most Pious and Prudent Wife, this Wife of his, one day met with *Susanna Martin;* but when she approach'd just unto her, *Martin* vanished out of sight, and left her extreamly affrighted. After which time, the said *Martin* often appear'd unto her, giving her no little trouble; and when she did come, she was visited with Birds, that sorely peck'd and prick'd her; and sometimes, a Bunch, like a Pullet's Egg, would rise in her Throat, ready to choak her, till she cry'd out, *Witch, you shan't choak me!* While this good Woman was in this extremity, the Church appointed a Day of Prayer, on her behalf; whereupon her Trouble ceas'd; and she saw not *Martin* as formerly; and the Church, instead of their Fast, gave Thanks for her Deliverance. But a considerable while after, she being Summoned to give in some Evidence at the Court, against this *Martin*, quickly thereupon this *Martin* came behind her, while she was milking her Cow, and said unto her, *For thy defaming me at Court, I'll make thee the miserablest Creature in the World.* Soon after which, she fell into a strange kind of distemper, and became horribly frantick, and uncapable of any reasonable Action; the Physicians de[75]claring, that her Distemper was preternatural, and that some Devil had certainly

probable Cause of Mrs. Brown's Languishment, every Ill being then attributed to the Devil or his Witches. It seems she never recovered from her Malady, whatever it was, but died on the 22d of Nov. of the same Year, (1692). He died in 1716.—See Quincy, *Hist. Har. Col.*, i, 418, and Savage's *Dictionary*, i, 279.

bewitched her; and in that condition ſhe now remained.

IX. *Sarah Atkinſon*[170] teſtify'd, That *Suſanna Martin* came from *Ameſbury* to their Houſe at *Newbury*, in an extraordinary Seaſon, when it was not fit for any to Travel. She came (as ſhe ſaid, unto *Atkinſon*) all that long way on Foot. She brag'd and ſhew'd how dry ſhe was; nor could it be perceived that ſo much as the Soles of her Shoes were wet. *Atkinſon* was amazed at it; and profeſſed, that ſhe ſhould her ſelf have been wet up to the knees, if ſhe had then came ſo far; but *Martin* reply'd, *She ſcorn'd to be Drabbled!* It was noted, that this Teſtimony upon her Trial, caſt her in a very ſingular Confuſion.

X. *John Preſſy*[171] teſtify'd, That being one Evening very unaccountably Bewildred, near a Field of *Martins*, and ſeveral times, as one under an Enchantment, returning to the place he had left, at length he ſaw a marvellous Light, about the bigneſs of an Half-buſhel, near two Rod out of the way. He went, and ſtruck at it with a Stick, and laid it on with all his might. He gave it near forty blows; and felt it a palpable ſubſtance. But going from it, his Heels were

170 Wife, perhaps, of the John Atkinſon mentioned previouſly.—See Coffin's *Newbury*, 293.

171 Perhaps the ſame as *Preſon*, or *Preſſon*. He is the *Preſſie* of Savage, no doubt, who ſays his Wife was Mary Gage, whom he married 30th Nov., 1665. I do not find among the Gages of Rowley or elſewhere, a Daughter married to a Preſſie. John *Preſſie* was of Ameſbury, 1677.—*N. E. H. G. Reg.*, vi, 202.

ftruck up, and he was laid with his Back on the Ground, fliding, as he thought, into a Pit; from whence he recover'd by taking hold on the Bufh; altho' afterwards he could find no fuch Pit in the place. Having, after his Recovery, gone five or fix Rod, he faw *Sufanna Martin* ftanding on his Left-hand, as the Light had done before; but they changed no words with one another. He could fcarce find his Houfe in his Return; but at length he got home extreamly affrighted. The next day, it was upon Enquiry underftood, that *Martin* was in a miferable condition by pains and hurts that were upon her.

It was further teftify'd by this Deponent, That after he had given in fome Evidence againft *Sufanna Martin*, many years ago, fhe gave him foul words about it; and faid, *He fhould never profper more;* particularly, *That he fhould never have more than two Cows; that tho' he was never fo likely to have more, yet he fhould never have them.* And that from that very day to this, namely for twenty years together, he could never exceed that number; but fome ftrange thing or other ftill prevented his having of any more.

XI. *Jervis Ring*[172] teftify'd, That about feven

172 Savage calls him *Jarvis* and has given him Wife, Hannah Fowler, 24th Dec., 1685; Son Jarvis, born 2d Oct., 1686; Daughters, Hannah, born 3d March, 1689, Elizabeth, 3d Sept., 1692, and Son Oliver, born 17th June, 1698. This was a Salifbury Family. The Jofeph Ring, mentioned in the next Section, was perhaps that *Jofeph* born the 3d of Auguft, 1664 (at Salifbury), Son of Robert. Inftead of this Robert *Ring* having come over in the Ship Bevis, in 1638, it

years ago, he was oftentimes and grievoufly oppreffed in the Night, but faw not who troubled him; until at laft he Lying perfectly Awake, plainly faw *Sufanna Martin* approach him. She came to him, and forceably bit him by the Finger; fo that the Print of the bite is now, fo long after, to be feen upon him.

XII. But befides all of thefe Evidences, there was a moft wonderful Account of one *Jofeph Ring*, produced on this occafion.

[76] This Man has been ftrangely carried about by *Dæmons*, from one *Witch-meeting* to another, for near two years together; and for one quarter of this time, they have made him, and keep him Dumb, tho' he is now again able to fpeak. There was one *T. H.* who having, as 'tis judged, a defign of engaging this *Jofeph Ring* in a fnare of Devillifm, contrived a while, to bring this *Ring* two Shillings in Debt unto him.

Afterwards, this poor Man would be vifited with unknown fhapes, and this *T. H.* fometimes among them; which would force him away with them, unto unknown Places, where he faw Meetings, Feaftings, Dancings; and after his return, wherein they hurried him along through the Air,

does not appear that any Perfon of the Name of Ring came at that Time in that Ship. Mr. Savage "ftrangely" fays Robert Ring came over in the Bevis of Northampton, and ftranger ftill there is no Robert *Ring* on *his own* Lift of Paffengers. For Robert *Knight* he copied (or fome one for him), Robert *Ringht!* Being unwilling to admit a new Name into his Dictionary, he has committed a more ferious Blunder. Mr. Lawfon fays he was prefent when Ring gave his Teftimony, and fully corroborates our Author's Statement.—*Lawfon,* 113.

he gave Demonſtrations to the Neighbours, that he had indeed been ſo tranſported. When he was brought unto theſe helliſh Meetings, one of the firſt Things they ſtill did unto him, was to give him a knock on the Back, whereupon he was ever as if bound with Chains, uncapable of ſtirring out of the place, till they ſhould releaſe him. He related, that there often came to him a Man, who preſented him a *Book*, whereto he would have him ſet his Hand; promiſing to him, that he ſhould then have even what he would; and preſenting him with all the delectable Things, Perſons, and Places, that he could imagin. But he refuſing to ſubſcribe, the buſineſs would end with dreadful Shapes, Noiſes and Screeches, which almoſt ſcared him out of his Wits. Once with the Book, there was a Pen offered him, and an Ink-horn with Liquor in it, that ſeemed like Blood: but he never toucht it.

This Man did now affirm, That he ſaw the Priſoner at ſeveral of thoſe helliſh Randezvouzes.

Note, this Woman was one of the moſt impudent, ſcurrilous, wicked Creatures in the World; and ſhe did now throughout her whole Tryal, diſcover herſelf to be ſuch an one. Yet when ſhe was aſked, what ſhe had to ſay for ſelf? Her chief Plea was, *That ſhe had led a moſt virtuous and holy Life.*

IV. *The Tryal of* Elizabeth How,[173] *at the Court of Oyer and Terminer, held by Adjournment at Salem June* 30, 1692.

I. E*LIZABETH HOW* pleading *Not Guilty* to the Indictment of Witchcrafts, then charged upon her; the Court, according to the usual Proceedings of the Courts in *England*, in such Cases, began with hearing the Depositions of several afflicted People, who were grievously tortured by sensible and evident *Witchcrafts*, and all complained of the Prisoner, as the cause of their Trouble. It was also found that the Sufferers were not able [77] to bear her *Look*, as likewise, that in their greatest Swoons, they distinguished her *Touch* from other Peoples, being thereby raised out of them.

And there was other Testimony of People to whom the shape of this *How*, gave trouble nine or ten years ago.

II. It has been a most usual thing for the bewitched Persons, at the same time that the *Spectres*, representing the *Witches*, troubled them, to be visited with Apparitions of *Ghosts*, pretending to have been Murdered by the *Witches* then represented. And sometimes the Confessions of the Witches afterwards acknowledged those very Murders, which these *Apparitions* charged upon

173 She belonged to Topsfield. There was an Ephraim Howe in that Town, possibly her Husband. Her Husband had a Brother, as will be seen, named John, but his Residence is not given.

them; altho' they had never heard what Informations had been given by the Sufferers.

There were such Apparitions of Ghosts testified by some of the present Sufferers; and the Ghosts affirmed, that this *How* had Murdered them: Which things were *fear'd* but not *prov'd.*

III. This *How* had made some Attempts of joyning to the Church at *Ipswich,* several years ago; but she was denyed an admission into that Holy Society, partly through a suspicion of Witchcraft, then urged against her. And there now came in Testimony, of preternatural Mischiefs, presently befalling some that had been Instrumental to debar her from the Communion whereupon she was intruding.

IV. There was a particular Deposition of *Joseph Safford,*[174] That his Wife had conceived an extream Aversion to this *How,* on the Reports of her Witchcrafts: But *How* one day, taking her by the Hand, and saying, *I believe you are not ignorant of the great Scandal that I lye under, by an evil Report raised upon me.* She immediately, unreasonably and unperswadeably, even like one Enchanted, began to take this Woman's part. *How* being soon after propounded, as desiring an Admission to the Table of the Lord, some of the pious Brethren were unsatisfy'd about her. The Elders appointed a Meeting to hear Matters objected against her; and no Arguments in the

174 This Name is erroneously printed *Stafford* in the London Edition. It was an Ipswich Family, of which many Items of its Members will be found in Dr. Phelps's *Hist. of that Town,* and a few in Savage's *Dict.*

World could hinder this Goodwife *Safford* from going to the Lecture. She did indeed promiſe, with much ado, that ſhe would not go to the Church-meeting, yet ſhe could not refrain going thither alſo. *How's* Affairs there were ſo canvaſed, that ſhe came off rather *Guilty* than *Cleared;* neverthelefs Goodwife *Safford* could not forbear taking her by the Hand, and ſaying, *Tho' you are Condemned before Men, you are Juſtify'd before God.* She was quickly taken in a very ſtrange manner, Frantick, Raving, Raging and crying out, *Goody* How *muſt come into the Church; ſhe is a precious Saint; and tho' ſhe be condemned before Men, ſhe is Juſtify'd before God.* So ſhe continued [78] for the ſpace of two or three Hours; and then fell into a Trance. But coming to her ſelf, ſhe cry'd out, *Ha! I was miſtaken;* and afterwards again repeated, *Ha! I was miſtaken!* Being aſked by a ſtander by, *Wherein?* ſhe replyed, *I thought Goody* How *had been a precious Saint of God, but now I ſee ſhe is a Witch: She has bewitched me, and my Child, and we ſhall never be well, till there be a Teſtimony for her, that ſhe may be taken into the Church.* And *How* ſaid afterwards, that ſhe was very ſorry to ſee *Safford* at the Church-meeting mentioned. *Safford,* after this, declared herſelf to be afflicted by the Shape of *How;* and from that Shape ſhe endured many Miſeries.

V. *John How*, Brother to the Huſband of the Priſoner teſtified, that he refuſing to accompany the Priſoner unto her Examination, as was by her deſired, immediately ſome of his Cattle were

Bewitched to Death, leaping three or four foot high, turning about, fpeaking, falling, and dying at once; and going to cut off an Ear, for an ufe that might as well perhaps have been omitted, the Hand wherein he held his Knife was taken very numb, and fo it remained, and full of Pain, for feveral Days, being not well at this very Time. And he fufpected this Prifoner for the Author of it.

VI. *Nehemiah Abbot*[175] teftify'd, that unufual and mifchievous Accidents would befal his Cattle, whenever he had any Difference with this Prifoner. Once, particularly, fhe wifhed his Ox choaked; and within a little while that Ox was choaked with a Turnip in his Throat. At another Time, refufing to lend his Horfe, at the Requeft of her Daughter, the Horfe was in a preternatural manner abufed. And feveral other odd things of that kind were teftified.

VII. There came in Teftimony, that one Goodwife *Sherwin*, upon fome Difference with *How*, was Bewitched; and that fhe dyed, charging this *How* with having an Hand in her Death. And that other People had their Barrels of Drink unaccountably mifchieved, fpoil'd and fpilt, upon their difpleafing of her.

The things in themfelves were trivial, but there

175 This Individual can be identified and traced in the Abbot *Genealogical Regifter*, and alfo in Savage's *Dictionary;* but more minute Information is given by his Kinfman, Abiel Abbot, A. M., in his *Hiftory of Andover*, Chap. x.; a valuable little Work by the Way, without either Heads of Chapters or Index.

being ſuch a Courſe of them, it made them the more to be conſidered. Among others, *Martha Wood*, gave her Teſtimony, That a little after her Father had been employed in gathering an account of *How's* Converſation, they once and again loſt great Quantities of Drink out of their Veſſels, in ſuch a manner, as they could aſcribe to nothing but Witchcraft. As alſo, That *How* giving her ſome Apples, when ſhe had eaten of them, ſhe was taken with a very ſtrange kind of Amaze, inſomuch that ſhe knew not what ſhe ſaid or did.

VIII. There was likewiſe a Cluſter of Depoſitions, That one *Iſaac Cummings*[176] refuſing to lend his Mare unto the Huſband of this *How*, the Mare was within a Day or two taken in a ſtrange condition: The Beaſt [79] ſeemed much abuſed, being bruiſed as if ſhe had been running over the Rocks, and marked where the Bridle went, as if burnt with a red hot Bridle. Moreover, one uſing a Pipe of Tobacco for the Cure of the Beaſt, a blew Flame iſſued out of her, took hold of her Hair, and not only ſpread and burnt on her, but it alſo flew upwards towards the Roof of the Barn, and had like to have ſet the Barn on Fire: And the Mare dyed very ſuddenly.

IX. *Timothy Perley*[177] and his Wife, teſtify'd, Not only unaccountable Miſchiefs befel their

[176] Probably of Topsfield.

[177] Of Ipſwich, ſuppoſed to be Son of that Allen *Perley*, who in 1635, came to New England from Hertfordſhire. See *Founders of New England*, 16. John *Pearly*, mentioned in the next Section was no Doubt of the ſame Family.

Cattle, upon their having of Differences with this Prisoner: but also that they had a Daughter destroyed by Witchcrafts; which Daughter still charged *How* as the Cause of her Affliction. And it was noted, that she would be struck down whenever *How* were spoken of. She was often endeavoured to be thrown into the Fire, and into the Water, in her strange Fits: Tho' her Father had corrected her for charging *How* with bewitching her, yet (as was testified by others also) she said, She was sure of it, and must dye standing to it. Accordingly she charged *How* to the very Death; and said, *Tho'* How *could afflict and torment her Body, yet she could not hurt her Soul:* And, *That the Truth of this matter would appear when she should be dead and gone.*

X. *Francis Lane*[178] testified, That being hired by the Husband of this *How* to get him a parcel of Posts and Rails, this Lane hired *John Pearly* to assist him. This Prisoner then told *Lane*, That she believed the Posts and Rails would not do, because *John Perly* helped him; but that if he had got them alone, without *John Pearlie's* help, they might have done well enough. When *James How* came to receive his Posts and Rails of *Lane*, *How* taking them up by the Ends, they, tho' good and sound, yet unaccountably broke off, so that *Lane* was forced to get thirty

178 To what Family this Francis Lane belonged I have not been able to determine. Perhaps he belonged to the Hampton Family.

or forty more. And this Prifoner being informed of it, ſhe ſaid, She told him ſo before, becauſe *Pearly* helped about them.

XI. Afterwards there came in the Confeſſions of ſeveral other (penitent) Witches, which affirmed this *How* to be one of thoſe, who with them had been baptized by the Devil in the River at *Newbury*-Falls: before which he made them there kneel down by the Brink of the River and worſhiped him.

V. *The Trial of* MARTHA CARRIER,[179] *at the Court of Oyer and Terminer, held by Adjournment at Salem, Auguſt* 2, 1692.

I. MARTHA CARRIER was Indicted for the bewitching of certain Perſons, according to the Form uſual in ſuch Caſes, pleading *Not Guilty*, [80] to her Indictment; there were firſt brought in a conſiderable number of the bewitched Perſons; who not only made the Court ſenſible of an horrid Witchcraft committed upon them, but alſo depoſed, That it was *Martha Carrier*, or her Shape, that grievouſly tormented them, by Biting, Pricking, Pinching and Choaking of them. It was further depoſed, That while this *Carrier* was on her Examination, before the Magiſtrates, the Poor People were ſo tortured

[179] She was of Andover, and the Copy of her Indictment is printed in full, in the Hiſtory of that Town. She was the Wife of Thomas Carrier of Andover, who died in Colcheſter, Ct., aged 109 Years. See Farmer, *Hiſt. Billerica*, 33. See alſo Calef, *More Wonders*, 136.

that every one expected their Death upon the very fpot, but that upon the binding of *Carrier* they were eafed. Moreover the Look of *Carrier* then laid the Afflicted People for dead; and her Touch, if her Eye at the fame time were off them, raifed them again: Which Things were alfo now feen upon her Tryal. And it was teftified, That upon the mention of fome having their Necks twifted almoft round, by the Shape of this *Carrier*, fhe replyed, *Its no matter though their Necks had been twifted quite off.*

II. Before the Trial of this Prifoner, feveral of her own Children had frankly and fully confeffed, not only that they were Witches themfelves, but that this their Mother had made them fo. This Confeffion they made with great Shews of Repentance, and with much Demonftration of Truth. They related Place, Time, Occafion; they gave an account of Journeys, Meetings and Mifchiefs by them performed, and were very credible in what they faid. Neverthelefs, this Evidence was not produced againft the Prifoner at the Bar, inasmuch as there was other Evidence enough to proceed upon.

III. *Benjamin Abbot*[180] gave in his Teftimony, That laft *March* was a twelvemonth, this *Carrier* was very angry with him, upon laying out fome Land, near her Hufband's: Her Expreffions in

[180] See *Hift. Andover,* 30, 168. He was Son of the firft George Abbot of Andover, and died in 1703, leaving Defcendants. His Wife Sarah, mentioned onward, was Daughter of Ralph *Farnum* or *Varnum* of Andover. Further of this in an enfuing Volume.

this Anger, were, *That ſhe would ſtick as cloſe to* Abbot *as the Bark ſtuck to the Tree; and that he ſhould repent of it afore ſeven Years came to an End, ſo as Doctor* Preſcot[181] *ſhould never cure him.* Theſe Words were heard by others beſides *Abbot* himſelf; who alſo heard her ſay, *She would hold his Noſe as cloſe to the Grindſtone as ever it was held ſince his Name was* Abbot. Preſently after this, he was taken with a Swelling in his Foot, and then with a Pain in his Side, and exceedingly tormented. It bred into a Sore, which was launced by Doctor *Preſcot*, and ſeveral Gallons of Corruption ran out of it. For ſix Weeks it continued very bad, and then another Sore bred in the Groin, which was alſo lanced by Doctor *Preſcot*. Another Sore then bred in his Groin, which was likewiſe cut, and put him to very great Miſery: He was brought unto Death's Door, and ſo remained until *Carrier* was taken, and carried away by the Conſtable, from which very Day he began to mend, and ſo grew better every Day, and is well ever ſince.

Sarah Abbot alſo, his Wife, teſtified, That her Huſ[41]band was not only all this while Afflicted in his Body, but alſo that ſtrange extraordinary and unaccountable Calamities befel his Cattel; their Death being ſuch as they could gueſs at no Natural Reaſon for.

IV. *Allin Toothaker*[182] teſtify'd, That *Richard*,

[181] Perhaps *Peter*, who lived in what is ſince Danvers.

[182] In the Liſt of Paſſengers who came to New England in the Ship

the fon of *Martha Carrier*, having fome difference with him, pull'd him down by the Hair of the Head. When he Rofe again, he was going to ftrike at *Richard Carrier;* but fell down flat on his Back to the ground, and had not power to ftir hand or foot, until he told *Carrier* he yielded; and then he faw the fhape of *Martha Carrier*, go off his breaft.

This *Toothaker*, had Received a wound in the *Wars;* and he now teftify'd, that *Martha Carrier* told him, *He fhould never be Cured.* Juft afore the Apprehending of *Carrier*, he could thruft a knitting Needle into his wound, four inches deep; but prefently after her being fiezed, he was thoroughly healed.

He further teftify'd, that when *Carrier* and he fometimes were at variance, fhe would clap her hands at him, and fay, *He fhould get nothing by it;* whereupon he feveral times loft his Cattle, by ftrange Deaths, whereof no natural caufes could be given.

V. *John Rogger*[183] alfo teftifyed, That upon the threatning words of this malicious *Carrier*, his Cattle would be ftrangely bewitched; as was more particularly then defcribed.

Hopewell from London, September, 1635, are the Names of Roger, Margaret, and Roger Toothaker, of Ages 23, 28 and 1 Years. Allen Toothaker above named was probably of this Family. He feems to have refided in Andover, or near his Tormenter.

183 Perhaps of the *Rogerfes* of Billerica; but it is about as uncertain to defignate among the John Rogerfes as among the John Smiths. See Farmer's *Hift. Billerica*, 13, 32-3.

VI. *Samuel Preſton*[184] teſtify'd, that about two years ago, having ſome difference with *Martha Carrier*, he loſt a *Cow* in a ſtrange Preternatural unuſual manner; and about a month after this, the ſaid *Carrier*, having again ſome difference with him, ſhe told him; *He had lately loſt a Cow, and it ſhould not be long before he loſt another*; which accordingly came to paſs; for he had a thriving and well-kept *Cow*, which without any known cauſe quickly fell down and dy'd.

VII. *Phebe Chandler*[185] teſtify'd, that about a Fortnight before the apprehenſion of *Martha Carrier*, on a Lordſday, while the Pſalm was ſinging in the *Church*, this *Carrier* then took her by the ſhoulder and ſhaking her, aſked her, *where ſhe lived:* ſhe made her no Anſwer, although as *Carrier*, who lived next door to her Fathers Houſe, could not in reaſon but know who ſhe was. Quickly after this, as ſhe was at ſeveral times croſſing the Fields, ſhe heard a voice, that ſhe took to be *Martha Carriers*, and it ſeem'd as if it [42] was over her head. The voice told her, *ſhe ſhould within two or three days be poiſoned.* Accordingly, within ſuch a little time, one half of her right hand, became greatly ſwollen, and very painful; as alſo part of her Face; whereof

184 Samuel Preſton was of Andover, where he died in 1738, aged 85. Hence he was born in 1653. See Abbot's *Hiſt. Andover*, for other Details of the family. We cannot make much out of Mr. Savage's Article in his *Dictionary*.

185 She was doubtleſs of the Andover Family of Chandler, but Data does not appear by which ſhe can be aſſigned to her Place in the Pedigree of that Family.

ſhe can give no account how it came. It continued very bad for ſome dayes; and ſeveral times ſince, ſhe has had a great pain in her breaſt; and been ſo ſiezed on her leggs, that ſhe has hardly been able to go. She added, that lately, going well to the Houſe of God, *Richard*, the ſon of *Martha Carrier*, look'd very earneſtly upon her, and immediately her hand, which had formerly been poiſoned, as is aboveſaid, began to pain her greatly, and ſhe had a ſtrange Burning at her ſtomach; but was then ſtruck deaf, ſo that ſhe could not hear any of the prayer, or ſinging, till the two or three laſt words of the Pſalm.

VIII. One *Foſter*,[186]. who confeſſed her own ſhare in the Witchcraft for which the Priſoner ſtood indicted, affirm'd, that ſhe had ſeen the priſoner at ſome of their *Witch-meetings*, and that it was this *Carrier*, who perſwaded her to be a Witch. She confeſſed, that the Devil carry'd them on a pole, to a Witch-meeting; but the pole broke, and ſhe hanging about *Carriers* neck, they both fell down, and ſhe then received an hurt by the Fall, whereof ſhe was not at this very time recovered.

IX. One *Lacy*,[187] who likewiſe confeſſed her ſhare in this Witchcraft, now teſtify'd, that ſhe

186 Perhaps of the Family of Ephraim Foſter of Andover, and if ſo, his Wife. Theſe were the Anceſtors of the diſtinguiſhed Theodore, and Dwight Foſter. See *Hiſt. Andover*, 38. Ephraim Foſter married Hannah, Daughter of Robert Eames, 1678.

187 There was a Family of Lacy at Andover at this Time. Lawrence Lacy was born there, according to Abbot, in 1683.

and the prifoner were once Bodily prefent at a *Witch-meeting* in *Salem Village;* and that fhe knew the prifoner to be a Witch, and to have been at a Diabolical facrament, and that the prifoner was the undoing of her, and her Children, by enticing them into the fnare of the Devil.

X. Another *Lacy*, who alfo confeffed her fhare in this Witchcraft, now teftify'd, that the prifoner was at the *Witch-meeting*, in *Salem Village*, where they had Bread and Wine Adminiftred unto them.

XI. In the time of this prifoner's Trial, one *Sufanna Sheldon*,[188] in open Court had her hands Unaccountably ty'd together with a Wheel-band, fo faft that without cutting, it could not be loofed: It was done by a *Spectre;* and the Sufferer affirm'd, it was the *Prifoners*.

Memorandum. This Rampant Hag, *Martha Carrier*, was the [43] perfon, of whom the Confeffions of the Witches, and of her own Children among the reft, agreed, That the Devil had promifed her, fhe fhould be *Queen of Hell*.[189]

HAVING thus far done the Service impofed upon me; I will further purfue it, by re-

188 This Perfon was of Billerica. John *Sheldon* was among the early Settlers of that Town, but had gone from there or was dead before 1700.—Farmer's *Billerica*, 34.

189 In the London Edition this Word was printed *Heb*, evidently a typographical Error. Poor Martha Carrier was executed, in purfuance of Evidence, than which nothing could be more childifh and meaninglefs ever heard of under "the Cope of Heaven." The poor old Mother to "be Queen of Hell"! The Author fhows his Depravity by extravagantly and barbaroufly denouncing her as a "Rampant Hag."

lating a few of those Matchless CURIOSITIES, with which the *Witchcraft* now upon us, has entertained us. And I shall Report nothing but with Good Authority, and what I would invite all my Readers to examine, while 'tis yet Fresh and New, that if there be found any mistake, it may be as willingly *Retracted*, as it was unwillingly *Committed.*

The First CURIOSITIE.

I. 'Tis very Remarkable to see what an Impious and Impudent *imitation* of Divine Things, is Apishly affected by the Devil, in several of those matters, whereof the Confessions of our *Witches*, and the Afflictions of our *Sufferers* have informed us.

That Reverend and Excellent Person, Mr. *John Higginson*, in my Conversation with him, Once invited me to this Reflection; that the Indians which came from far to settle about *Mexico*, were in their Progress to that Settlement, under a Conduct of the *Devil*, very strangely Emulating what the Blessed God gave to *Israel* in the Wilderness.

Acosta,[190] is our Author for it, that the Devil in ' their Idol *Vitzlipultzli*,[191] governed that mighty

[190] A learned Jesuit, and as superstitious as he was learned. The Work out of which the Extract is made, is entitled the *Natural and Moral History of the West Indies.* Then (1591) a *History of the West Indies* included America.

[191] According to Clavigero, the

'Nation. He commanded them to leave their 'Country, promiſing to make them *Lords* over all 'the Provinces poſſeſſed by *Six* other Nations of 'Indians, and give them a Land abounding with 'all precious things. They went forth, carrying 'their Idol with them, in a Coffer of *Reeds*, ſup-'ported by Four of their Principal *Prieſts;* with 'whom he ſtill *Diſcourſed* in ſecret, Revealing to 'them the Succeſſes, and Accidents of their way. 'He adviſed them, when to *March*, and where to '*Stay*, and without his Commandment they 'moved not. The firſt thing they did, wherever 'they came, was to Erect a *Tabernacle*, for their 'falſe god; which they ſet always in the midſt 'of their Camp, and there placed the *Ark* upon 'an *Alter*. When they, Tired with pains, talked 'of, *proceeding no further* in their Journey, then a 'certain pleaſant Stage, whereto they were arrived, 'this Devil in one night, horribly kill'd them 'that [44] had ſtarted this Talk, by pulling out 'their Hearts. And ſo they paſſed on till they 'came to *Mexico*.

The Devil which *then* thus imitated what was in the Church of the *Old Teſtament*, now among *Us* would Imitate the Affairs of the Church in the *New*. The *Witches* do ſay, that they form themſelves much after the manner of *Congregational Churches;* and that they have a *Baptiſm*

God the moſt celebrated in Mexico was *Huitzilopochzli.—Hiſt. Mexico*, Cullen's Tranſlation, i, 259. See alſo the Plate, *ib.*, 279.

and a *Supper*, and *Officers* among them, abominably Resembling those of our Lord.[192]

But there are many more of these Bloody *Imitations*, if the Confessions of the *Witches* are to be Received; which I confess, ought to be but with very much of Caution.

What is their stricking down with a fierce *Look?* What is their making of the Afflicted *Rise*, with a touch of their *Hand?* What is their Transportation thro' the *Air?* What is their Travelling *in Spirit*, while their Body is cast into a Trance? What is their causing of *Cattle* to run mad and perish? What is their Entring their Names in a *Book?* What is their coming together from all parts at the Sound of a *Trumpet?* What is their Appearing sometimes Cloathed with *Light* or *Fire* upon them? What is their Covering of themselves and their Instruments with *Invisibility?* But a Blasphemous Imitation of certain Things recorded about our Saviour or His Prophets, or the Saints in the Kingdom of God.[193]

192 It is certainly singularly noteworthy that the Devil and his Throng of Witches should adopt the Forms and Practices of the Churches of the Author's own Order. One would naturally suppose that they would have chosen those of the primitive Churches.

193 It is as much easier, as it is safer to answer these Questions now than in Dr. Mather's Time. Everybody is born in the same Ignorance as in those Days, but fortunately we of this Day are surrounded by a lighter Age, and hence grow up with more Knowledge. And yet *our* Age of Light is Light only by Comparison.

A Second CURIOSITIE.

II. In all the *Witchcraft* which now Grievously Vexes us, I know not whether anything be more Unaccountable, than the Trick which the Witches have to render themſelves, and their Tools *Inviſible.* *Witchcraft* ſeems to be the Skill of Applying the *Plaſtic Spirit* of the World, unto ſome unlawful purpoſes, by means of a Confederacy with *Evil Spirits.* Yet one would wonder how the *Evil Spirits* themſelves can do ſome things: eſpecially at *Inviſibilizing* of the Groſſeſt Bodies. I can tell the Name of an Ancient Author, who pretends to ſhow the *way,* how a man may come to walk about *Inviſible,* and I can tell the Name of another Ancient Author, who pretends to Explode that way. But I will not ſpeak too plainly Leſt I ſhould unawares Poiſon ſome of my *Readers,* as the pious *Hemingius*[194] did one of his *Pupils,* when he only by way of Diverſion recited a *Spell,* which, they had ſaid, would cure *Agues.* This much I will ſay; The notion of procuring *Inviſibility,* by any *Natural Expedient,* yet known, is, I Believe, a meer PLINYISM;[195] How far it may be [45] obtained by a *Magical Sacrament,* is beſt known to the Danger-

194 Nicholas *Hemmingius,* I ſuppoſe, a native of the Iſland of Laland, born in 1513. His Buſineſs was that of a Smith, but taking to Learning, he ſtudied with the celebrated Melancthon, and became a Profeſſor of Hebrew at Copenhagen. He died in the Year 1600.

195 A Word not found in the Dictionaries. Perhaps it may be defined by the Readers of the Works of the elder Pliny.

ous Knaves that have try'd it. But our *Witches* do ſeem to have got the knack: and this is one of the Things, that make me think, *Witchcraft* will not be fully underſtood, until the day when there ſhall not be one Witch in the World.

There are certain people very *Dogmatical* about theſe matters; but I'll give them only theſe three Bones to pick.

Firſt, One of our bewitched people, was cruelly aſſaulted by a *Spectre*, that, ſhe ſaid, ran at her with a *ſpindle:* tho' no body elſe in the Room, could ſee either the *Spectre* or the *ſpindle*. At laſt, in her miſeries, giving a ſnatch at the *Spectre*, ſhe pull'd the *ſpindle* away, and it was no ſooner got into her hand, but the other people then preſent, beheld, that it was indeed a Real, Proper, Iron *ſpindle*, belonging they knew to whom; which when they lock'd up very ſafe, it was neverthelefs by *Demons* unaccountably ſtole away, to do further miſchief.[196]

Secondly, Another of our bewitched people, was haunted with a moſt abuſive *Spectre*, which came to her, ſhe ſaid, with a *ſheet* about her. After ſhe had undergone a deal of Teaze, from the Annoyance of the *Spectre*, ſhe gave a violent ſnatch at the ſheet that was upon it; wherefrom ſhe tore a corner, which in her hand immediately became *Viſible* to a Roomful of Spectators; a

196 This Story of the iron Spindle is briefly told by Lawſon, who probably took it from our Author. See Lawſon's Work, P. 102-3 of the London Edition. It is not in the original (Boſton) Edition.

palpable Corner of a Sheet. Her Father, who was now holding her, catch'd that he might keep what his Daughter had ſo ſtrangely ſeized, but the unſeen *Spectre* had like to have pull'd his hand off, by endeavouring to wreſt it from him; however he ſtill held it, and I ſuppoſe has it ſtill to ſhow; it being but a few hours ago, namely about the beginning of this *October*, that this Accident happened; in the family of one *Pitman*,[197] at *Mancheſter*.

Thirdly, A young man, delaying to procure Teſtimonials, for his Parents, who being under confinement on ſuſpicion of *Witchcraft*, required him to do that ſervice for them, was quickly purſued with odd Inconveniences. But once above the Reſt, an Officer going to put his *Brand* on theHorns of ſome *Cows*, belonging to theſe people, which tho' he had ſeiz'd for ſome of their debts, yet he was willing to leave in their poſ-ſeſſion, for the ſubſiſtance of the poor Family; this young man help'd in holding the Cows to be thus branded. The three firſt *Cows* he held well enough; but when the hot Brand was clap'd on the Fourth, he *winc'd* and *ſhrunk* at ſuch a Rate, as that he could hold the Cow no longer. Being afterwards Examined about it, he confeſſed, that at that very inſtant when the *Brand* entered the *Cow's Horn*, exactly the like [46] burning *Brand*

[197] There were Pitmans at Marblehead, and Salem at this Time. Mancheſter was then included in Salem. There was a Thomas Pitman hung there not long before the Witch Caſes occurred.

was clap'd upon his own Thigh; where he has expoſed the laſting marks of it, unto ſuch as aſked to ſee them.

Unriddle theſe Things,—*Et Eris mihi magnus Apollo.*

A Third CURIOSITIE.

III. If a Drop of *Innocent Blood* ſhould be ſhed, in the Proſecution of the *Witchcrafts* among us, how unhappy are we! For which cauſe, I cannot expreſs my ſelf in better terms than thoſe of a moſt Worthy Perſon, who lives near the preſent Center of theſe things.[198] *The Mind of* God *in theſe matters, is to be carefully lookt into, with due Circumſpection, that Satan deceive us not with his Devices, who transforms himſelf into an Angel of Light, and may pretend juſtice and yet intend miſchief.* But on the other ſide, if the ſtorm of Juſtice do now fall only on the Heads of thoſe guilty *Witches* and *Wretches* which have defiled our Land, *How Happy!*

The Execution of ſome that have lately Dyed, has been immediately attended, with a ſtrange Deliverance of ſome, that had lain for many years, in a moſt ſad Condition, under, they knew not whoſe *evil hands.* As I am abundantly ſatisfy'd, That many of the Self-Murders committed here, have been the effects of a Cruel and Bloody *Witchcraft*, letting fly *Demons* upon the miſerable

198 Perhaps Mr. John Higginſon.

Seneca's; thus it has been admirable unto me to see, how a Devilish *Witchcraft*, sending Devils upon them, has driven many poor people to *Despair*, and persecuted their minds, with such Buzzes of *Atheism* and *Blasphemy*, as has made them even run *distracted with Terrors:* And some long *Bow'd* down under such a *spirit of Infirmity*, have been marvellously Recovered upon the death of the Witches.

One *Whetford*[199] particularly ten years ago, challenging of *Bridget Bishop* (whose Trial you have had) with steeling of a Spoon, *Bishop* threatned her very direfully: presently after this, was *Whetford* in the Night, and in her Bed, visited by *Bishop*, with one *Parker*, who making the Room light at their coming in, there discoursed of several mischiefs they would inflict upon her. At last they pull'd her out, and carried her unto the Sea-side, there to *drown* her; but she calling upon God, they left her, tho' not without Expressions of their Fury. From that very time, this poor *Whetford* was utterly spoilt, and grew a Tempted, Froward, Crazed sort of a Woman; a vexation to her self, and all about her; and many ways unreasonable. In this Distraction she lay, till those women were Apprehended by the Authority; *then* she be[47]gan to mend; and upon their Execution, was presently and perfectly Recovered, from the ten years madness that had been upon her.

199 There was a Family of *Whitfords* in Salem at this Time.

A Fourth CURIOSITIE.

IV. 'Tis a thousand pitties, that we should permit our Eyes to be so *Blood-shot* with passions, as to loose the sight of many wonderful things, wherein the Wisdom and Justice of God, would be Glorify'd. Some of those things, are the frequent **Apparitions** of Ghosts, whereby many Old **Murders** among us, come to be considered. And, among many Instances of this kind, I will single out one, which concerned a poor man, lately *Prest* unto Death, because of his Refusing to *Plead* for his Life.[200] I shall make an Extract of a Letter, which was written to my Honourable Friend, *Samuel Sewal*, Esq.; by Mr. *Putman*, to this purpose;

'The Last Night my Daughter *Ann*, was 'grievously Tormented by Witches, Threatning 'that she should be *Pressed* to Death, before *Giles* '*Cory*. But thro' the Goodness of a Gracious 'God, she had at last a little Respite. Where-'upon there appeared unto her (she said) a man 'in a Winding Sheet, who told her that *Giles* '*Cory* had Murdered him, by *Pressing* him to 'Death with his Feet; but that the Devil there

200 The shocking Barbarity employed in the Execution of this "poor Man" can only find a Parallel in an Age as benighted as this of 1692. A more diabolical Depravity could never exhibit itself in human Nature. The next Story seems to be introduced to lessen the Odium which it is probable the Author thought might attach itself to the Affair. It is wonderful indeed, that a foul Murder should have been kept so still, and then, at a late Day, to come out in a Dream.

'appeared unto him, and Covenanted with him, 'and promiſed him, *He ſhould not be Hanged.* 'The Apparition ſaid, God Hardned his heart; 'that he ſhould not hearken to the Advice of the 'Court, and ſo Dy an eaſy Death; becauſe as it 'ſaid, *It muſt be done to him as he has done to me.* 'The Apparition alſo ſaid, That *Giles Cory*, was 'carry'd to the Court for this, and that the Jury 'had found the Murder, and that her Father 'knew the man, and the thing was done before 'ſhe was born. Now Sir, This is not a little 'ſtrange to us; that no body ſhould Remember 'theſe things, all the while that *Giles Cory* was in 'Priſon, and ſo often before the Court. For all 'people now Remember very well, (and the Re- 'cords of the Court alſo mention it,) That about 'Seventeen Years ago, *Giles Cory* kept a man in 'his Houſe, that was almoſt a Natural Fool: 'which Man Dy'd ſuddenly. A Jury was im- 'pannel'd upon him, among whom was Dr. *Ze- 'robbabel Endicot*;[201] who found the man bruiſed 'to Death, and having clodders of Blood about 'his Heart. The Jury whereof ſeveral are yet 'alive brought in the man Murdered; but as if 'ſome Enchantment had hindred the Proſecution 'of the Matter, the Court Proceeded not againſt '[48] *Giles Cory*, tho' it coſt him a great deal of 'Mony to get off. Thus the Story,

201 A Son of the firſt Governor of the Colony, John Endicott. He reſided a conſiderable Period in Boſton. See *Hiſtorical and Gen. Regiſter*, i, 335, *et ſeq.* He died in the Spring of 1684.

THE Reverend and Worthy Author, having at the Direction of His Excellency *the Governour, so far Obliged the Publick, as to give some Account of the Sufferings brought upon the Countrey by* Witchcraft; *and of the Tryals which have passed upon several Executed for the Same:*

Upon Perusal thereof, We find the Matters of Fact and Evidence, Truly reported. And a Prospect given, of the Methods of Conviction, *used in the Proceedings of the Court at* Salem.

Boston Octob. 11. 1692. William Stoughton Samuel Sewall.

BUT is *New-England*, the only Christian Countrey, that hath undergone such Diabolical Molestations? No, there are other Good people, that have in this way been harassed; but none in circumstances more like to *Ours*, than the people of God, in *Sweedland*. The story is a very Famous one; and it comes to Speak English by the Acute Pen of the Excellent and Renowned Dr. *Horneck.*[202] I shall only single out a few of the more Memorable passages therein Occurring; and where it agrees with what happened among ourselves, my Reader shall understand, by my inserting a Word of every such thing in **Black Letter.**

I. It was in the Year 1669. and 1670. That at

[202] Anthony Horneck. The original Work was written in High Dutch. The Author's Name does not appear. We have the Work appended to the fourth Edition of Glanvil's *Sadducismus Triumphatus*, 1726. Dr. Mather has given but a brief Abstract.

Mobra in *Sweedland*, the **Devils** by the help of **Witches**, committed a moft horrible outrage. Among other Inftances of Hellifh Tyranny there exercifed, one was, that Hundreds of their Children, were ufually in the Night fetcht from their Lodgings, to a Diabolical Rendezvouz, at a place they called, *Blockula*, where the Monfters that fo Spirited them, **Tempted** them all manner of Ways to **Associate** with them. Yea, fuch was the perillous Growth of this *Witchcraft*, that Perfons of Quality began to fend their Children into other Countries to avoid it.

II. The Inhabitants had earneftly fought God by **Prayer**; and **Yet** their Affliction **Continued**. Whereupon **Judges** had a Special **Commission** to find and root out the Hellifh Crew; and the rather, becaufe another County in the Kingdom, which had been fo molefted, was delivered upon the Execution of the *Witches*.

III. The **Examination**, was begun with a Day of **Humiliation**; appointed by Authority.[203] Whereupon the Commiffioners **Consulting**, how they might refift fuch a Dangerous Flood, the **Suffering Children**, were firft Examined; and tho' they were [49] Queftioned **One** by **One** apart, yet their **Declarations All Agreed**. The **Witches** Accuf'd

203 It does not appear that a Thankfgiving was appointed, but the King appointed Commiffioners to examine into the Matter. Thofe Commiffioners proceeded to the Town, and at once entered upon an Inveftigation; "to whom both the Minifter and feveral of the People of Fafhion complained with Tears in their Eyes, of the miferable Condition they were in."—*Ibidem*, 484.

in these Declarations, were then Examined; and tho' at first they obstinately **Denied**, yet at length many of them ingenuously **Confessed** the Truth of what the children had said; owning with Tears, that the **Devil**, whom they call'd *Loeyta*, had **stopt** their **Mouths**; but he being now **Gone** from them, they could **No Longer Conceal** the Business. The things by them **Acknowledged**, most wonderfully **Agreed** with what other Witches, in other places had confessed.

IV. They confessed, that they did use to **Call upon** the **Devil**, who thereupon would **Carry** them away, over the Tops of Houses, to a Green Meadow, where they gave themselves unto him. Only one of them said, That sometimes the *Devil* only took away her **Strength**, leaving her **Body** on the ground; but she went at other times in **Body** too.

V. Their manner was to come into the **Chambers** of people, and fetch away their children upon Beasts, of the Devils providing: promising **Fine Clothes** and other Fine Things unto them, to inveagle them. They said, they never had power to do thus, till of late; but now the Devil did **Plague** and **Beat** them, if they did not gratifie him, in this piece of Mischief. They said, they made use of all sorts of **Instruments** in their Journeys! Of **Men**, of **Beasts**, of **Posts**; the *Men* they commonly laid asleep at the place, whereto they rode them; and if the children mentioned the **Names** of them that stole them away, they were miserably **Scourged** for it, until some of them were killed. The **Judges** found the marks of the Lashes on some of them; but the Witches said, **They would Quickly vanish**. Moreover the Children would be in **Strange Fits**, after they were brought Home from these Transportations.

VI. The **First Thing**, they said, they were to do at *Blockula*, was to give themselves unto the Devil, and **Vow** that they would serve him. Hereupon, they **cut their Fingers**, and with **Blood** writ their **Names** in his **Book**. And he also caused them to be **Baptised** by such **Priests**, as he had, in this Horrid company. In **some** of them, the **Mark** of the **cut Finger** was to be found; they said, that the Devil gave **Meat** and **Drink**, as to *Them*, so to the Children they brought with them: that afterwards their Custom was to *Dance* before him; and *swear* and *curse* most horribly; they said, that the Devil show'd them a great Frightful, Cruel *Dragon*, telling them, **If they confessed any Thing**, he would let loose that Great Devil upon them; they added, that the Devil had a **Church**, and that when the **Judges** were coming, he told them **he would** [50] **kill them all**; and that some of them had **Attempted to Murder the Judges** but **could not**.

VII. Some of the **Children**, talked much of a **White Angel**, which did use to **Forbid** them, what the Devil had bid them to do, and **Assured** them that these doings would **Not last long**; but that what had been done was permitted for the wickedneſs of the People. This **White Angel**, would ſometimes reſcue the Children, from **Going in**, with the Witches.

VIII. The Witches confeſſed many miſchiefs done by them, declaring with what kind of **Enchanted Tools**, they did their Miſchiefs. They ſought eſpecially to **kill the Minister** of *Elfdale*, but could not. But ſome of them ſaid, that ſuch as they wounded, would **Be recovered**, upon or before their Execution.

IX. The **Judges** would fain have ſeen them ſhow ſome of their **Tricks**; but they Unanimouſly declared, that, **Since they had confessed**, all, they found all their **Witchcraft** gone; and the Devil then **Appeared very Terrible** unto them, threatning with an **Iron Fork**, to thruſt them into a Burning Pit, if they perſiſted in their Confeſſion.

X. They were diſcovered no leſs than *three-ſcore and ten* Witches in One Village, **three and twenty** of which **freely confessing** their Crimes, were condemned to dy. The reſt, (**One** pretending ſhe was with Child) were ſent to *Fahluna*, where moſt of them were afterwards executed. Fifteen Children, which confeſſed themſelves engaged in this Witchery, dyed as the reſt. Six and Thirty of them between *nine* and *ſixteen* years of Age, who had been leſs guilty, were forced to run the Gantlet, and be laſhed on their hands once a Week, for a year together; twenty more who had leſs inclination to theſe Infernal enterpriſes, were laſhed with Rods upon their Hands for three Sundays together, at the Church door; the number of the ſeduced Children, was about three hundred. This courſe, together with **Prayers** in all the Churches thro' the Kingdom, iſſued in the deliverance of the Country.[204]

XI. The moſt Accompliſhed Dr. *Horneck* inſerts a moſt wiſe caution, in his preface to this Narrative, ſaies he, *there is no Public Calamity, but ſome ill people, will ſerve themſelves of the ſad providence and make uſe of it for their own ends; as* Thieves *when an houſe or town is on Fire, will ſteal what they can.* And he mentions a Remarkable Story of a young Woman, at *Stockholm*, in the year 1676, Who accuſed her own Mother of being a Witch; and ſwore poſitively, that ſhe had carried her away in the Night; the poor Woman was burnt upon it: profeſſing her innocency to the laſt. But tho' ſhe had been an Ill Woman, yet it afterwards prov'd that ſhe was not *ſuch* an one; for her Daughter came to the Judges [51] with hideous Lamentations, Confeſſing, That ſhe

204 The Doctor omits ſome of the beſt Parts of theſe Stories. One or two will more than ſuffice probably. "Thoſe [Witches] of Elfdale confeſſed, That the Devil uſed to play upon an Harp before them, and afterwards to go with them that he liked beſt, into a Chamber, where he committed venerous Acts with them; and this indeed all confeſſed; That he had carnal Knowledge of them, and that the Devil had Sons and Daughters by them, which he did marry together, and brought forth Toads and Serpents."—*Page* 491.

"They [the bewitched] ſaid they had ſometimes ſeen a very great Devil like a Dragon, with Fire round about him, and bound with an iron Chain; and the Devil that converſes with them tells them, that if they confeſs anything, he will let that great Devil looſe upon them, whereby all Sweedland ſhall come into great danger."—*Page* 492.

had wronged her Mother, out of a wicked fpite againft her; whereupon the Judges gave order for her Execution too.

But, fo much of thefe things; and, now, *Lord, make thefe Labours of thy Servant, Profitable to thy People!*

[205] *Matter Omitted in the Trials.*

NINETEEN Witches have been Executed at *New-England*, one of them was a Minifter, and two Minifters more are Accuf'd. There is a hundred Witches more in Prifon, which broke Prifon, and about two Hundred more are Accuf'd, fome Men of great Eftates in *Bofton*, have been accuf'd for *Witchcraft*. Thofe Hundred now in Prifon accuf'd for Witches, were Committed by fifty of themfelves being *Witches*, fome of *Bofton*, but moft about *Salem*, and the Towns Adjacent. Mr. *Increafe Mather* has publifhed a Book[206] about *Witchcraft*, occafioned by the late Trials of Witches, which will be fpeedily printed in *London* by *John Dunton*.

THE DEVIL DISCOVERED.

2 Cor. II. 11. *We are not Ignorant of His* DEVICES.

OUR Bleffed Saviour has bleffed us, with a counfil, as Wholfome and as Needful as any that can be given us, in Math. 26. 41. *Watch and Pray, that yee Enter not into Temptation.* As there is a Tempting *Flefh*, and a Tempting *World*, which would feduce us from Our Obedience to the Laws of God, fo there is a Bufy *Devil*, who

[205] The following Paragraph is not in the firft Edition.

[206] Entitled " A Further Account of the Tryals of the New England Witches. . . . . . . To which is added Cafes of Confcience concerning Witchcrafts and Evil Spirits perfonating Men. Written at the Requeft of the Minifters of New England."

is by way of Eminency called, *The Tempter;* becauſe by him, the Temptations of the *Fleſh* and the *World* are managed.

It is not *One Devil* alone, that has Cunning or Power enough to apply the Multitudes of *Temptations,* whereby Mankind is daily diverted from the Service of God; No, the *High Places* of Our Air, are Swarming full of thoſe *Wicked Spirits,* whoſe Temptations trouble us; they are ſo many, that it ſeems no leſs than a *Legion,* or more than twelve thouſands may be ſpared, for the Vexation of one miſerable man. But becauſe thoſe Apoſtate Angels, are all *United* under one Infernal Monarch, in the Deſigns of Miſchief, 'tis in the Singular Number, that they are ſpoken of. Now, the *Devil* whoſe Malice and Envy, prompts him to do what he can, that we may be as unhappy as himſelf, do's ordinarily uſe more *Fraud* than *Force,* in his aſſaulting of us; he that aſſail'd our Firſt Parents, in a *Serpent,* will ſtill Act *Like a Serpent,* rather than a *Lion,* in proſecuting of his wicked purpoſes upon us, and for us to guard againſt the Wiles of the *Wicked One,* is one of the greateſt cares, with which our God ha's charged us.

We are all of us liable to various *Temptations* every day, whereby if we are carried aſide from the ſtrait *Paths of Righteouſneſs,* we get all ſorts of wounds unto our ſelves. Of *Temptations,* I may ſay, as the Wiſe Man ſaid, of *Mortality; there is no diſcharge from that war.* The *Devils* fell hard upon both *Adams*, nor may [52] any among the Children of both, imagine to be excused. The *Son* of God Himself, had this *Dog* of Hell, barking at Him; and much more may the Children of *Men*, look to be thus Visited; indeed, there is hardly any *Temptation*, but what is, *Common to Man*. When I was considering, how to spend one Hour in Raising a most Effectual and Profitable *Breastwork*, against the inroads of this Enemy, I perceived it would be done, by a short answer to this

CASE.

What are those Usual Methods *of* Temptation, *with which the Powers of Darkness do assault the Children of Men?*

The *Corinthians*, having upon the Apostles Direction, Excommunicated one of their Society, who had married his Mother-in-law, & this, as it is thought, while his own Father was Living too; the Apostle encourages them to Re-admit that man, upon his very deep and sharp *Repentance*. He gives divers Reasons of his propounding this unto them; whereof one is, *Lest Satan should get advantage of them;* for, had the man miscarried, under any Rigour of the Sentence continued upon him, after his *Repentance*, 'tis well if the Church itself had not quickly fallen to pieces thereupon; besure, the Success of the Gospel had been more than a little Incommoded. The Apostle upon this Occasion, intimates, That *Satan* has his *Devices;* by which word are meant, Artifices or Contrivances uſed for the *Deceiving* of thoſe that are Treated with them well, But what ſhall *we do* that we may come to this *Corinthian Attainment, We are not Ignorant of Satan's Devices?* [*Non cuivis homini Contingit!*]

Truly, the Devil has *Mille Nocendi Artes;* and it will be impoſſible for us, to run over all the *Stratagems* and *Policies* of our Adverſary. I ſhall only attempt a few Obſervations upon the *Temptations* of our Lord Jeſus Chriſt: who was *Tempted in all things like unto us, except in our Sins.* When we read the *Temptations* of our Lord Jeſus Chriſt, in the Fourth Chapter of *Matthew* There, Thence, you will underſtand, what was once counted ſo difficult; Even, *The way of a Serpent upon the Rock.* There are certain Ancient and Famous *Methods* which the Devil in his *Temptations,* does moſtly accuſtome himſelf unto; which is not ſo much from any Barrenneſs, or Sluggiſhneſs in the Devil, but becauſe he has had the Encouragement of a, *Probatum eſt,* upon thoſe horrid Methods. How did the Devil aſſault the Firſt *Adam?* It was with Temptations drawn from *Pleaſure,* and *Profit,* and *Honour,* which, as the Apoſtle notes, in 1 Joh. 2, 16. are, *All that is in the World.* [53] With the very ſame temptations it was, that he fell upon the Second *Adam* too. Now, in thoſe *Temptations,* you will ſee the more *Uſual Methods,* whereby the *Devil* would be Enſnaring of us; and I beſeech you to attend unto the following Admonitions, as thoſe *Warnings* of God, which the Lives of your ſouls depend upon your taking of.

There were eſpecially Three *Remarkable* Aſſaults of *Temptations*, which the *Devil* it ſeems, viſibly made upon our Lord; after he had been more inviſibly for Forty dayes together *Tempting* of that Holy One; and we may make a few diſtinct *Remarks* upon them all.

§ The firſt of our Lords three Temptations is thus related, in Mat. 4, 3. *He was an Hungry; and when the Tempter came to him, he ſaid, If thou be the Son of God, Command that theſe Stones be made Bread.*

From whence, take theſe *Remarks*.

I. The Devil will ordinarily make our *Conditions*, to be the Advantages of his *Temptations*. When our Lord was *Hungry*, then *Bread! Bread!* ſhall be all the Cry of his Temptation; the Devil puts him upon a wrong ſtep, for the getting of *Bread*. There is no Condition, but what has indeed ſome *Hunger* accompanying of it; and the Devil marks what it is, that we are *Hungry* for. One mans Condition makes him *Hunger* for Preferments, or Employments, another mans makes him *Hunger* for Caſh or Land, or Trade; another mans makes him *Hunger* for Merriments, or Diverſions: And the Condition of every Afflicted Man, makes him *Hunger* with Impatience for Deliverance. Now the Devil will be ſure to ſuit his Perſwaſions with our *Conditions.* When he has our *Condition* to ſpeak with him, & for him, then thinks he, *I am ſure this man will now hearken to my Propoſals!* Hence, if men are in *Proſperity,* the Devil will tempt them to Forgetfulneſs of God; if they are in *Adverſity,* he will tempt them to Murmuring at God; in all the expreſſions of thoſe impieties. Wiſe *Agur* was aware of this; in *Prov.* 30, 9. ſays he, if a man be *Full,* he ſhall be tempted, *to deny God, and ſay who is the Lord?* if a man be Poor, he ſhall be tempted, *to ſteal, and take the Name of God in vain.* The Devil will talk ſuitably; if you ponder your Conditions, you may expect you ſhall be tempted agreeably thereunto.

II. The Devil does often manage his *temptations,* by urging of our *Neceſſities.* Our Lord, was thus by the Devil bawl'd upon; *You want Bread, and you'll ſtarve, if in my way you get it not.* The Devil will ſhow ſome forbidden thing unto us, and plead concerning it, as of *Bread* we uſe to ſay, *it muſt be had. Neceſſity* has a wonderful compulſion in it. You may ſee what *Neceſſity* will do, if you read in Deut. 28. 56. *the tender and the delicate Woman among you, her eye ſhall be evil towards the Children that ſhe ſhall bear, for ſhe ſhall eat them for want of all things.* The Devil will perſwade us that there is a *Neceſſity* of our doing what he does propound unto us; and then tho' the *Laws* of God about us were ſo many *Walls* of Stone, yet we ſhall break [54] through them all. That little inconvenience, of our coming to beg our *Bread,* O what a fearful Reprefentation does the Devil make of it! and when once the Devil fcares us to think of a finful thing, *it muft be done,* we foon come to think, *it may be done.* When the Devil has frighted us into an Apprehenfion, that it is a *Needful* thing which we are prompted unto, he prefently Engages all the Faculties of our Souls, to prove, that it may be a *Lawful* one; the Devil told *Efau, You'll dye if you don't fell your Birthright;* the Devil told *Aaron, You'll pull all the people about your ears, if you do not countenance their fuperftitions;* and then they comply'd immediately. Yea, fometimes if the Devil do but Feign a Neceffity, he does thereby *Gain* the Hearts of Men; he did but feign a Need, when he told *Saul, the Cattel muft be fpared, and the facrifice muft be precipitated,* and he does but feign a Need, when he tells many a man, *if you do no fervile work on the* Sabbath-day, *and if you don't Rob God of his evening,*[207] *you'll never fubfift in the world.* All the denials of God, in the world, ufe to be from this Fallacy impof'd upon us. It never can be neceffary for us to violate any Negative Commandment in the Law of our God; where God fays, *thou fhalt not,* we cannot upon any pretence reply, I *muft.* But the

[207] It was long a Cuftom among fome of the New England People to keep Saturday Evening as though it were a Part of Sunday. Others did not regard that Evening, but kept Sunday Evening. The former claimed that Sunday began at Sunfet.

Devil will put a moſt formidable and aſtoniſhing face of neceſſity upon many of thoſe *Abominable things, which are hateful to the ſoul of God.* He'll ſay nothing to us about, the one thing needful; but the petite and the ſorry *Need-nots* of this world, he'll ſet off with moſt bloody Colours of *Neceſſity.* He will not ſay, *'tis neceſſary for you to maintain the Favour of your God, and ſecure the* welfare of your Soul; but he'll ſay, *'tis neceſſary for you to keep in with your Neighbours; and that you and yours may have a good Living among them.*

III. The Devil does inſinuate his moſt Horrible *Temptations,* with pretence, of much *Friendſhip* and *Kindneſs* for us. He ſeemed very unwilling that our Lord ſhould want any thing that might be comfortable for him; but, he was a *Devil* ſtill! The *Devil* flatters our Mother *Eve,* as if he was deſirous to make her more Happy than her Maker did; but there was the *Devil* in that flattery. *Sub Amici fallere Nomen,*——to Salute men with profers to do all manner of Service for them; and at the ſame time to Stab them as *Joab* did *Abner* of old; this is juſt like the *Devil,* and the *Devil* truly has many Children that Imitate him in it. Some very Affectionate Things were ſpoken once unto our Lord; *Lord, be it far from thee, that thou ſhouldeſt ſuffer any Trouble!* But our Lords Anſwer was, in Mat. 16. 23. *Get thee behind me Satan.* The Devil will ſay to a man, *I would have thee to Conſult thy own Intereſt, and I would have Trouble to be far from thee.* He ſpeaks theſe *Fair Things*, by the Mouths of our profeſſed Friends unto us, as he did by the Tongue of a Speckled Snake unto our Deluded Parents at the firſt. But all this while, 'tis a Direction that has been wiſely given us; *When he ſpeaks fair, Believe him not, for there are ſeven Abominations in his Heart.*

IV. Things in themſelves *Allowable* and *Convenient*, are oftentimes turned into ſore *Temptations* by the Devil. He preſſ'd our Lord unto the mak[55]ing of *Bread;* Why, that very thing was afterwards done by our Lord, in the Miracles of the *Loaves;* and yet it is now a motion of the *Devil, Pray, make thy ſelf a little Bread.* The Devil will frequently put men by, from the doing of a *ſeaſonable Duty;* but how? Truly by putting us upon another *Duty*, which may be at that juncture a moſt *Unſeaſonable* Thing. It is ſaid in Eccl. 8. 5. *A Wiſe Mans heart diſcerns both Time and Judgment.* The *Ill-Timing* of good Things, is One of the chief Intregues, which the Devil has to Proſecute. The Devil himſelf, will Egg us on to many a *Duty;* and why ſo? But becauſe at that very Time a more proper and Uſeful Duty, will have a *Superſedeas* given thereunto. And, thus there are many Things, whereof we can ſay, though no more than this, yet ſo much as this, *They are Lawful ones*, by which Lawful Things——*Perimus Omnes.* Where ſhall we find that the Devil has laid our moſt fatal Snares? Truly, our Snares are on the *Bed*, where it is

Lawful for us to Sleep; at the *Board*, where it is *Lawful* for us to Sit; in the *Cup*, where 'tis *Lawful* to Drink; and in the *Shops*, where we have *Lawful* Bufinefs to do. The *Devil* will decoy us, unto the utmoft Edge of the *Liberty* that is *Lawful* for us; and then one Little pufh, hurries us into a Tranfgreffion againft the Lord. And the *Devil* by Inviting us to a *Lawful* thing, at a wrong time for it, Layes us under further Entanglement of Guilt before God. 'Tis *Lawful* for People to ufe Recreations; but in the Evening of the Lords Day, or the Morning of any Day, how Enfnaring are they! The *Devil* then too commonly bears part in the Sport. If *Promifcuous Dancing* were Lawful; though almoft all the Chriftian Churches in the World, have made a Scandal of it; yet for Perfons to go prefently from a *Sermon* to a *Dance*, is to do a thing, which Doubtlefs the *Devil* makes good Earnings of.

V. To *diftruft* Gods Providence and Protection, is one of the worft things, into which the Devil by his *Temptations* would be hurrying of us. He would fain have driven our Lord unto a Sufpicion of Gods care about Him, faid the Devil, *You may dy for lack of Bread, if you do not look better after your felf, than God is like to do for you.* It is an ufual thing for Perfons to difpair of Gods *Fatherly Care* Concerning them; they torture themfelves with diftracting and amazing Fears, that they fhall come to want before they dy; Yea, they even fay with *Jonas*, in Chap. 2. 4. *I am caft out of the sight of God;* He wont look after me! But it is the Devil that is the Author of all such Melancholly Suggestions in the minds of men. It is a thought that often raises a Feaver in the Hearts of *Married* Persons, when Charges grow upon them; *God will never be able in the way of my calling, to feed and cloath all my Little Folks.* It is a Thought with which *Aged* persons are often tormented, *Tho' God has all my dayes hitherto supplied me, yet I shall be pinched with Straits before I come to my Journeys end.* 'Tis a malicious Devil that raises these *Evil surmisings* in the hearts of Men. And sometimes a distemper of Body affords a Lodg[56]ing for the Devil, from whence he shoots the cruel Bombs of such *Fiery Thoughts* into the minds of many other persons. With such thoughts does the Devil choose to persecute us; because thereby we come to *Forfeit* what we *Question.* We *Question* the Care of God, and so we *Forfeit* it, until perhaps the Devil do utterly *drown us in Perdition.* Our God says, *Trust in the Lord, and do good, and verily thou shalt be fed.* But the Devil says, *don't you trust in God; be afraid that you shall not be fed;* and thus he hinders men from the *doing of Good.*

VI. There is nothing more Frequent in the *Temptations* of the Devil, then for our *Adoption* to be doubted, because of our *Affliction.* When our Lord was in his Penury, then says the Devil, *If thou be the Son of God;* he now makes an *If,* of it; *What? the Son of God, and yet not be able to*

Command a Bit of Bread! Thus, when we are in very Afflictive Circumſtances, this will be the Devils Inference, *Thou art not a Child of God.* The Bible ſays in Heb. 12. 7. *If you are Chaſtened, it is a ſhrow'd ſign that you can't be Children.* Since he can't Rob us of our *Grace,* he would Rob us of our *Joy;* and therefore having Accuſed us unto God, he then Accuſes God unto us. When *Iſrael* was weak and faint in the Wilderneſs, then did *Amalek* ſet upon them; juſt ſo does the Devil ſet upon the people of God, when their Loſſes, their Croſſes, their Exerciſes have Enfeebled their Souls within them; and what ſays the Devil? E'en the ſame that was mutter'd in the Ear of the Afflicted *Job, Is not this the Uprightneſs of thy Ways? Remember, I pray thee, who ever periſhed, being Innocent? If thou wert a Child of God, He would never follow thee, with ſuch Teſtimonies of his Indignation.* This is the *Logic* of the Devil; and he thus interrupts that patience and that Chearfulneſs wherewith we ſhould *ſuffer the will of God.*

VII. To diſpute the Divine Original and Authority of *Gods Word,* is not the leaſt of thoſe *Temptations* with which the Devil troubles us. God from Heaven, had newly ſaid unto our Lord, *this is my Beloved Son;* but now the Devil would have him to make a diſpute of it, *If thou be the ſon of God.* The Devil durſt not be ſo Impudent, and Braſen fac'd, as to bid men uſe *Pharaohs* Language, *Who is the Lord, that I ſhould obey his voice?* But he will whifper into our Ears, what he did unto our Mother *Eve* of old, *It is not the Lord that hath fpoken what you call his Word.* The Devil would have men fay unto the *Scripture*, what they faid unto the *Prophet*, in Jer. 43. 2. *Thou fpeakeft falfely; the Lord our God hath not fent thee to fpeak what thou fayeft unto us;* & he would fain have fecret & curfed Mifgivings in our hearts, *that things are not altogether fo as the Scripture has reprefented them.* The Devil would with all his heart make one huge Bonefire of all the Bibles in the world; & he has got Millions of perfecutors to *affift him in the fuppreffion of that miraculous book. It was the* devil *once in the tongue of a Papift*, that cry'd out, *A plague on this bible; this 'tis that* [89] *does all our mifchief.* But becaufe he can't *Suppress* this Book, he fets himfelf, to *Difgrace* it all that he can. Altho' the Scripture carries its *own Evidence* with it, and be all over, fo pure, fo great, fo true, and fo powerful, that it is impoffible it fhould proceed from any but God alone; yet the Devil would gladly bring fome Difcredit upon it, as if it were but fome *Humane Contrivance;* Of nothing, is the Devil more defirous, than this; That we fhould not count, *Chrift* fo precious, *Heaven* fo Glorious, *Hell* fo Dreadful, and *Sin* fo odious, as the Scripture has declared it.

§. The Second of our Lords Three Temptations, is related after this manner, in Mat. 4. 5, 6. *Then the Devil taketh him up, into the Holy City, and ſetteth him upon a Pinacle of the Temple; and ſaith unto him, if thou be the Son of God, caſt thy ſelf down; for it is written, He ſhall give his Angels charge concerning thee, and in their Hands, they ſhall bear thee up, leſt at any time thou daſh thy Foot againſt a Stone.*

From whence take theſe *Remarks.*

I. The places of the greateſt *Holineſs* will not ſecure us from Annoyance by the *Temptations* of the Devil, to the greateſt wickedneſs. When our Lord was in the *Holy City,* the Devil fell upon him there. Indeed, there is now no proper *Holineſs* of *Places* in our Days; the Signs and Means of Gods more ſpecial Preſence are not under the Goſpel, ty'd unto any certain *places:* Neverthelesſ there are *places,* where we uſe to enjoy much of God; and where, altho' God viſit not the *Perſons* for the ſake of the *Places,* yet he viſits the *Places* for the ſake of the *Perſons.* But, I am to tell you that the Devil will viſit those *Places* and beſt *Perſons* there. No *Place,* that I know of, has got ſuch a *Spell* upon it, as will always keep the Devil out. The *Meeting-Houſe* wherein we Aſſemble for the Worſhip of God, is fill'd with many Holy People, and many Holy Concerns continually; but if our Eyes were ſo refined as the Servant of the Prophet had his of old, I ſuppoſe we ſhould now ſee a Throng of *Devils* in this very place. The Apoſtle has intimated, that Angels come in among us; there are Angels it ſeems that hark, how I *Preach,* and how you

Hear, at this Hour. And our own ſad Experience is enough to intimate, That the *Devils* are likewiſe Rendevouzing here. It is Reported, in *Job* 1. 5. *When the Sons of God came to preſent themſelves before the Lord, Satan came alſo among them.* When we are in our Church-Aſſemblies, O how many *Devils*, do you imagine, [90] croud in among us! There is a *Devil* that rocques one to Sleep, there is a *Devil* that makes another to be thinking of, he ſcarce knows what himſelf; and there is a *Devil*, that makes another, to be pleaſing himſelf with wanton and wicked Speculations. It is alſo poſſible, that we have our *Cloſets*, or our *Studies*, glorioufly perfumed with Devotions every day; but alas, can we ſhut the Devil out of them? No, Let us go where we will, we ſhall ſtill find a Devil nigh unto us. Onely, when we come to Heaven, we ſhall be out of his reach for ever; *O thou foul Devil; we are going where thou canſt not come!* He was hiſſed out of *Paradeſe*, and ſhall never enter it any more. Yea, more than ſo, when the *New Jeruſalem* comes down into the *High Places* of our Air, from whence the Devil ſhall then be baniſhed, there ſhall be no Devil within the Walls of that Holy City. *Amen. Even ſo Lord Jeſus, Come quickly.*

II. Any other acknowledgments of the Lord Jeſus Chriſt, will be permitted by the Temptations of the Devil, provided thoſe Acknowledgments of him, which are *True* and *Full*, may be thereby prevented. What was it, that the Devil hurried our Lord Jeſus Chriſt unto the Top of the *Temple* for? Surely it could not meerly be to find *Precipices;* any part of the Wilderneſs would have afforded *Them.* No, it was rather to have *Spectators.* And why ſo, Why, the carnal Jews had an Expectation among them; that *Elias* was to fly from Heaven to the Temple; and the Devil ſeems willing, that our Lord ſhould be cry'd up for *Elias,* among the giddy multitude; or any thing in the World, tho never ſo conſiderable otherwiſe, rather than to be received as the Chriſt of God. The Devil will allow his Followers to think very highly of the Lord Jeſus Chriſt; O but he is very lothe to have them think, *All.* We read in Col. 1. 19. *It has pleaſed the Father, that in him there ſhould all Fullneſs dwell.* But it is pleaſing to the Devil that we deny ſomething of the Immenſe *Fullneſs,* which is in our Lord. The Devil would confeſs to our Lord, *Thou art the Holy one of God!* but then he claps in, *Thou art Jeſus of Nazareth;* which was to conceal our Lords being *Jeſus of Bethlehem,* and ſo his being, *The True Meſſiah.* All the *Hereſies,* and all the Perſecutions, that ever plagued the Church of God, have ſtill been, to ſtrike at ſome *Glory* of our Lord Jeſus Chriſt. A CHRIST Entirely Acknowledged, will ſave the Souls of them that ſo Acknowledge Him; but, ſays the Devil, *Whatever I muſt not give way to that.* As they ſay, the Devil [91] makes Witches unable to utter all the *Lords Prayer,* or ſome ſuch Syſtem of

Religion, without ſome Deprevations of it; thus the Devil will conſent that we may make a very large Confeſſion of the Lord Jeſus Chriſt; only he will have us to deprave it, at leaſt in ſome one Important Article. Some one Honour, ſome one Office, and ſome one *Ordinance* of the Lord Jeſus Chriſt, muſt be always left unacknowledged, by thoſe that will do as the Devil would have them.

III. *High Stations* in the Church of God, lay men open to violent and peculiar *Temptations* of the Devil. When our Lord was upon the *Pinacle*, that is not the *Fane*, or *Spire*, but the *Battlements* of the *Temple*, there did the Devil peſter him, with ſingular Moleſtations, and he therein ſeems to intend an Entanglement for the Jews, as well as for our Lord. Believe me they that ſtand High, cannot ſtand ſafe. The Devil is a *Nimrod*, a mighty Hunter; and common or little Game, will not ſerve his Turn: he is a *Leviathan*, of whom we may ſay, as in *Job*. 41. 34. *He beholds all high things.* Men of high Attainments, and Men of high Employments, in the Church of God, muſt look, like *Peter* to be more *Sifted*, and like *Paul*, to be more *Buffeted* than other Men. *Feriunt Summos Fulmina Montes.*——The Devil can raiſe a Storm, when God permitteth it, but as for thoſe Men that ſtand near Heaven, the Devil will attack them with his moſt cruel ſtorms of Thunder and Lightening. It was ſaid, *let him that ſtands take heed*; but we may ſay, *They that ſtand moſt high, have cauſe to take moſt heed.* The

Devil is a *Goliah ;* and when he finds a *Champion,* he'l be ſure moſt fiercely to Combate ſuch a Man. He is for, *Killing many Birds with one ſtone ;* and he knows that he ſhall hinder a world of *Good,* and produce a world of *Ill,* if once he can bring a Man Eminently Stationed into his Toyls. Hence 'tis that the *Miniſters* of God, are more dogg'd by the Devil, than other perſons are. Eſpecially ſuch *Miniſters,* as move in the higheſt Orb of Serviceableneſs; and moſt of all ſuch *Miniſters* as have ſpent many years in Laudable Endeavours to be ſerviceable; Thoſe Miniſters are the *Stars* of Heaven, at which the *Tayl* of the *Dragon,* will give the moſt ſweeping and moſt ſtinging ſtrokes; the Devil will find that for them, that ſhall make them *Walk ſoftly* all their Days. . Theſe are the Men, that have creepled, and vexed the Devil more than other Men; for which the Devil has an old Quarrel with them. O Neighbours, little do you think, what black Days of Mourning, and Faſting, and Praying before the Lord, a Raging Devil does fill the lives of ſuch *Men of God* withall.

[92] IV. The Devil will make a deceitful and unfaithful uſe of the *Scriptures* to make his *Temptations* forceable. When the Devil Solicited our Lord, unto an evil thing, he quoted the *Ninty Firſt* Pſalm unto him, tho' indeed he fallaciouſly clip'd it, and maim'd it, of one clauſe very material in it. O never does the Devil make ſuch dangerous Paſſes at us, as when he does wreſt our

own *Sword* out of our Hands, and push *That* upon us. We have to defend us, that Weapon in *Eph.* 6. 16. *The Sword of the Spirit, which is the word of God;* but when the Devil has that very Weapon to fight us with, he makes terrible work of it. When the Devil would poyson men with false *Doctrines*, he'l quote Scriptures for them; a *Quaker* himself, will have the First Chapter of *John* always in his mouth. When the Devil would perswade men to vile *Actions*, he'l quote Scriptures for them; he'l encourage men to go on in Sin, by showing them, where 'tis said, *The Lord is ready to Pardon.* I say this, The one story of *Davids* Fall, in the Scripture, has been made by the Devil an Engine for the Damnation of many Millions. The Devil will fright men from doing those things, that are, *the Things of their Peace;* but How? He'l turn a *Scripture* into a *Scare-crow* for them. The Devil will fright them from all constant Prayer to God, by quoting that Scripture, *The Sacrifice of the Wicked, is an Abomination to the Lord;* the Devil will fright them from the Holy Supper of God, by quoting that Scripture, *He that Eats and Drinks unworthily, Eats and Drinks damnation to himself.* And thus the Devil will by some abused Scripture, Terrifie the Children of God; the Scripture is written as we are told, *For our Comfort;* but it is quoted by the Devil, *for our terror.* How many Godly Souls have been cast into sinful Doubts and Fears, by the Devils foolish glosses upon that Scripture, *He that doubts is damned;* and that, *the fearful ſhall have their portion in the burning Lake:* The Devil ſometimes has play'd the *Preacher*, but I ſay, *Beware all ſilly Souls when ſuch a Fool is Preaching.*

V. Grievous and Pulling Hurries to *Self-Murder* are none of the ſmalleſt outrages, which the Devil in his *Temptations* commits upon us. Why, did the Devil ſay to our Lord, *Caſt thy ſelf down*, but in hopes that our Lord would have broke his Bones, in the fall? The Devil is an *Old Murtherer;* and he loves to *Murder* men; but no *Murder* gives him ſo much ſatisfaction, as that which at his inſtigation, men perpetrate upon themſelves. We [93] ſee that ſuch as are *Bewitched* and *Poſſeſſed* by the Devil, do quickly lay violent hands upon themſelves, if they be not watched continually, and we ſee that when perſons have begun that *Unnatural* buſineſs of *killing themſelves*, there is a *Preternatural* Stupendious Prodigious Aſſiſtance, by the Devil given thereunto. When people are going to Harm themſelves, we call upon them, like thoſe to the Jailor, in *Acts* 16. 28. *Do thy ſelf no harm!* And we have this Argument for it, *It is the Devil that is dragging of you to this miſchief; but will you believe, will you obey ſuch an one as the Devil is?* What was it that made *Judas* to ſtrangle himſelf? We read it was when the *Devil was in him.* I ſuppoſe there are few *ſelf-murderers*, but what are firſt very ſtrangely fallen into the Devils hands; and poſſibly, 'tis by ſome Extraordinary *Diſcon-*

tent, againft God, or *back-fliding* from him, that the Devil firft entred into thofe difturbed Souls. Indeed, fome very great Saints of God, have fometimes had hideous Royls raifed by the Devil in their minds; untill they have e'en cry'd out with *Job*, *I choofe ftrangling rather than life;* and fometimes the ill Humours or Vapours in the Bodies of fuch Good Men, do fo harbour the Devil that they have this woful motion every day thence made unto them; *You muft kill your felf! you muft! you muft!* But it is rarely any other than a *Saul*, an *Abimelek*, an *Achitophel*, or a *Judas;* rarely any other, than a very Reprobate, whom the Devil can drive, while the man is *Compos Mentis*, to Confummate fuch a Villany. Yea, no Child of God, in his Right Senfes can go fo far in this impiety, as to be left without all Time and Room for true *Repentance* of the Crime; 'tis *thus* done, by none but thofe that go to the Devil. A *felf-murder*, acted by one that is upon other accounts a Reafonable man, is but fuch an attempt of Revenge upon the God that made him, as none but one full of the Devil can be guilty of. If any of you are Dragoon'd by the Devil, unto the murdering of your felves, my Advice to you is, *Difclofe it*, *Reveal it*, *make it known immediately*. One that Cut his own Throat among us, Expired crying out, *O that I had told! O that I had told.* You may fpoil the Devil, if you'l *Tell* what he is a doing of.

VI. Prefumptuous and Unwarrantable *Trials* of

the Bleſſed God, are ſome of thoſe things whereinto the Devil would fain hook us with his *Temptations.* This was that which the Devil would have brought our Lord unto, even, *A tempting of the Lord our God.* It is the charge of our God upon us, in *Deut.* 6. 16. *Thou ſhalt not tempt the Lord thy God.* But that which the Devil *Tries,* is, to put us upon *Trying* in a ſinful way whether God be ſuch a God as indeed he is. [94] 'Tis true as to the ways of Obedience, our God ſays unto us, *Prove me, in thoſe ways; Try, whether I won't be as good as my Word.* But then there are ways of *Preſumption,* wherein the Devil would have us to trie, what a God it is, *With whom we have to do.* The Devil would have us to trie the Purpoſe of God, about our ſelves or others; but how? By going to the *Devil* himſelf; by Conſulting *Aſtrologers,* or *Fortune Tellers;* or perhaps by letting the Bible fall open, to ſee what is the firſt Sentence we light upon. The Devil would have us trie the Mercy of God, but how? By running into *Dangers,* which we have no call unto. He would have us trie the Power of God; but how? By looking for good things, without the uſe of Means for the getting of them. He would have us trie the Juſtice of God; but how? By venturing upon Sin in a *Corner,* with an Imagination that God will never bring us out. He would have us trie the Promiſe of God; but how? By *Limiting* the Lord, unto ſuch or ſuch a way of manifeſting Himſelf, or elſe believing of nothing at all. He would have us trie the Threatning of God; but how? By going on impenitently in thoſe things, for which the *Wrath of God comes upon the Children of Diſobedience.* Thus would the Devil have us to affront the Majeſty of Heaven every day.

VII. The *Temptations* of the Devil, aim at puffing and bloating of us up, with *Pride;* as much perhaps as any one iniquity. The Devil would have had Our Lord make a *Vain glorious* Diſcovery of himſelf unto the World, by *Flying in the air,* ſo as no mortal can. *Hoc Ithacus velit*— the Devil would have us to ſoar aloft, and not only to be above other men, but alſo to *know* that we are ſo, *Pride* is the Devils own ſin; and he affects eſpecially to be, *The King over the Children of Pride,* it is a caution in 1 Tim. 3. 6. A Paſtor muſt not be *A Novice; Leſt being lifted up with Pride, He fall into the condemnation of the Devil.* (*Summo ac Pio cum Tremore Hunc Textum Legamus nos Miniſtri Juvenes!*) Accordingly, the Devil would have us to be inordinately taken and moved with what *Excellencies* our God has beſtowed upon us. If our *Eſtates* riſe, he would have us riſe in our Spirits too. If we have been bleſſed with Beauty, with Breeding, with Honour, with Succeſs, with Attire, with Spiritual Priviledges, or with Praiſe-worthy Performances; Now ſays the Devil, *Think thy ſelf better than other Men.* Yea, the Devil would have us arrogate unto our ſelves, thoſe *Excellencies* which really we never were owners of; and *Boaſt of a falſe Gift*. He would have us moreover to Thirſt after Applauſe among others that may ſee Our *Excellencies!* and be impatient if we are not accounted *ſome-body*. He would have us further[95]more, to aſpire after ſuch a *Figure*, as God has never yet ſeen fitting for us; and croud into ſome *High Chair* that becomes us not. Thus would the Devil Elevate us into the *Air*, above our Neighbours; and why ſo? 'Tis that we may be puniſhed with ſuch *Falls*, as may make us cry out with *David, O my Bones are broken with my Falls!* The Devil can't endure to ſee men lying in the *Duſt;* becauſe there is no falling thence. He is a *Fallen Spirit* himſelf, and it pleaſes him to ſee the *Falls* of men.

§. The Third of our Lords Three Temptations, is related in ſuch Terms as theſe. Matth. 4. 8, 9. *Again the Devil taketh him up, into an exceeding High Mountain, and ſheweth him all the Kingdoms of the world, and the glory of them: and ſaith unto him, all theſe things will I give thee, if thou wilt fall down and Worſhip me.* From whence take theſe Remarks.

I. The Devil in his *Temptations* will ſet the Delight of this world before us; but he'll ſet a fair, and a falſe *Varniſh* upon thoſe Delights. They were ſome unknown *Perſpectives*, which the Devil had, both for the Refracting of the *Medium*, and for the Magnifying of the *Object*, whereby he gave our Lord at once a proſpect of the whole Roman Empire; but what was it? It was the *World*, and the *Glory* of it; he ſays not a word of the *World*, and the *Trouble* of it. No ſure; not a word of that; the Devil will not have his Hook ſo barely expoſ'd unto us. The Devil ſets off the Delights of Sin, which he offers unto us, with a ſtretched and raiſed Rhetorick; but he will not own, *That in the midſt of our Laughter, our Heart ſhall be ſorrowful;* and *That the end of our Mirth ſhall be Heavineſs.* There is but one Glaſs in the Spectacles, with which the Devil would have us to read, thoſe paſſages in *Eccles.* 11. 9. *Rejoyce O young Man in thy youth, and let thy Heart chear thee in the Dayes of thy youth, and walk in the ways of thy Heart, and in the ſight of thine Eyes.* Thus far the Devil would have us to Read; and he'll make many a fine Comment upon it; he'll tell us, That if we'll follow the Courſes of the World, we ſhall ſwim in all the Delights of the World. But he is not willing you ſhould Read out the next words; *But know thou, that for all theſe things God ſhall bring thee into judgment.* O he's loth we ſhould be aware of the dreadful Iſſues, and Reckonings that our Worldly Delights will be attended with. He ſets before us, *the Pleaſures of Sin;* but he will not ſay, *Theſe are but for a Seaſon.* He ſets before us, *The ſweet Waters of Stealth?* but he will not ſay, *There is Death in the Pot.* He is a *Mountebank*, that will beſtow nothing but Romantic Praiſes upon all that he makes us the Offers of.

[96] II. There are moſt Helliſh *Blaſphemies* often buzz'd by the *Temptations* of the Devil, into the minds of the beſt Men alive. What a moſt Execrable Thing was here laid before our Lord Himſelf: Even, To own the *Devil* as *God!* a thing that can't be uttered, without unutterable Horror of Soul. The beſt man on earth, may have ſuch *Fiery Darts* from Hell ſhot into his mind. One that was acted by the *Devil,* had the impudence to propound this unto ſuch a good man as *Job, Curſe God.* And the Devil pleaſes himſelf, by chafing the Hearts of good men, with his baſe Injections, *That there is no God,* or, *That God is not a Righteous God;* and a thouſand more ſuch things, too Deviliſh to be mentioned. A good man is extreamly grieved at it, when he hears a *Blaſphemy* from the mouth of another man; ſaid the Pſalmiſt, in Pſal. 44. 15, 16. *My Confuſion is continually before me, for the voice of him that Blaſphemeth.* But much more when a good man finds a *Blaſphemy* in his own Heart; O it throws him into moſt Fevouriſh Agonies of Soul. For this cauſe, a miſchievous Devil will *Flie blow* the Heart of ſuch a man, with ſuch Blaſphemous Thoughts, as make him crie out, *Lord I am e'n weary of my life.* Yea, the Devil ſerves the man juſt as the Miſtreſs of *Joſeph* dealt with him; he importunes the man to think wickedly from Day to Day; and if the man re-

fuſe, he cries out at laſt, *Behold what wicked thoughts this man has lodging in him.* Sayſt thou ſo? *Satan!* No, they are Brats of thy own; and at thy Door alone ſhall they be laid for ever.

III. There is a ſort of Witchcrafts in thoſe things, whereto the Temptations of the Devil would inveigle us. To worſhip the Devil is Witchcraft, and under that notion was our Lord urged unto ſin. We are told in 1 *Sam.* 15. 23. *Rebellion is as the ſin of Witchcraft:* When the Devil would have us to ſin, he would have us to do the things which the forlorn Witches uſe to do. Perhaps there are few perſons, ever allured by the Devil unto an Explicit Covenant with himſelf. If any among ourſelves be ſo, my councel is, that you hunt the Devil from you, with ſuch words as the Pſalmiſt had, *Be gone, Depart from me, ye evil Doers, for I will keep the Commandments of my God.* But alas, the moſt of men, are by the Devil put upon doing the things that are Analagous to the worſt uſages of Witches. The Devil ſays to the ſinner, *Deſpiſe thy Baptiſm, and all the Bond of it, and all the Good of it.* The Devil ſays to the ſinner, *Come, caſt off the Authority of God, and, and refuſe the Salvation of Chriſt for ever.* Yea, the Devil who is called, *The God of this World,* would have us to take Him for our God, and rather Hear Him, Truſt Him, Serve Him, than the God that formed us.

[97] IV. The *Temptations* of the Devil do Tug and Pull for nothing more, than that the Rulers

of the World may yield Homage unto him. Our Lord has had this by his Father Engag'd unto him, *That he ſhall one day be Governour of the Nations.* The Devil doe's extreamly dread the approach of that Illuſtrious time, when *The Kingdom of God ſhall come and his Will be done, as in Heaven, and on Earth.* For this cauſe it was that he was deſirous, Our Lord ſhould rather have accepted of him, that Kingdom, which *Antichriſt* afterwards accepted of him, for the Eſtabliſhment of *Devil-worſhip,* in the World. I may tell you, The Devil is mighty unwilling, that there ſhould be one *Godly Magiſtrate* upon the face of the Earth. Such is the influence of *Government,* that the Devil will every where ſtickle mightily, to have that ſiding with him. What *Rulers* would the Devil have, to command all mankind, if he might have his will? Even, ſuch as are called in Pſal. 94. 20. *The throne of iniquity, which frames miſchief by a Law;* ſuch as will promote Vice, by both Connivance and Example; and ſuch as will oppreſs all that ſhall be *Holy, and Juſt, and Good.* All men have cauſe therefore to be jealous, what Uſe the Devil may make of them, with reference to the Affairs of Government; but Rulers may moſt of all think, that the Lord Jeſus from Heaven calls upon them, *Satan has deſired that he might Sift you, and have you; O Look to it, what ſide you take.*

Thus have you in the Temptations of our Lord, ſeen the principal of thoſe Devices, which the

Devil has to Entrap our Souls. But what ſhall we now do, that we may be fortified againſt thoſe Devices? O that we might be well furniſhed with the *Whole Armour of God!* But me thinks, there were ſome things attending the Temptations of our Lord, which, would eſpecially Recommend thoſe few Hints unto us for our Guard.

Firſt, If you are not fond of Temptation, be not fond of Needleſs, or Too much Retirement. Where was it, that the Devil fell upon our Lord? it was when he was Alone in the Wilderneſs. We ſhould all have our Times to be Alone every Day; and if the Devil go to ſcare us out of our Chambers, with ſuch a Bugbear, as that he'll appear to us, yet ſtay in ſpite of his teeth, ſtay to finiſh your Devotions; he Lyes, he dare not ſhew his head. But on the other-ſide by being too ſolitary, we may lay our ſelves too much open to the Devil; You know who ſays, *Wo to him that is alone.*

[98] Secondly, Let an *Oracle* of God be your defence againſt a *Temptation* of *Hell.* How did our Lord ſilence the *Devil?* It was with an, *It is written!* And *all* his Three Citations were from that one Book of *Deuteronomy.* What a *full* Armoury then have we, in *all* the ſacred Pages that lie before us? Whatever the Words of the *Devil* are, drown them with the words of the *Great God.* Say, *It is Written* The *Belſhazzar* of *Hell* will Tremble and Withdraw, if you ſhow theſe *Hand-Writings* of the Lord.

Laſtly, Since the Lord Jeſus Chriſt has conquered all the *Temptations* of the Devil, Flie to that Lord, Crie to that Lord, that He would give you a ſhare in his Happy Victory. It was for Us that our Lord overcome the Devil: and when he did but ſay, *Satan, Get hence,* away preſently the Tygre flew: Does the Devil moleſt Us? Then let us Repair to our Lord, who ſays, *I know how to ſuccour the Tempted.* Said the *Pſalmiſt, Pſal.* 61. 2. *Lead me to the Rock that is higher than I.* A Woman in this Land being under the Poſſeſſion of Devils, the Devils within her, audibly ſpoke of diverſe Harms they would inflict upon her; but ſtill they made this anſwer, *Ah! She Runs to the Rock! She Runs to the Rock!* and that hindered all. O this *Running to the Rock;* 'tis the beſt Preſervation in the World; the *Vultures* of *Hell* cannot prey upon the *Doves* in the *Clefts* of that *Rock.* May our God now lead us thereunto.[207]

207 The Editor feeling quite confident, that the Reader, by this Time, has got enough of the Devil, will forbear making any Remarks or Comments. Why the Author ſhould place his "Diſcovery" at the End of his Book the Reader is as well qualified to judge as the Editor, and he will only add, that it is a Pity that he (the Author) had not made the Diſcovery ſooner, if by that Diſcovery the poor Witches had been let alone, and left out of the Queſtion, as no real Uſe of them is conceivable, when, in Reality the Devil could and actually did do all the Miſchief himſelf.

As has been before intimated, Dr. Mather was not alone in his Eſtimation of the Importance of the Devil. Mr. Lawſon, in his Sermon at Salem Village, before referred to, among other Paſſages, ſaid to his Hearers (who were above a thouſand): "It is Matter of TERROR, *Amazement, and Aſtoniſhment, to all ſuch wretched Souls,* (if there be any here in the Congregation, and

God grant that none of you may ever be found as fuch) *as have given up their Names, and* Souls *to the Devil:* Who by Covenant have bound themfelves to be his Slaves and Drudges, confenting to be Inftruments, in whofe Shapes, he may torment and afflict their Fellow-creatures, to the amazing and aftoning of the Standers by."—*Page* 64.

Similar Extracts might be made from many of the Writings of that Day, but Time and Space are inadequate, and the Reader, who may now incline to a better Acquaintance with the Devil, than thefe Pages afford him, muft be referred to Dr. Mather's Cotemporaries.

In clofing thefe Notes it fhould be mentioned that the Text of this Edition of the *Wonders of the Invifible World* has been fet up from the lateft London Edition of that Work, as mentioned in the Preface to this Edition. When that Preface was written it was not contemplated to ufe the Original Edition in reading the Proofs. But it was finally decided to read by the Original. By this Courfe the Text has been to fome Extent improved. Yet no Difference of Importance was found. The Departures of the London Publifher were only verbal—never altering the Senfe. At the Expenfe of a little tautological Verbiage the whole has been made conformable to the original Edition —manifeft typographical Errors excepted.

[END OF THE WONDERS OF THE INVISIBLE WORLD AND OF THE FIRST VOLUME.]

www.ingramcontent.com/pod-product-compliance
Lightning Source LLC
LaVergne TN
LVHW010200110826
845151LV00002B/571
* 9 7 8 1 4 2 5 5 3 6 6 4 0 *